Understanding MPEG-4

Understanding
MPEG-4

Klaus Diepold
Sebastian Moeritz

AMSTERDAM • BOSTON • HEIDELBERG • LONDON
NEW YORK • OXFORD • PARIS • SAN DIEGO
SAN FRANCISCO • SINGAPORE • SYDNEY • TOKYO

Focal Press is an imprint of Elsevier

Focal Press is an imprint of Elsevier
200 Wheeler Road, Burlington, MA 01803, USA
Linacre House, Jordan Hill, Oxford OX2 8DP, UK

∞ Recognizing the importance of preserving what has been written, Elsevier prints
its books on acid-free paper whenever possible.

Library of Congress Cataloging-in-Publication Data
Application submitted.

British Library Cataloguing-in-Publication Data
A catalogue record for this book is available from the British Library.

For information on all Focal Press publications
visit our website at www.focalpress.com

04 05 06 07 08 10 9 8 7 6 5 4 3 2 1

Printed in the United States of America

Contents

CHAPTER 1

Introduction

1.1. Scanning the Issue

MPEG-4, the multimedia standard that allows us to create, deliver, and consume audio-visual content in various qualities for various devices, and the only standard that offers the opportunity to create interactive content, has arrived, and is playing a significant role in today's technology landscape.

After years of work by many dedicated engineers and scientists in the standardization bodies, a big chunk of media-compression technology has been standardized and published. But it isn't over yet. MPEG-4, the international open standard still continues to grow, new technologies are continuously added, and new application possibilities are envisioned. At the same time, it is now the task of even more engineers and developers to combine the bits and pieces of specified technology and continue turning the standard into profitable products and services. To make this commercialization process successful, it is of the utmost importance that marketing strategists and business executives pick up a basic understanding of the technical opportunities offered by MPEG-4, in order to actively contribute their visions and to spawn their business ideas.

It is, however, not an easy task for people who are not concerned with developing media-compression technology on a daily basis to see all the potential and business opportunities slumbering in the technology that has been standardized. Not everyone has an engineering or science degree or has the time to stick her nose into literally hundreds of pages of specification documents. Picking up magazines and reading articles and press releases doesn't necessarily help much, either, when it comes to better understanding MPEG-4. The entire specification of MPEG-4 has turned into an enormous body of work, which is difficult to master, answering questions concerning the practical merits offered by the standard. Furthermore, a lot of confusing statements have been published about MPEG-4, some in favor of the standard, and some carrying a lot of criticism, either expressed openly or compressed between the lines. Wild and sometimes puzzling performance claims have been made, mostly for the compression performance of video codecs. All sorts of rumors and opinions are circling around, originating from sources whose credibility is compromised by conflicting interests or questionable motivations (in fact, you would not believe how popular the element of gossip is in the jungle of technology media). All this together creates a situation that makes MPEG-4 an interesting media standard whose application benefits and business impact turn out to be difficult to understand, although some are in fact pretty evident and possible to describe.

Try picking up some technical papers and books to learn about MPEG-4 or even buy yourself a copy of the standards document from the International Organization for Standardization. Chances are that things will get even more confusing. One reason may be the sheer amount of new terminology, the excessive use of abbreviations, and the introduction of entirely new concepts that are difficult to evaluate and understand. The amount of technological items that have gone into the MPEG-4 toolbox is vast.

In reality, you do not need to be an algorithm impresario or compression guru to understand MPEG-4 and take advantage of it. As with many things in life, MPEG-4 is really about common sense. What many people do not realize is that not all pieces of the standard are equally valuable for building new products or any type of business. The big questions are how to navigate through this techno-jungle, and what choices are there for you to make. If you approach this as you would anything else in your "regular" professional life, you would ask yourself questions like, "How much does it cost, and how much can we make with it, and when?"; "How do we develop a gut feeling of what business opportunities MPEG-4 enables?''; ''How can the imagination of my product specialists soar and create new ideas if MPEG-4 is so hard to understand?''; ''Can we easily check if the wonderful ideas for new products and services product specialists have developed will benefit from the existence of the standard?''; ''Are there alternative technologies that we can use?''; ''Why should we base our products on an international and open standard in the first place?''.

In our business, we hear a lot of questions like, ''What are the first applications that benefit from the new standard and when will they be available?'' The first good news is that quite a few applications are already available, and are being deployed in a number of different industries covering a broad range of services with an enormous market potential. The second good news is that MPEG-4 as a standard is continuously being improved over time, which will guarantee competition, quality, markets and revenue potential. The products based on MPEG-4 standard will also continuously improve over time as companies and research institutions keep pushing the envelope to reach the theoretical as well as the practical limits of compression technology for all sorts of multimedia data. In coming chapters, we will elaborate more on this last aspect, which turns out to be important for appreciating the value that comes from having a standard.

1.2. Why Write Another Book on MPEG-4?

In fact, there are quite a number of excellent books that have been published recently, covering various technological aspects of MPEG-4 with varying level of detail. There are certainly a few books and publications to come in the near future, dealing with new technical aspects of the standard. However, most of those books focus on providing a detailed description of the technologies included in the MPEG-4 standard. Many technical articles have been published on the subject as well. However, the target audience for those more scientific articles is developers of hardware or software systems, undergraduate and graduate students of engineering schools, and other technologists who want to learn about the wealth of new technologies in MPEG-4.

Besides this technically oriented readership, there are business and press people, marketers, content creators, and artists, as well as analysts and other people who have a strong interest in technology and the markets driven or affected by media technologies. In other words, at the same time that technology professionals require well-founded information for their field of engagement, business professional require the same, but on a less technical, more explanatory and illustrative basis. Our target readers are such professionals that originally come from diverse markets, such as telecommunications, computers, consumer electronics, digital media business, and media production, to name just the more dominant examples.

It is necessary and helpful for all participants in the value creation chain to have a basic understanding of what a new technology can actually provide in terms of business-relevant features and benefits. It is also necessary to be able to distinguish between the true merits and the limitations of a standard such as MPEG-4, as well as to know the pitfalls and recognize the hype. This book tries to offer insights into the whys and hows of the standard and what impact MPEG-4 has on various businesses and markets. The authors provide basic technical insights, spiced up with personal views, comments and opinions on how to look at the various technological gems in MPEG-4 from a business-oriented viewpoint.

That is, this book does not contain mathematical formulas or detailed technical descriptions of the standard. This is no handbook to read while the soldering iron is heating up or while your compiler is powering up as you start building things. We are trying to provide a sense of the scope and the various capabilities and opportunities the standard offers. The book tries to embody what we like to call "the sauna approach," that is, explaining things in an easy-to-understand manner so that you can chat about MPEG-4 while sitting in a sauna, which we all probably should do more often. Overall, we are trying to make our contribution to avoiding the next Internet bubble blast, by going behind the scenes of MPEG-4 and providing an understandable illustration of this exciting multimedia standard.

Finally, we would like to offer some personal views on what may happen in the future with MPEG-4 and with international standardization in general, a look at the threads and the opportunities.

1.3. Understanding Technology

Executives, by the nature of their job, need to make business-relevant decisions. In this context, it is obviously advantageous to be informed or briefed about the matter at hand so that a coherent judgment can be made. Executives do not need to know, for example, all the mysterious secrets of the MPEG-4 standard; they merely need a well-founded, basic, but precise knowledge of the standard, and they especially need to know what sort of business-relevant features and benefits there will potentially be. Another requirement for business executives is to be able to differentiate between the merits and the limitations of a standard such as MPEG-4, as well as to know where to expect potential problems. The emphasis of this book, therefore, is on offering some insights on why the standard is the way it is and what impact MPEG-4 has on various businesses and markets.

1.4. Acknowledgments

The authors wish to thank the members of the MPEG community, more specifically, Olivier Avaro, Vittorio Baroncini, Ulrich Benzler, Karlheinz Brandenburg, Mark Buxton, Leonardo Chiariglione, Stephan Herrman, Carsten Herpel, Andreas Hutter, André Kaup, Rob Koenen, Peter Kuhn, Didier LeGall, Tobias Oelbaum, Fernando Perreira, Thomas Sikora, Gerhard Stoll, Gary Sullivan, T. K. Tan, C. J. Tsai, and Michael Wollborn.

The authors would also like to acknowledge the support and multiple teachings of Steve Edelson, Manuel Cubero, Joe Hahn, Ivar Formo, Gude Gudesen, Hans Herrmann Horn, Martin Jacklin, Stephan Keszler, Philipp Kraetzer, Fadi Malak, Harald Martens,

Birger Nergaard, David Price, Thomas Ramm, Jan Otto Reberg, Klaas Schüür, Peter Schuster, and Bene Wiedenmann.

Finally, we would like to thank our editor, Joanne Tracy, for her continued encouragement, and patience.

CHAPTER 2
MPEG—Organization and Standard

You may have heard or read the abbreviation "MPEG." You may have various associations attached to this four-letter term. Chances are that the associations you have are either with video on DVDs or with digital broadcast television. Other people immediately think about audio files on the Web or Napster or similar MP3 file-sharing systems. People think of all sorts of things when they hear the term MPEG. However, the truth about what MPEG actually stands for and what it represents is not generally known. And for the average consumer, there is no immediate need to. Many people don't understand how a mobile phone works in detail or what GSM stands for and they can still make use of these technologies. This is somewhat the same with MPEG. It's mostly invisible to the end consumer.

However, if one is doing business in a marketplace where MPEG represents a relevant technology, more knowledge about the facts behind this famous abbreviation are necessary. MPEG stands for "Moving Picture Expert Group." In order to better understand any of the MPEG standards and MPEG-4 in particular, it is helpful to have some insights into what sort of animal MPEG is as an organizational body, how it works, where it lives, and—you get the idea.

In this chapter, we will elaborate on the organizational concepts behind MPEG. In order to better grasp MPEG-4, it is helpful to have a basic understanding of how and why the MPEG standards were created, and who is actually pushing for those standards. So we will begin to describe MPEG in terms of organizational entities.

2.1. MPEG—the Standardization Body

In public discussion, the label MPEG is used to denote completely different things. For some people, MPEG is a standard for video compression or just a compression technology; for others it is a file format for audio and video. Still others think of MPEG as a group, or a company, or an organization. Some people may have no clear picture of what MPEG actually is, and consider those who use it to be a funky crowd of video aficionados. In this section, we attempt to shed some light on different aspects of MPEG, when considering it as an organization.

2.1.1. Structure of ISO

Let's start with the meaning of the abbreviation, which stand for "**M**oving **P**icture **E**xperts **G**roup." MPEG is actually a nickname for a working group of the International Organization for Standardization, abbreviated as ISO (notice the flipping of the letters in the abbreviation). If you want to spend some time browsing through the ISO's Web site, you can find it under www.iso.ch [1]. The ISO's Web site provides a neat explanation of why the letters in the abbreviation ISO appear to be mixed up. Because "International Organization for Standardization" would have different abbreviations in different languages (for example, IOS in English; OIN in French, for Organization Internationale de Normalisation), it was decided at the outset to use a word derived from the Greek "*isos*," meaning "equal." Thus, whatever the country, whatever the language, the short form of the organization's name is always ISO.

Furthermore, from the Web site you can learn that the ISO is a network of the national standards institutes, from 147 member bodies. A *member body* of ISO is the national body "most representative of standardization in its country." Only one such body for each country is accepted for membership of the ISO. Member bodies are entitled to participate and exercise full voting rights on any technical committee and policy committee of ISO. A *correspondent member* is usually an organization in a country that does not yet have a fully-developed national standards activity. Correspondent members do not take an active part in the technical and policy development work, but they are entitled to be kept fully informed about the work that is of interest to them. *Subscriber membership* has been established for countries with very small economies. Subscriber members pay reduced membership fees that nevertheless allow them to maintain contact with international standardization. ISO has its Central Secretariat in Geneva, Switzerland, which coordinates the organization. ISO is a non-governmental organization (NGO). Therefore, unlike the United Nations, the national members of ISO are not delegations of the governments of those countries but come from public and private sectors. It is important that the ISO be an NGO because many of its members are part of the governmental structure of their respective countries, or are mandated by their government. Other members have their roots uniquely in the private sector, having been set up by national partnerships of industry associations. The following are a few examples of members in the ISO: Japan is represented by the JISC (Japanese Industrial Standards Committee), the U.S. is represented by ANSI (American National Standards Institute), and Germany by the DIN (Deutsches Institut für Normung). ISO's national members pay subscriptions that meet the operational cost of ISO's Central Secretariat. The dues paid by each member are in proportion to the country's GNP and trade figures. Another source of revenue is the sale of standards, which covers 30% of the budget. However, the operations of the central office represent only about one fifth of the cost of the system's operation. The main costs are borne by the organizations that manage the specific projects or loan experts to participate in the technical work. These organizations are, in effect, subsidizing the technical work by paying the travel costs of the experts and allowing them time to work on their ISO assignments.

Each of those national standards organizations establishes its own set of rules on who can be a member and how to join and how the national standardization work is administered. In many cases, it is the companies residing in a country which are the paying members of the national standards organization. The representatives of the companies working in standardization on a national level will get accredited by the national organization to participate in the international MPEG meetings and have access to the corresponding documentation, which is shared among the members of MPEG.

In the course of finalizing and publishing an international ISO standard, various ballots are held in which the ISO members, i.e., the national organizations, can vote to either accept the standard or reject it. Each country has just one vote. Therefore, the companies engaged in MPEG standardization have to discuss and agree on a national level in order to cast a vote for or against the adoption of a standard. This can lead to interesting situations when different parts of a multinational corporation participate in ballots as part of different national organizations. Wouldn't it be ironic if, say, Siemens in Germany would have to go with a national vote submitted by the DIN, which is different than the vote submitted by the ANSI, which represents the U.S. branch of the company?

The final draft International Standard (FDIS) is circulated to all ISO member bodies by the ISO Central Secretariat for a final Yes/No vote within a period of 2 months. The text is approved as an International Standard if a $\frac{2}{3}$ majority of the P-members of the TC/SC are in favor and not more than $\frac{1}{4}$ of the total number of votes cast are negative. If these approval criteria are not met, the standard is referred back to the originating Technical Committee for reconsideration in light of the technical reasons submitted in support of the negative votes received.

Within the ISO organization, MPEG is more formally referred to as "Coding of Moving Pictures and Audio," which is a slightly less appealing name for the group. However, since ISO is less concerned with finding appealing names than with being well organized, MPEG is referred to by the string ISO/IEC/JTC1/SC29/WG11. This string describes the route one has to take through the organizational chart of the ISO to arrive at the Working Group 11, which is MPEG. But let's see what additional information about the structure of ISO the route down the organizational chart reveals.

ISO/IEC has a Joint Technical Committee—JTC1—which deals with standardization in the field of information technology (IEC is yet another standardization body). The ISO has more than 200 technical committees dealing with all sorts of standardization activities. For example, there is TC176, which deals with quality management and quality assurance. This is where the ISO9000 suite of standards originates from. On the next level, we see SC29—Subcommittee 29—which deals with "coding of audio, picture, multimedia and hypermedia information." A parallel subcommittee is SC24, which handles computer graphics and image processing. SC24 has issued standards such as VRML (Virtual Reality Modeling Language). Finally, we arrive at the Work Group level, abbreviated WG. MPEG is assigned to WG11. MPEG is not alone; sibling working groups exist, such as WG1—coding of still pictures—and WG12 multimedia and hypermedia. (Refer to Figure 2.1 to get a visual overview of the organizational structure.) These working groups are better known by their corresponding nicknames, such as "JPEG—Joint Photographic Experts Group" or "MHEG—Multimedia and Hypermedia Experts Group," respectively.

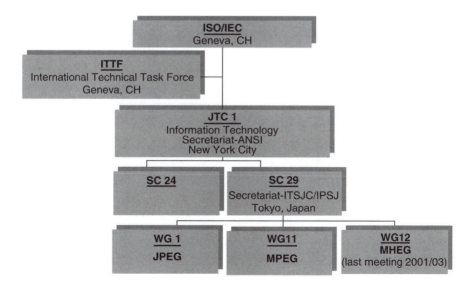

Figure 2.1 Organizational overview of ISO and MPEG.

2.1.2. MPEG—the Agenda

What is MPEG as a group actually doing? What is it producing? As a partial answer, let's have a look at the official description of MPEG's "Area of Work," which reads as follows:

Development of international standards for compression, decompression, processing, and coded representation of moving pictures, audio, and their combination, in order to satisfy a wide variety of applications.

In other words, MPEG creates a technical specification for the (de)compression of all sorts of audio-visual data. MPEG is not concentrating on one particular field of application, but rather tries to supply standardized technology at a fairly generic level in order to embrace as many application fields as possible.

The program of work for the MPEG working group, as taken from the "Terms of Reference," to found at the ISO Web site reads as follows:

- MPEG shall serve as the responsible body within ISO/IEC for recommending a set of standards consistent with the Area of Work. MPEG shall cooperate with other standardization bodies dealing with similar applications.
- MPEG shall consider requirements for interworking with other applications such as telecommunications and broadcasting, with other image coding algorithms defined by other SC29 working groups and with other picture and audio coding algorithms defined by other standardization bodies.
- MPEG shall define methods for the subjective assessment of quality of audio, moving pictures, and their combination for the purpose of the area of work. MPEG shall assess characteristics of implementation technologies realizing coding algorithms of audio, moving picture, and their combination. MPEG shall assess characteristics of digital storage and other delivery media targets of the standards developed by WG11.
- MPEG shall develop standards of coding of moving pictures, audio, and their combination, taking into account quality of

coded media, effective implementation, and constraints from delivery media.

- MPEG shall propose standards for the coded representation of moving picture and audio information, and information consisting of moving pictures and audio in combination. MPEG shall propose standards for protocols associated with coded representation of moving pictures, audio, and their combination.

2.1.3. MPEG Meetings

In order to fulfill its mission as stated in the program of work, MPEG holds meetings about four times a year, in locations that are scattered around the world. An average MPEG meeting consists of 250 to 350 participants from more than 20 countries. The meetings serve as a point of personal communication and cooperation to fuse the many results that have been created all over the world. Most importantly, consensus on all technical questions must be achieved to actually generate a final product, which is an MPEG standard. A typical MPEG meeting lasts 5 days, starting on a Monday morning and ending on a Friday night—days that are packed with activities and concentrated work to seriously push ahead on the progress toward finalizing a standard. The work continues between the meetings as the delegates return to their companies, research organizations, or universities. For this purpose, each meeting creates a list of so-called ad-hoc groups. Each ad-hoc group is convened by a chairman. The purpose of the ad-hoc group is to work on specific problems or questions that need to be resolved or answered until the next meeting. The goal of the ad-hoc group is formulated as a mandate. Whoever feels entitled and competent to contribute can join the ad-hoc group. Most of the correspondence for the ad-hoc group is handled via e-mail reflectors and occasionally meetings are held. E-mail reflector and meetings are organized by the chairman, who is mostly an acclaimed expert for the particular issue at hand. By the time the next MPEG meeting is held, the ad-hoc group needs to present a written report about the findings and discussions. The report is expected to contain recommendations for MPEG to be accepted or discussed during the meeting. An ad-hoc group officially ceases to exist as soon as the next MPEG meeting begins. However, it may well be the case that the ad-hoc group is instantiated again at the end of this meeting since the problem or issue is not fully resolved and needs further work. In fact, a lot of work towards the standard is done under the umbrella of ad-hoc groups. There are somewhere between 10 and 20 ad-hoc groups established at the end of each meeting.

2.1.4. MPEG Subgroups

We have arrived at the Work Group level within the ISO org chart, and MPEG has been identified as WG11. The actual group counts several hundred people worldwide, actively contributing to the creation of MPEG standards. An MPEG meeting of 250 to 350 people is too big a group to be convened as one single crowd, and the topics dealt with are quite diverse and not of interest to all participants. Therefore, MPEG itself is subdivided into subgroups. Each of the subgroups deals with a specific topic and includes all the experts in that particular field. A subgroup is managed by a chairman, who convenes the subgroup meetings and reports to the MPEG convener. While the individual chairpersons change over time, the MPEG convener, Leonardo Chiariglione, has been a constant throughout the years since he started MPEG in the late 80s. More information on Leonardo Chiariglione and his involvement with multimedia standards can be looked up in the article [2]. In Figure 2.2 the various subgroups of MPEG are graphically depicted.

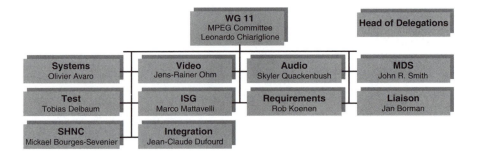

Figure 2.2 Subgroups of MPEG.

The following sections describe the subgroups in MPEG and their respective agendas.

2.1.4.1. Requirements Subgroup

The task of the requirements group is to collect the technical requirements that the new standard shall satisfy. This sounds rather modest, but there are MPEG delegates who consider the requirements group as the head (though not the brain) of MPEG. The requirements group also deals heavily with strategic questions. Profiling policies are discussed within this group, as are the definitions of the profiles. Profiling discussions typically occur toward the end of a standardization campaign, since the technical groups need to first conclude much of their technical work. We will go over the concept of profiles and levels in a later chapter.

Requirements are also the group that collects new ideas and suggestions for new work items or emerging application domains that may require standardization of technology. In addition, this group gathers experts from various fields (audio, video, systems, etc.) to discuss the overall strategy and decision-making procedures and policies for activities such as establishing profiles. Even though the requirements group produces quite a number of documents throughout the process, none of these documents will become a part of the finished standard.

2.1.4.2. Video Subgroup

The video subgroup combines all technical experts who are concerned with video signal processing. This is where the new video compression technologies are actually proposed, discussed, and tested, and where the technical decisions are made about which video coding technology will make it into the standard. The video group is responsible for the technical content that is specified in Part 2, the visual part of the MPEG standard. (We will tell you more about the individual parts of MPEG standards in a later chapter of this book.) Traditionally, the video subgroup is the largest group in MPEG.

2.1.4.3. Audio Subgroup

The audio subgroup is very similar to the video group, i.e., it is a gathering of internationally acclaimed technical experts. The group deals with all aspects of audio coding and audio-signal processing. Note that this is the group where MP3, the Internet surfers' favorite music file format, has been specified, among other technologies in the field. Hence, the audio subgroup is responsible for the text of the standards document that contains the audio specification (typically Part 3 of an MPEG standard but also Part 10 in MPEG-2).

2.1.4.4. Systems Subgroup

The third big technical group is the systems subgroup. This group also consists of international experts who deal with all technical questions concerning the combination and the packeting of audio and visual data along with other ancillary data. Part 1, the systems part of most MPEG standards, is produced by the systems group. Traditionally, the results from the systems group are extremely important for things like getting a TV system actually going. However, the public relations for the systems group has not always reflected the importance of its accomplishments.

2.1.4.5. Test Subgroup

The test group is another example of a technical subgroup whose accomplishments are publicly underrepresented. Nevertheless, since MPEG puts an emphasis on thoroughly assessing the quality of their work, testing the standardized technology in order to verify that the requirements are met by the new standard is another essential part of MPEG. The test subgroup is responsible for designing, specifying, and actually performing and evaluating various types of testing activities of MPEG. As a major responsibility, the test group issues Part 4 of the MPEG standards, which describes the methodology to test for compliance with the specifications in the video, audio, and systems parts of the standard. Part 4 of the standards is traditionally one of the last parts to be issued and published, because the test group has to wait until the other technical groups are done with their job and until the requirements subgroup has concluded its profiling discussion.

Since testing is not necessarily a field where companies and individuals can position their Intellectual Property Rights (IPR) or patents, this is a group where the head count of participants is always subject to variations.

2.1.4.6. Implementation Study Group

The implementation study group (ISG) is another technical subgroup. Its task is to advise the big technical groups regarding implementation questions. A typical question ISG deals with is which algorithm is more complex, A or B, and by how much is it more complex? Often this question comes up, for example, if the audio or video group needs to make a decision on which algorithm to pick for the specification, in particular if both alternatives produce about the same result in terms of coding performance. Other than that, ISG does not produce a normative part of an MPEG standard. As part of the MPEG-4 activities, ISG creates a technical report, which includes a reference hardware description for various coding tools.

2.1.4.7. Synthetic Natural Hybrid Coding (SNHC) Subgroup

MPEG-4 contains technologies that process synthetic visual data. Synthetic in this context includes techniques from computer graphics and animation, that is, from a field where the moving pictures and images are synthesized by the computer rather than captured by a camera. It has been found in the course of the MPEG-4 project that this domain is characterized by different experts, a different culture, and other technical features when compared to the video subgroup. Those differences made it beneficial to combine all efforts and experts for synthetic visual data in a separate subgroup. The resulting SNHC subgroup does not issue a separate part of the MPEG standard. SNHC instead merges the results and specifications with the work of the video subgroup to jointly create the visual part of MPEG.

2.1.4.8. Liaison

MPEG as a standards work group is not alone in the world of technology standards. There are numerous organizations and technical groups, which deal with topics related to the MPEG work items. In order to avoid duplicated efforts and conflicting specifications, MPEG has created liaisons to those organizations. A typical example is the liaison to DVB (Digital Video Broadcast) or SMPTE (Society of Motion Picture and Television Engineers). Both organizations are creating specifications for their particular field of application. Those specifications use MPEG standards as building blocks. It is important for all parties involved to stay tuned, in order to foster the development and adoption of complementary standards and to avoid conflicts or mismatches. Another very important task for the liaison group is to coordinate the cooperation with the Video Coding Experts Group (VCEG), a separate video-coding experts group under the control of the ITU (International Telecommunications Union). VCEG has created the other family video coding standards, denoted by abbreviations like H.261, H.262, H.263, and more recently, H.264. Traditionally, there has been a kind of cooperation/competition between MPEG and VCEG. The constructive cooperation between the two groups is evidenced by the fact that H.262 and the video part of MPEG-2 actually contain identical text, which has been developed jointly. The competition part is represented by the race for the best video coding technology during the MPEG-4 project, where the VCEG has won the beauty contest against the MPEG-4 codec with the development of their H.26L technology. Based on this result, VCEG and MPEG joined forces to establish the joint video team (JVT), which further progressed on the H.26L design to arrive at what is now MPEG-4 AVC (Advanced Video Coding) in the ISO world and H.264 in the ITU world.

2.1.4.9. Head of Delegations

Each national delegation participating in MPEG assigns a head of delegation (HoD). All those HoDs meet in an assembly to discuss and decide on various logistical and organizational matters of relevance to running MPEG. HoDs also have the pleasure of deciding on future meeting locations.

2.1.5. Other Standardization Organizations

In addition to the ISO, there is the ITU (formerly CCIR), the IEEE (Institute for Electrical and Electronics Engineers), the ETSI (European Telecommunication Standards Institute) at the international level, as well as national standardization bodies such as DIN and ANSI.

Parallel to those standards bodies, there are quite a number of industry consortia, which are also pushing actively for standardized technology, mostly for particular fields of applications or markets. Examples are the DVB (Digital Video Broadcasting) project, DAVIC (Digital Audio Video Council), the DVD-Forum, IETF (Internet Engineering Task Force), Web3D, W3C, DMTF (Distributed Management Task Force), 3GPP (3rd Generation Partner Project) and ISMA (Internet Streaming Media Alliance), to name just a few.

In some cases, standards are set by individual companies when they release products that turn out to be so successful that they reach the status of a de-facto standard. Examples of this type of standard are the audio cassette as introduced by Philips, the Audio Compact Disk (CD) as proposed by Philips and Sony, analog VCR introduced by JVC, and finally, the Windows operating system by Microsoft. Alternatively, a company can submit its technology to a standards body such as ISO and ask if it can be standardized. Sun Microsystems with Java is an example of this last procedure.

2.2. MPEG—the Standardization Process

There exist quite a number of de-facto standards and specifications in the audio-visual field. Most of them have been developed and deployed by companies to serve the needs of a particular industry. There are other cases where the standard is the result of one product being successfully introduced to the market where it has become universally accepted. Take the Philips compact audio tape format as a classic example. For the most part, this style of standardization has resulted in products, services, and applications pertaining to one industry not being interoperable with those of another industry. As long as the borders between industries are clear, this has not constituted a major problem. Such borders are built on a tight integration of services and technology, i.e., a particular technology is intimately tied to one particular service. This was particularly true in the good old days of analog technology. Take for example the standard telephone system which, way back when, was used almost exclusively for voice communications. Only later, with the advent of analog modems, did the telephone networks come to be used for transmitting faxes or other data services. Today, digital audio and video content is communicated as digital signals, or bits. The bare bits can be transmitted over any type of transmission channel, including telephone networks, which increasingly have transformed into data networks. The Internet is a packet-switched data transmission network, which doesn't care what the transported bits are actually representing. It could be voice data (IP telephony), or video (media streaming) or just plain old file transfer—audio and video are used in multiple instances. This is a major problem for those producing content, those consuming it, and the service providers in between. The problem originates from the fact that the universality of digital data networks removes the traditional separation between media, services, industries, and even products.

In former times, a telephone network was only a telephone network and was entirely distinct from a television network, which again was entirely different from a radio network. This also translates to different technologies being used for each of such networks. This was even more true for the companies and industries associated with the networks. On one hand, there was a telephone network company taking care of the telephone network and the pertaining voice service. This business was completely different from operating a television network. A telephone network operator was not in competition with a television network operator. A TV set was usable for watching TV or videos exclusively. With digital technology, all those boundaries are vanishing. A telephone network operator can start to distribute video and audio content through his network, just as much as a television network operator can think about offering competitive telecommunication services based on his infrastructure. If a consumer owns a computer it is possible to use it for watching movies, listening to music, sending e-mails or even do long-distance phone calls over the Internet. More problems come from the possibility to copy digital data without any loss of fidelity or quality. This taps into yet another topic—the field of digital rights management, which we will not cover here.

From its earliest stages, MPEG has taken a distinguished approach. When developing a standard, participation of all industries potentially affected by the new technology has been sought and obtained. Look at the large number of individuals from diverse industries attending MPEG meetings and subscribing to MPEG e-mail reflectors. Requirements from a wide range of industries have been collected and a set of commonly shared technologies capable of satisfying the fundamental requirements of all participating industries has been developed and standardized.

As explained in the previous section, MPEG can rightfully be considered as a group. However, MPEG also incorporates a specific standardization program or process. This process has been shaped through years of intense standardization work practiced by the many MPEG colleagues. In particular, the MPEG Convener has initiated and brought forward this process by means of his dedication and vision. Therefore, the acronym MPEG is intimately connected to the name of Leonardo Chiariglione.

Let's have a look at the process that has ultimately led to successful media standards such as MPEG-1, MPEG-2, and, of course, MPEG-4. There is no such thing as MPEG-3. Why this is will be explained a little later in this book. But before we dive into the description of the standardization process, we will discuss briefly the challenges standardization has to face. The MPEG process will then be shown as one method of coping with those challenges.

2.2.1. Challenges for the Standardization Process

Any standardization process, and MPEG is no exception, is exposed to a number of challenges, which make standardization a difficult and sometimes frustrating endeavor. The thing that makes MPEG particularly challenging is the fact that it is located in the field of information technology, which can be characterized by extremely fast innovation cycles and a global approach to developing products and services. Keep this in mind as you read the following sections.

2.2.1.1. Frozen Technology

Formulating a standard implies that the parties agree on a set of technological features, which will be subsequently specified in detail and kept fixed over some period of time. Any selection of technological features for the standard represents a mere snapshot of the technology available at the time the standard is crafted. This may lead to a situation in which the standard consists of frozen technology that no longer follows the most recent trends in research and advanced development. The result is that the standard is not adopted by industry, since complying with the standard cuts the industry off from further improvements.

2.2.1.2. Obsolete Technology

The challenge of obsolete technology being adopted as part of a standard is very closely related to the case described in the previous subsection. This can happen if the finalization of the standardization process is delayed unduly until the technology selected has turned stale and obsolete. Timeliness of publication for a new standard is therefore of prime importance. Again, the above situation will lead to the standard not being adopted, since nobody wants to have products and services which are tied to a standard embodying last year's technology.

2.2.1.3. Premature Technology

A standards body may be tempted to select premature technology in a misled effort to escape the problem of adopting technology that will be obsolete by the time the standard is published. Premature technology means that it becomes evident after the standardization campaign is finished that the stuff won't work the way it was expected. The result is that the standard will not be used since nobody wants to build products based on a standard that doesn't work.

2.2.1.4. Over- and Under-Specification

If a standard is tuned to match a particular application field, then it may turn out that the technology tries to fix too many details of the application field. Therefore, it can't live outside of the original target market and application, which unnecessarily limits the applicability and success of the standard. This situation represents a case of over-specification.

Underspecification refers to too many options to choose from. The implementer has a long list of options to choose from or a substantial number of loose ends. Expressed in other words, the standard does not provide sufficient technical detail that allows the implementation of standards compliant products without making additional design choices. This way, interoperability between products is sacrificed, and the standard suffers from underspecification. Another case of underspecification is given if the standard comprises many alternative solutions for achieving a particular functionality. These alternatives are also often called "options," where the implementer either makes a choice for one solution or opts for implementing all options. The first situation again puts interoperability in jeopardy while the second approach tends to make products unnecessarily costly.

2.2.1.5. Timeliness of a Standard

Information technology is a fast-moving field. This sounds like a fairly obvious statement. However, from a standards point of view this fact makes standardization a difficult task. Besides the challenges mentioned so far, it is also important to have a standard that will allow the industry to begin building products and setting up services by the time the markets are in existence. It is definitely too late to start a standardization effort once the selling of potentially incompatible products has started. At that point, a product or a product family would need to be adopted that could serve as a de facto standard. It is therefore important to have the standards ready in time, which implies that standards people need to have a magic crystal ball to foresee future opportunities, predict the upcoming technologies, and thus begin the standards development process early enough.

2.2.2. Patents and Intellectual Property Rights

Standards and patents—a contradiction? This is a tricky subject, which we will shed some light on in the chapter dealing with the business interface. ISO, and hence MPEG, acknowledge the existence of Intellectual Property Rights (IPRs) and patents. Here we are talking about the patents and IPRs associated with the technology contained in the standard. There are also IPRs and copyrights associated with media items such as a movie or a piece of music. We will defer the latter discussion to another chapter.

To date, ISO has not dealt with issues of licensing of MPEG technology, as this is certainly outside of the jurisdiction of such an organization. Licensing of technology is a subject that should be addressed and handled by the companies or individuals involved. However, ISO does have a policy to deal with patents. This policy requires companies who have actively contributed technology to the standard to sign a so-called "Patent Statement." This document simply states that the respective company will grant access to the patents associated with the standard on non-discriminatory and reasonable terms. This only applies to products that claim to be compliant with MPEG.

Times are changing, and so are the established patterns of doing business, due to new technical means and a changing environment. This also creates a new challenge for standardization. Until recently, traditional communication standards were implemented in terms of physical devices (i.e., the technology was embodied in hardware implementations). The pertaining intellectual property rights are associated with the hardware device carrying the technology, which is protected by patents. With the advent of more recent digital technologies, a standard is likely to be implemented by a processing algorithm that runs on a programmable device, i.e., the implementation takes place via a software application executed on a PC or a similar programmable device. Actually, the standard becomes a piece of computer code whose IPR protection is achieved by protecting the copyright of the source code. Digital networks, such as the Internet or wireless communication networks, are pervasive, and it is possible for a PC or a PDA to run a multiplicity of algorithms downloaded from the network.

According to the traditional pattern of the ISO dealing with IPRs, a patent holder is supposed to grant fair, reasonable, and non-discriminatory terms to a licensee. However, there are significant possibilities for the patent holder to actually discriminate against the licensee. The discrimination occurs because the patent holder is assuming a certain business model that is based on the existence of hardware, whereas the licensee may have a completely different model that is based on the existence of a programmable device and software. Questions naturally arise concerning how to interpret the notion of "fair, reasonable and non-discriminatory" in this context and how the environment for such policies has changed through the advance of technology.

There are more changes that create new challenges for standardization. Digital technologies cause convergence. In the analog domain, there is a clear separation between the devices and systems that make communication possible and the messages themselves. Take rental videos as an example. When a video cassette is rented by a consumer for use on a home video player, a remuneration is paid to the holders of the copyright for the movie. The holders of patent rights for the video recording system receive a remuneration at the time the player is purchased. In the digital domain, an audio-visual presentation may be composed of some digitally encoded pieces of audio and video, text, and drawings. There is a software application that manages the user interaction and the access to the different components of the presentation. If the application runs on a programmable device, the intellectual property can only be associated with the bits—the digital content and the executable program code, which may have been downloaded from the network. Since, in a digital world, the play-back device, (i.e., the software application) as well as the content (i.e., the movie) are nothing but bits, they can easily be copied without loss of functionality or quality and distributed to other consumers. This can happen without creating a stream of money to remunerate neither the implementer of the playback software nor the creator of the digital media item. This is the root for all activities to prevent piracy of software, video, or audio. The case for the MP3 audio format serves as a good example for both aspects. The software players for MP3 audio files were distributed freely until the inventors of the technology stepped in and asked for patent licenses. The fair remuneration for the content owners in this context is still an ongoing discussion.

2.2.3. Principles of MPEG Standardization

Since the technological landscape changed from analog to digital, with all the associated implications, it was essential that standard makers modify the way by which standards are created. Standards must offer interoperability, across countries, services, and applica-tions, and not a "system-driven approach" in which the value of a standard is limited to a specific, vertically integrated system. This brings us to the toolkit approach in which a standard must provide a minimum set of relevant tools, which, after assembled according to industry needs, provide the maximum interoperability at a min-imum of complexity and cost. The success of MPEG standards is mainly based on this toolkit approach, bounded by the "one func-tionality, one tool" principle. In conclusion, MPEG wants to offer the users interoperability and flexibility, at the lowest cost and level of complexity.

In the previous section, we listed a number of challenges the stand-ardization process has to face. MPEG—or Leonardo Chiariglione, the MPEG convener—has developed a vision and an approach that apparently circumvents possible pitfalls and shortcomings. The current subsection presents a list of concepts by which MPEG is governed to produce successful standards.

2.2.3.1. A Priori Standardization

If a standards body is to serve the needs of a community of industries, it must start the development of standards well ahead of the time the standard will be needed. This requires a fully functioning and dedicated strategic planning function, totally up to date on the evolution of the technology and the state of research.

2.2.3.2. Systems vs. Tools

Many industry-specific standards bodies create standards that fail because they attempt to specify complete systems to completely match specific applications at hand. As soon as such applications are slightly transformed, the corresponding standard may lose its validity. Furthermore, each industry then requests its particular set of standards. This hampers economy of scale as well as the quick adaptation of technology to new product trends and innovative applications.

For a standard to supply longevity of the specification and to support economy of scale, the responsible standards bodies should collect different industries under one umbrella, where each industry needs standards based on the same technology. The target products and services of course may differ from industry to industry. This goal is accomplished if a standard like MPEG comes in individual components that are commonly referred to as "tools." Each industry then has the choice to pick tools from the standard and combine them according to the needs originating from the application. This way a hierarchy of standards can be created using lower-level specifications as fixed building blocks. As a good example of this concept, consider the Digital Video Broadcasting system specification, which builds on top of the MPEG-2 standard as a basic building block for audio and video coding.

2.2.3.3. Specify the Minimum

When standards bodies are made up of a single industry, it is very convenient to add to a standard those nice little aspects that bring it nearer to a product specification. This is the case with industry standards or standards used to enforce the concept of "guaranteed quality" so dear to broadcasters and telecommunication operators because of their "public service" nature. To guard against the threat of over-specification, only the minimum that is necessary for interoperability should be specified. The extra elements that are desirable for an industry may be unnecessary for—or even alienate—another industry.

2.2.3.4. One Functionality—One Tool

This is a strict rule within MPEG, which is based on common sense. Too many failures in standards are known to have been caused by too many options. The reader may wonder why the existence of options and choice is considered to be detrimental to the quality of a standard, when this is usually taken as a bonus. If there is choice in tools for the same functionality, how would all the receivers out in the field know which choices have been taken by the transmitters at the sending side? As a solution to this dilemma, a receiver has to either incorporate all alternative tools for one functionality, or the designer himself has to make a choice. In the one case, the receiver device is unnecessarily burdened by superfluous tools and thus is overly expensive. In the other case, no one can guarantee that there is interoperability between receivers and transmitters of different manufacturers.

2.2.3.5. Relocation of Tools

When a standard is defined by a single industry, there is generally a certain agreement about where a given functionality resides in the system. In a multi-industry environment, this is usually not the case because the location of a function in the communication chain is often associated with the value added by a certain industry. The technology must be defined not only in a generic way, but also in such a way that the technology can be located at different points in the system.

2.2.3.6. Verification of the Standard

It is not enough to produce a standard and collect cool technology. After the work is completed, evidence must be given to the industry that the work done indeed satisfies the requirements originally agreed upon, which may be considered as "product specification" for standardization. This is obviously also an important promotional tool for the acceptance of the standard in the marketplace.

At the end of a standardization campaign, the new standard will be verified by formal tests. Besides the verification of functionalities, the verification tests include the assessment of the coding performance for video and audio codecs. To this end, the new codecs are compared with previous versions of MPEG standards or carefully selected reference codecs. Setting up and performing meaningful verification tests can be a challenge and can require substantial effort and know-how. The MPEG group also has the ambition for its tests to be as objective and unbiased as possible. This is considered the only feasible way for the standard to gain credibility in the marketplace.

The challenge is to not test just one particular implementation of the standard and compare it to one particular product. More specifically, MPEG doesn't want to test the performance of a particular encoder, as this is not covered by the standard. Comparing optimized commercial encoders with reference implementation doesn't give meaningful results. If you have ever tried to make sense out of results originating from, for example, a test performed by press people, you may have an idea how difficult this can be. Results of MPEG tests can be found on MPEG's home page http://www.chiariglione.com [3].

2.2.4. What Is Actually Standardized by MPEG?

Standardization in general and MPEG in particular are facing a whole collection of challenges, which have been listed previously. One fundamentally important approach taken by MPEG to deal with those challenges is that it refrains from specifying a video or audio encoding machinery. To some people, that's surprising. However, this fact has to be stressed and underlined several times as it is an essential aspect for any MPEG standard.

MPEG only specifies the bit stream syntax and the decoder semantics. MPEG specifies the bit stream by setting the rules for how to line up the ones and zeros in a sequence, in order to form a legal serial bit stream that carries the compressed media data. Specifying the decode semantics means that MPEG specifies the meaning of those bits so that a decoder unambiguously knows how to process the incoming serial bit stream in order to recreate the original video data.

The actual encoding process, that is, the mechanism for creating the bits for the compressed representation of the original video data, is not covered by the standard. This holds for any type of visual data as well as for audio. Similar concepts are employed for other types of media standards as well, such as JPEG, JPEG2000, and the family of ITU video codecs denoted by H.26x.

This concept of seemingly restricted standardization enables the further progress of encoding technology. The lack of encoder specification allows for competition around who has the best encoder (best image quality for the bit), the fastest encoder, or the cheapest encoder. Competition on the decoder side concerns price, performance, and features of the decoding device.

How does this concept then play out? Everybody can create an encoder to his or her liking. In theory, you can even use a text editor to create a legal video file that can be played back on a compliant decoder. The only requirement is that the created bit stream has its syntax bits set according to the specification. Nowhere in the standard does it say anything about the pictures needing to look good. The fact that a coded bit stream adheres to the specification set out by MPEG does not automatically mean that the decoded images will look good when played back by a decoder and watched on a screen. The achievable quality of the decoded audio or video streams is determined by the capabilities of the encoder. And the encoder can be anything from a very simple and cheap piece of software that has to rely on manual interaction from a human operator, resulting in very slow encoding process, to a highly sophisticated real-time–capable device that has gone through many cycles of optimization.

The MPEG-4 standard opens new frontiers in the way users will play with, create, re-use, access, and consume audiovisual content. The MPEG-4 object-based representation approach, where a scene is modeled as a composition of objects, both natural and synthetic, with which the user may interact, is at the heart of the MPEG-4 technology.

2.2.5. The Standardization Process

MPEG follows a development process, the major steps of which will be explained in the next subsections.

2.2.5.1. Exploration Phase

MPEG is regularly exploring new fields of application in order to plan for new work items. In an initial step for strategic planning, MPEG members are asked for input in order to identify relevant new applications. Members understand "relevance" to mean that the applications feature properties that make it necessary or at least beneficial to develop a standard for these markets to unfold. This is a point that needs careful consideration by the group as a whole to avoid launching work items that will lead nowhere.

Through a sequence of technical discussions, MPEG identifies the technical functionalities that are needed by the applications taken into consideration. This discussion takes place in open seminars and workshops where industry experts are invited to present and discuss their subjects. The exploration phase typically lasts for about 6 to 12 months, depending on the extent of the search.

2.2.5.2. Requirements Phase

Based on those identified functionalities, MPEG collects and describes the technical requirements in such a way that a set of requirements can be identified that are common for different applications across the areas of interest. MPEG also identifies requirements that are not common but still relevant. In this phase, a scope of work is established.

As a final step in this phase, a public call for proposals is issued, asking all interested parties to submit relevant technology to fulfill the identified requirements and functionalities. The development of the requirements takes about 6 to 12 months, which somewhat parallels the exploration phase.

2.2.5.3. Competitive Phase

In the competitive phase, all submitted proposals are evaluated for their technical merits and compared to each other. The evaluation is done in a well-defined, adequate, and fair evaluation process. The "beauty contest" can entail subjective testing, objective comparisons (e.g., coding performance and complexity), and evaluation by experts to fully assess the strengths and weaknesses of the submissions. In any case, the detailed evaluation process has been developed by MPEG members a priori, and is published openly, together with the call itself. This way all submitters of new technology know in advance how performance of proposals will be assessed. As a result of the evaluation, the technology best addressing the requirements is selected as a starting solution for the standard base on which further development efforts towards the final standard will emerge. The competitive phase covers about 3 to 6 months, which partly overlaps with the requirements phase.

2.2.5.4. Collaborative phase

During the collaborative phase, all the MPEG members collectively improve and complete the most promising tools identified at the evaluation. The group identifies the individual pieces of technology that offer excellent solutions to certain elements of the requirements. Those pieces are identified, and are subsequently integrated into the starting solution, which has been selected by the end of the competitive phase. So begins a collaborative process to draft and improve the standard. The collaboration includes the definition and improvement of a "Working Model," which embodies an early version of the standard. The Working Model evolves by comparing different alternative tools with those already in the Working Model. This process is based on the so-called "Core Experiments" (CE), which will be explained in more detail.

The collaborative phase is the major strength of the MPEG process—hundreds of the top experts in the world, from dozens of companies and universities, work together for a common goal. It is therefore no surprise that this super-team traditionally achieves excellent technical results, justifying the need for most companies to at least follow the process, even if they cannot be directly involved.

The collaborative phase lasts for 1 year following the completion of the competitive phase. The total process up to this point takes about 2 years.

2.2.6. Further Steps and Updates

The standardization process doesn't actually end with the publication of the agreed-upon standard. The standard and its parts are a living thing that continues to develop even after it has "grown up." This occurs by means of updates to the standard. These can be done in various ways, depending on the type of update. However, special emphasis is given to maintaining backward compatibility of the specification whenever this is a viable option, although it is not always possible. The latest addition of video coding technology to the visual part of MPEG-4 is commonly referred to as MPEG-4 AVC (Advanced Video Coding) or H.264 alternatively. This is an example of how the standard can be updated while sacrificing backward compatibility in favor of significant technical improvements. A similar process has taken place in the audio coding regime, where AAC (Advanced Audio Coding) has been added to MPEG-2 as a separate part, which is not backward compatible to formats such as MP3.

The options for updating the standard allow new technology to be added as it becomes available and as it shows significant performance gains over the existing specification.

Another need to change the standard originates from the detection of errors in the specification after its completion. There is a particular process to amend the standard or to correct errors in the specification that are detected after completion and publication of the documents. To this end, MPEG issues Corrigenda to include the fixes in an updated version of the standard. A Corrigendum is a particular type of document to describe fixes for technical problems that have been detected in an already finalized and published part of a standard.

MPEG always keeps its door open and is alert to monitor the progress made in the ongoing search for technology enhancements. To aid in this process, MPEG issues "Calls for Evidence," which allow interested parties to present new/improved technologies within the scope of work covered by MPEG's charter. The new technology needs to demonstrate significant benefits to trigger new standardization actions. Those actions may include issuing amendments to the existing standards or initiating an entirely new standard.

2.2.7. Standardization Work in the Collaborative Phase

The previously described process is not rigid. Some steps may be taken more than once and iterations are sometimes needed. This was the case during the MPEG-4 project. The time schedule, however, is always closely observed by MPEG, and the convener in particular. Although all technical decisions are made by consensus, the process keeps running at a fast pace, allowing MPEG to timely deliver technical solutions and a stable standard.

As stated above, two working tools play a major role in the collaborative development phase that follows the initial competitive phase: the Working Model and Core Experiments (CE). Both elements will be described in more detail below.

2.2.7.1. Working Model

In MPEG-1, the (video) working model was called Simulation Model (SM); in MPEG-2, the (video) working model was called Test Model (TM). Every once in a while, you may run across a statement that tests whether MPEG-2 video coding has been done on the basis of

TM-5. This refers to the MPEG-2 Test Model version 5, which was the final version of the test model during MPEG-2. This version has been implemented in software for test purposes. It is freely available as open-source software and is sometimes loosely referred to as the "Eckard coder," named after Stefan Eckard, a PhD student at Technische Universität München (TUM), who was responsible for a substantial part of the software implementation work.

In MPEG-4, the various working models were called "Verification Models" (VM). Besides the VMs for video, there were independent VMs for the audio, SNHC, and systems developments. A Verification Model consists of a textual description of the current version of the respective system, as well as a corresponding software implementation such that experiments performed by multiple independent parties will be based on a common framework. Hence, the experiments should produce essentially identical results. The VMs enable the checking of the relative performance benefits of different tools, as well as the measuring of performance improvements of selected tools.

The first MPEG-4 VMs were built after screening the submissions that came in answer to the call for proposals. The first VM (for each technical area) was not the best proposal but a combination of the best tools, independent of the proposal that they belonged to. Each VM includes an encoder (non-normative tools) as well as a corresponding decoder (normative tools). Even though the encoder will not be standardized, it is needed in order to create the common framework that allows the performing of adequate evaluation and comparison of coding tools. The goal is to continuously include in the VM the incremental improvements of the technology. After the first VMs were established, new tools were brought to MPEG-4 and were evaluated inside the VMs following a core experiment procedure. The VMs evolved through various versions as core experiments verified the inclusion of new techniques, or proved that included techniques should be substituted. At each version, only the best performing tools were part of the VM. If any part of a proposal was selected for inclusion, the proposer had to provide the corresponding source code for integration into the VM software under the conditions specified by MPEG.

2.2.7.2. Core Experiments

Now let's clarify the term "Core Experiment," which was mentioned above. The improvement of the VMs starts with a first set of core experiments defined at the conclusion of the evaluation of the proposals. The core experiments process allows for multiple, independent, directly comparable experiments to be performed to determine whether or not a proposed tool has merit. Proposed tools target the substitution of a tool in the VM or the direct inclusion in the VM to provide a new relevant functionality. Improvements and additions to the VMs are decided based on the results of core experiments. A core experiment has to be completely and uniquely defined, so that the results are unambiguous. In addition to the specification of the tool to be evaluated, a core experiment also specifies the conditions to be used, again so the results can be compared. A core experiment is proposed by one or more MPEG experts and is accepted by consensus, providing that two or more independent experts agree to perform the experiment.

It is important to realize that neither the Verification Models, nor any of the Core Experiments, will end up in the standard itself, as these are just working tools to ease the development process. Although it is not easy at this stage to tell how many core experiments have been performed in MPEG-4—dozens, for certain—it is safe to say that the group reached its goal by continuously improving upon the technology to be included in the standard.

2.2.8. Interoperability and Compliance

One of the major reasons to create standards is to achieve interoperability. This term appears in any discussion dealing with standards. Interoperability should be seen as closely related to the topic of compliance. Let's discuss both those concepts, since they are central to any MPEG standard and MPEG-4 in particular.

2.2.8.1. Interoperability

A standard specifies technology for use in devices. If the devices are implemented according to the standard specification, all devices, irrespective of the specific manufacturer, are working more or less in the same way, or at least in a specified way. This implies that devices originating from different manufacturers can be interchanged without interrupting the functionality offered by the device. If this sort of exchangeability is achieved, we call the individual devices "interoperable." Note that interoperability does not imply that the products of all manufacturers are identical. This would preclude competition, which is certainly not the intention of MPEG. However, there must be a minimum set of rules that every product or device is complying with, such that products originating from different companies can work together in a seamless fashion. That's what a user expects from his or her cell phone or TV set, or even from the paper he or she puts into a printer or copy machine; that is, irrespective of who has manufactured the phone, the user would like to be able to place or receive calls without even thinking of the type of telephone his or her communication partner on the other end is using.

In the context of this book, we talk about interoperability if the encoder device of company A produces bit streams such that the decoder for company B can decode those streams correctly. Decoding correctly means that the decoder for company B can create a reconstruction of the original media data that is practically identical to the reconstruction generated by the decoder of company A. Devices are truly interoperable if this scenario also works the other way round; i.e., decoder A can reproduce the media data that have been created by encoder B so that they are practically identical to the decoding of the same data by decoder B.

If there are only two parties involved, then this doesn't appear to be a significant challenge for either company A or company B. However, consider the real world for a second, where there are many solution providers offering their products in the marketplace. It is a challenge then to make sure that all decoders from all companies can decode each other's streams successfully. It is hardly possible that all companies can cooperate at a level to achieve a complete mutual testing. Imagine how difficult it might be if the companies are competitors.

As end users, we are used to buy cell phones, for example, from a wide range of companies. We expect that we can use any of those phones, which are labeled as implementing the GSM standard, to perform mobile communications in any GSM network. We don't care who is building the GSM network components used in the telephone infrastructure, nor do we care which company's cell phone our communication partner is using—and we shouldn't have to. This is what the standard is supposed to achieve—true interoperability, which does not come for free.

2.2.8.2. Compliance

Interoperability is achieved by requesting the devices to be compliant with the standard. But what does compliance mean and how is it achieved? First, recall that the standard only specifies the bit stream syntax and the decoder. Thus, we talk about compliant bit streams and compliant decoders. Strictly speaking, there is no such thing as a compliant encoder. However, we may use this term loosely if we agree that a compliant encoder is a device that is producing legal and thus compliant bit streams.

To make a bit stream compliant, the standard defines which syntactic elements are allowed to appear in a stream. For a decoder to be compliant, the standard defines how the decoder is supposed to act on the received bit stream of digital data offered to the input.

The standard specifies so-called "conformance points." Each conformance point consists of two ingredients: 1) the list of syntactic elements that are admissible in a stream; and 2) quantitative bounds on parameters like maximum permissible image size, frame rate, bit rate, and sampling rate or similar. Such conformance points are defined by the profiles and levels of specification, which we will discuss in more detail in a later chapter.

The decoder that is compliant with a given conformance point must be able to decode all compliant bit streams, i.e., all bit streams that stick to the specified syntax and the specified upper bounds of some quantitative parameters, such as maximum bit rate, maximum image size, and other parameters of that type. In other words, the decoder has to implement *all* decoding tools that the standard requests, and provide at least as much memory and processing power as necessary. The decoder can offer additional features and capabilities and provide more computing power or offer abundant memory without causing a problem. In other words, the decoder may be capable of doing more than the specification requires, but in no cases can it do less in order to be compliant. See Figure 2.3 for a graphic representation of this.

As mentioned before, the encoder is not explicitly addressed by the standard. However, the encoder is not allowed to produce bit streams that exceed the specified capabilities of a compliant decoder, but to this end the encoder need not incorporate all coding tools that are specified. In Figure 2.4, a scenario is depicted schematically in which the decoder fails to be compliant and the encoder fails to produce compliant bit streams.

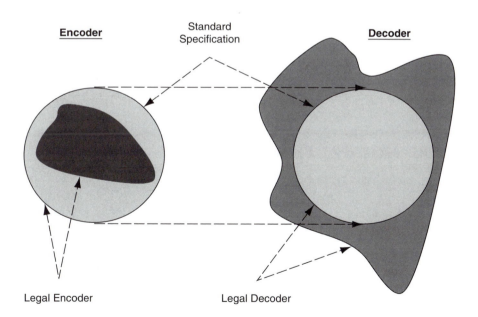

Figure 2.3 Concept of a compliant decoder and a matching encoder.

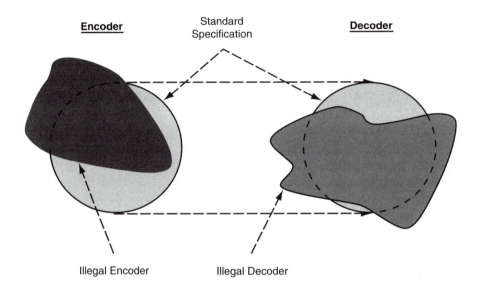

Figure 2.4 Violation of the concept of a compliance.

2.2.9. Examples of Successful Standards

Let us give you a few examples of successful standards that have shaped the technology scene and provided stable technology, helping to enable a sustained market growth and long-term business development.

2.2.9.1. NTSC/PAL Broadcast Television

NTSC and PAL are standards for analog color television predominantly in the U.S. and Europe, respectively. The NTSC standard was finalized and implemented in 1953, while PAL started in 1961 with black and white pictures and turned into a color TV standard by 1968. Both standards are still used today. There are billions of TV sets around the world—probably even more TV sets than telephones. Business has been good and competition fierce, while the technology has been kept transparent to the end users, in spite of technical improvements to the TV sets as well as the TV cameras and the sender infrastructure. If you happen to still own an operational NTSC TV set from the 1950s, it probably still produces good pictures today. Longevity and widespread use of the standard helped both to develop markets by bringing the cost for end consumers down, and to guarantee the longevity of the investment for the operators.

2.2.9.2. GSM—Mobile Cell-Phones

Telecommunications is a domain in which many standards were developed and deployed over a long period of time. The telecommunications services and markets would not have evolved without the existence of standards. In particular, consider the case of GSM—a European standard for mobile communications, which is used in most countries around the world. A user can take his GSM cell phone from Germany to Australia, and still be reachable at his regular phone number without having to know how it actually works. It is conceivable that the mobile communications market would not have lifted off the ground with this incredible speed and worldwide success without the existence of such a standard. Here are just a few additional facts to demonstrate the enormous success of the GSM standard:

- GSM has about 1 billion users worldwide.
- GSM can be used in 200 countries around the world. To offer some perspective, note that McDonald's is present in 100 countries, Coca Cola in 130 countries, and the United Nations in 180 countries.
- At its peak, the income for the EU by exporting GSM equipment throughout the world exceeded the revenues made by selling cars!

There are several factors that were responsible for this huge success of GSM, such as the technical quality of the standard, which was fostered by the joint willingness of all participating parties to come to an agreement (strong Memorandum of Understanding) through cooperation, and to standardize the result as an open specification. Also, the roll-out of GSM was not seriously slowed by patent issues. The existence of the GSM standard was the single most important reason for the explosion of the mobile communication market as we have experienced it throughout the last decade.

If you happen to still own a GSM cell phone of the first generation, you may notice that it still works flawlessly in today's system. The people responsible for the standard were very professional in formulating upgrade policies that guaranteed the backward compatibility of the latest systems with previous versions. This professionalism is responsible for the longevity of the GSM standard. This longevity in turn makes long-term investments in GSM infrastructure economically reasonable. Finally, there is no shortage of competition at the service and application level as well as on the manufacturer's side. All this competition helped to shape the market and to make mobile communication a compelling offering to the general public. In contrast to this, think of the situation when dealing with updates and upgrades in the PC world, or the evolution of streaming media in terms of market sizes and revenues. In both cases it can be recognized what a difference it makes to not have a commonly accepted standard, which provides longevity and broad market acceptance.

A standards story that makes worthwhile reading is the development of the DVB standard (Digital Video Broadcast) for building digital TV systems in Europe. A good starting point to learn more about the DVB project is the Web site www.dvb.org.

2.2.9.3. Paper Formats, ASCII, and Programming Languages

The existence of the DIN standard for document sizes, be it A formats or B formats, is yet another example of a successful standard. Based on the standardized document formats, it is easy to exchange documents, to build printers, copy machines, and so on. It is so omnipresent that we do not actively think about the benefits originating from such a standard.

Similar statements are true when it comes to the ASCII code or to the standardization of programming languages such as ANSI C to achieve portability of source code.

There are many more such examples of successful standards in our daily lives.

2.3. The MPEG Saga So Far

Before going further with the topic of MPEG-4, we would like to review the MPEG saga so far. As mentioned previously, there are other standardization organizations dealing with compression technology, most notably the ITU, which has a working group called the VCEG (Video Coding Experts Group). The official name of the group is ITU-T Study Group 16. There is both cooperation and competition between MPEG and the ITU when it comes to coding video. In this section, we will highlight the connections between the two groups regarding video coding. The ITU is more concerned with standards for communications applications. The main focus for the ITU has been on video conferencing or video telephony, whereas MPEG is more concerned with, but not confined to, consumer applications and consumer electronics.

2.3.1. Pre-MPEG Accomplishments

There have been standards for compression before the existence of MPEG. MPEG actually started in 1988. Before the first MPEG standard was completed, there was another very successful standard published—JPEG (Joint Photographic Experts Group), which specifies compression for still images. JPEG is also a standard issued by the ISO, by Working Group 1 of SC29. Think of JPEG as the older brother of the MPEG standards.

Besides the ISO, there are also a number of excellent standards in the field of audio-visual compression issued by the ITU. The ITU's video coding standards are typically named H.26x, where x stands for digits currently ranging from 1 up to 4. The first real video coding standard predating the first MPEG standard was the H.261 standard. This standard already comprised the fundamental concept of a motion-compensated hybrid video codec, which is the basis of all video coding standards to date. This basic concept has been improved over time by new standards and adapted to certain application domains to get better and better available compression. H.261 target bit rates for compressed video lie in the range between 64 kbit/s and 2Mbit/s. In fact, the standard is sometimes referred to as k×64, since the target bit rate steps are in multiples of 64 kbit/s. Interestingly enough, the development of this standard was largely driven by the vision of teleconferencing over ISDN channels. Note that ISDN channels can be bundled in steps of multiples of 64 kbit/s. The H.261 standard is still used today, largely due to the fact that it has simple encoding and a very simple decoding algorithm.

Various software implementations as open source code are available on the Web. The technology is conceptually simple and already includes many of the fundamental principles for coding video. H.261 was first published in 1990. The fact that the teleconferencing business did not really take off was another motivation for researchers around the world to find even better video and audio compression, as well as to enable the video telephony business.

2.3.2. MPEG-1: Coding for Digital Storage Media

The MPEG saga officially began with the development of the MPEG-1 standard, which is officially referred to as ISO/IEC 11192. MPEG-1 was designed with the target in mind of storing and retrieving video and audio on a compact disc (CD). The standardization effort was finished in November 1992, when MPEG-1 was approved. The speed of CD-ROM drives at that time was limited to a bit rate of about 1.5 Mbit/s. This is why MPEG-1 is usually only credited with supporting bit rates up to 1.5 Mbit/s for video and audio. However, note that MPEG-1 is not actually constrained to this bit rate, but can be used for higher bit rates and image sizes. For example, DirecTV started out with their direct satellite-based broadcasting service using MPEG-1 codecs for compressing standard TV resolution images. They later switched to MPEG-2, as soon as the new standard was finished and corresponding products were available. MPEG-1 audio coding has been employed to take care of compression affairs as part of the DAB (Digital Audio Broadcast) system, which is a terrestrial transmission system for delivering digital radio services as a replacement for conventional FM systems.

The Video CD (VCD) uses the MPEG-1 standard, which has turned out to be a success mainly in China, where the format is often used to distribute movie material. The distribution model didn't include a working royalty system and the recognition and protection of copyrights. However, in spite of this deficiency, decoder hardware manufacturers didn't complain about the business. MPEG-1 has also been used as a format for video clips on the Web in its early days. So far in China alone, more than 70 million Video CD players have been sold.

MP3 (MPEG-1 Audio Layer III) has turned into a buzz word to denote high-quality audio on the Web for downloading music, sharing music over peer-to-peer networks. It has changed forever the way people experience music. MP3 files are small enough to be downloaded from the Internet or stored on small mobile devices, while offering stereo audio of acceptable quality. In this regard, MP3 audio coding technology has created a new market and a new paradigm for content use. With peer-to-peer file-sharing systems such as Napster and Gnutella, it is clear that MP3 also has changed the world for people in the music business. This is a somewhat two-edged success story for the MPEG-1 standard. Whatever the business implications are, the technology opened up a completely new way of dealing with high-quality audio material, most notably with music on the Internet. The case of copyrights on music and illegal copying and distribution of music titles is still open and widely discussed. Once the rights of consumers and copyright holders find a point of equilibrium, the future of MP3-coded digital music will be ensured.

Personal computers using the Microsoft Windows operating system have a native MPEG-1 player installed. In addition, many compact and lightweight portable MPEG-1 cameras exist, which have become increasingly popular. MPEG-1 audio and video compression is still in use due to the wide availability of hardware and software solutions, and the familiarity of developers and users alike with the technology and products.

It is also still in use among video hobbyists and students for the distribution of downloaded movie material, much to the dismay of the major studios in Hollywood. The format is being used for creating low-budget CDs to store and play movies instead of using more costly DVDs. VCDs can be played back on most DVD players. SVCD is an extension of the VCD, which uses MPEG-2 codecs instead of MPEG-1. Other than the above examples, the MPEG-1 video system business appears to be on the decline.

All in all, MPEG-1 has been a substantial success, even though it has been used for a number of applications which were not necessarily envisioned at the time the standard was developed. It is actually not so unusual for technology to be developed for a certain application domain, only to find use in another field, as well.

2.3.3. MPEG-2/H.262 Coding for Digital TV and DVD

Two years after MPEG-1 was released, in November 1994, MPEG delivered its next stellar product, the MPEG-2 standard, which is officially referred to as ISO/IEC 13818. The driving force behind MPEG-2 and the main motivation was to offer compression technology to support the migration to digital television services. MPEG-2 is the result of cooperation between the ITU and MPEG. Thus, the same technology has been standardized by the ITU under the title H.262. The creation of an entire new industry—digital television—has been triggered by the arrival of this standard. DirecTV, Canal+, and Premiere, for instance, are all digital television broadcast services that are based on the MPEG-2 standard.

In Europe this industry is founded on the DVB (Digital Video Broadcasting) standard, which specifies complete transmission systems for television broadcast via satellite, cable, or terrestrial channels, to name a few examples. DVB prescribes the use of the entire MPEG-2 suite. Digital News Gathering Systems are based on MPEG-2 compression technology. Furthermore, HDTV services in the U.S. are built on the basis of MPEG-2 video compression in combination with Dolby Digital for coding the audio tracks with surround sound. This is the ATSC (Advanced Television Systems Committee) standard, which competes with its European counterpart, DVB. While ATSC is pushing for distribution of HDTV content in the United States, DVB has opted mainly for distribution of standard definition television services offering an increased number of channels to the end users. In Europe, HDTV was not expected to be a commercial success in the future. But it seems now that this opinion is beginning to change.

Today, the world has more than 80 million set-top boxes serving the cable, satellite, and terrestrial TV broadcasting businesses. In addition, the DVD has turned out to be the legitimate successor of the celebrated Audio Compact Disc. Not much more needs to be said about the overwhelming rise of the DVD, which is killing the business of analog VHS video formats even faster than the audio CD killed the vinyl records business for music. The DVD uses MPEG-2 video coding, and MPEG-2 audio, along with Dolby Digital (formerly AC-3) and MPEG-2 systems. MPEG-2 audio was chosen initially for the European markets and AC-3 was considered an option for the United States. However, by now most DVD players support both audio formats, whereas we haven't seen a DVD using MPEG-2 audio in a long time. But that only proves the point of the modularity of the MPEG standard. Application development can choose its favorite technology. Today, endless numbers of hardware and software DVD players are sold and distributed worldwide, now in excess of tens of millions of units, and we are still counting.

Finally, in 1996, MPEG received an Emmy for developing the MPEG-2 standard, as shown in Figure 2.5.

2.3.4. MPEG-4: Coding of Audio-Visual Objects

Discussions about MPEG-4 started as early as May 1991. It was not until September 1993 that MPEG-4 was formally on the agenda. The main task then was to identify the applications and requirements relevant for a video coding solution to be developed by MPEG, which was focusing on very low bit-rate coding. This scope of work was stated in the initial MPEG-4 project description. Parallel to the activities in MPEG, the near-term hybrid coding solution being developed within the ITU-T, the LBC (Low Bitrate Coding) group started producing the first results. This turned out later to be the ITU-T H.263 standard. The experts at that time were generally of the opinion that those results were close to the performance limit that could be obtained by block-based hybrid DCT/motion compensation video coding schemes.

At the MPEG meeting in Grimstad (Norway) in July 1994, MPEG decided on a major change in the direction of the MPEG-4 project. So far the main goal for MPEG-4 had been to offer coding technology with a significantly better compression ratio than could be achieved by conventional techniques such as MPEG-1 or MPEG-2. The majority of the video coding experts didn't believe that it was possible, within a time frame of 5 years, to bring about enough improvements in coding performance over the H.263 standard to justify a new standard that offered only "pure compression" at a mildly improved performance level. So MPEG started a soul-searching activity—an in-depth analysis of the audio-visual technology trends, based on the expected convergence of the seemingly separate worlds of TV/film/entertainment, computing, and telecommunications. Ultimately, MPEG decided to broaden the objectives of the emerging MPEG-4 coding standard, to support content-based access and manipulation of digital audio-visual objects.

Following this change of direction, the vision behind the MPEG-4 standard was explained through the eight "new or improved" functionalities described by MPEG. These eight functionalities came from an assessment of the functionalities that would be useful in future applications, but were not supported or not *well* supported by the available coding standards. The eight "new or improved" MPEG-4 functionalities were clustered in three classes according to the aforementioned three worlds, the convergence of which MPEG-4 wanted to address:

- Content-based interactivity: content-based multimedia data access tools, content-based manipulation and bit stream editing, hybrid natural and synthetic data coding, improved temporal random access. These concepts were driven by the vision of the anticipated advent of interactive television, combined with the interactive experience coming from computer games, together with the more traditional TV scenario.
- Compression: improved coding efficiency, coding of multiple concurrent data streams. This is actually where the heart of most MPEGers is beating—compression of multimedia data streams covering as many potential applications as possible. Compression has been, is, and will be a fundamental technology for the foreseeable future. However, few skeptics exist who believe that the age of compression will soon be over once we have ubiquitous broadband access—fiber to the brain, so to say. Concerning this latter point, please consult the chapter on business aspects, where we discuss this in more detail.
- Universal access: robustness in error-prone environments, content-based scalability. This set of functionalities originates from the desire of people in the information age to be increasingly mobile. Of course, part of this mobility implies that we have universal access not only to our e-mail box, but to all sorts of media information, such as video and audio.

The first MPEG-4 Call for Proposals was issued in July 1995. The call asked for relevant technology addressing the eight MPEG-4 functionalities. The technology received in response to the call was evaluated by means of subjective tests for complete algorithms and expert panels for single tools. In the case of algorithms proposed for the eight MPEG-4 functionalities, three functionalities (one per class) were selected as representative—content-based scalability, improved compression efficiency, and robustness in error-prone environments—and formal subjective tests were conducted for those. For the other five functionalities, proposals were evaluated by expert panels. The promising proposals were also subsequently thoroughly examined using the core experiments procedure.

The subjective tests for video coding were performed in November 1995 at the premises of Hughes Aircraft Co., in Los Angeles. The subjective tests for audio were performed in December 1995 at CCETT, Mitsubishi, NTT, and Sony. The video expert panel's evaluation was performed in October 1995 and January 1996.

After the evaluation of the submitted technology, choices were made and the collaborative phase started with the most promising tools. In the course of developing the standard, additional calls for proposals were issued, as not enough technology was available within MPEG to meet the requirements. For example, in March 1996, a call was issued for coding tools for synthetic data. When MPEG is missing technology to meet its objectives and good technology exists outside it, issuing calls is a typical approach taken by the MPEG group.

In January 1996, at the MPEG meeting in Munich, the first MPEG-4 Video Verification Model (VM) was defined. In this VM, a video scene was represented as a composition of "Video Object Planes" (VOPs), which is new-speak within MPEG-4 for the good old video frames. This first MPEG-4 Video VM used coding tools taken from the ITU-T H.263 standard. In addition to the H.263 tools, new shape-coding tools were selected to allow for the coding of arbitrarily shaped video objects. A similar process took place for audio.

Following this initial phase, several MPEG-4 VMs evolved by using the core experiments process, as described above. Finally, the various VMs were turned into the MPEG-4 specifications.

In December 1998 came the first serving of the new MPEG-4 standard, and additional helpings have been served since then. MPEG-4 is aimed at defining an audio-visual coding standard to address the converging needs of the communication, interactive, and broadcasting service models as well as the mixed-service models resulting from their technological convergence. The MPEG-4 standard opens new frontiers in the way users will play with, create, re-use, access, and consume audio-visual content. MPEG-4 is an object-based approach to the representation of audio-visual content. This object orientation is at the heart of MPEG-4 technology. Object-based representation means that a scene, which is to be viewed on a screen, is modeled as being composed of audio-visual objects. Those audio-visual objects can be natural and/or synthetic. The object-based concept allows for the user to interact with the content. How this interaction may work will be discussed to some extent in the next chapter. Also, let's defer the discussion of what natural and synthetic audio-visual objects actually are to the next chapter, where the technology will be discussed more deeply.

The most recent addition to the MPEG-4 standard is called AVC or H.264 (on the ITU side), where AVC stands for Advanced Video Coding. AVC is the result of the cooperation between video coding experts from MPEG and ITU. MPEG had concentrated on specifying video coding technology to enable new functionalities such as coding of arbitrarily shaped video objects. Companies and organizations outside of MPEG were claiming that if one drops the idea of shaped video objects that new coding tools were available that promised to give substantial gains in coding efficiency. It was furthermore claimed that MPEG-4 Visual was not competitive anymore with the latest developments. In the year 2000, this discussion about achievable improvements for video coding led MPEG to the decision to issue a "Call for Evidence." All interested parties around the world were invited to come to MPEG and to show-case their latest and hottest video coding technology. It was the goal for MPEG to learn if there has been progress in this field of research, which proves to be substantial enough to be considered for inclusion in future version of the standard.

The quality of the contributions in response to this call made MPEG issue a call for proposals for new video coding technology in order to improve coding efficiency for rectangular shaped video. All the submitted proposals were thoroughly tested for their merits. The proposal that was submitted from the video coding experts group (VCEG) of the ITU turned out to be the best proposal, clearly outperforming the best MPEG-4 codec at this point. The project name for the ITU's activities was H.26L, where the "L" stands for "Long Term." This way, H.26L was adopted as a starting solution for a new standardization campaign in MPEG-4. To this end a new group was formed which joined the forces of the MPEG experts and the ITU experts in the so-called Joint Video Team (JVT). The JVT then worked jointly to produce the two new

Figure 2.5 MPEG as a group won an Emmy in 1996 for the development of MPEG-2.

standards AVC for MPEG and H.264 for the ITU. Both new standards were finalized in 2004 and 2003, respectively. For more details and facts on the technical benefits of AVC, please consult the later chapters in this book.

Finally, let's have a bit of future talk to close the section. There is an ongoing discussion concerning the specification of the HD-DVD, which is the next-generation DVD offering high-definition video. Currently it looks as if HD-DVD will be using MPEG-4 AVC as the standard for compressing video. At least, this was the gist of arguments used at NAB'03, when the test results of the DVD forum were discussed. More recently, AVC is in fierce competition with Microsoft's VC-9 video coding technology, which is currently a candidate to become an SMPTE (Society of Motion Picture and Television Engineers) recommendation for coding High Definition TV signals. This was a hot topic during NAB 2004 in Las Vegas. Current thinking in the industry is to avoid any further delays and uncertainties and simply accept both formats in parallel. Whether this is a good approach will be seen in the future.

MPEG standards can be bought from ISO by sending an e-mail to sales@iso.ch. Notably, the complete software for MPEG-4 can be purchased on a CD-ROM for 56 Swiss Francs. It can also be downloaded for free from ISO's web site (www.iso.ch/ittf)—look under "publicly available standards" and then "14496-5" [1]. This software is free of copyright restrictions when used for implementing MPEG-4-compliant technology. (This does not mean that the software is free of patents, however.)

2.3.5. What Happened to the Number 3, 5, and 6?

This is a question that comes up regularly whenever someone is reviewing the MPEG numerology. Here is a short explanation of how the MPEG numbers came into being.

Originally, MPEG-3 contained technology for dealing with high-definition television (HDTV), which seemed a natural extension of the scope of MPEG-2 (standard television) at the time. As a contrast to targeting higher resolutions and higher bit rates and quality levels, MPEG-4 was set up in 1993 to target very low bit rate coding, supporting narrowband applications. Some time later, the experts realized that there was no need to specify MPEG-3, since MPEG-2 already comprised everything that was needed for supporting HDTV. So the MPEG-3 work item was dropped. However, MPEG-4 had already started, even though this project was re-oriented later. That's when MPEG ended up with the sequence of numbers, 1-2-4. The next time MPEG started the discussion about a new work item, the question of which number to assign it arose. For a very short time, the new work item was nick-named MPEG-8 within the MPEG group (actually, that was only for 3 days during the MPEG meeting in Chicago in 1996). At the end of the initial meeting on the subject, which went late into the night, the idea was born to call the new work item MPEG-7. The main reason was to not do the obvious. Sometimes even those serious coding experts get tired, hungry, grumpy, and even goofy. That's how the numbers 5 and 6 got dropped.

You can use MPEG numerology to disqualify the clueless, if a person starts to talk about MPEG-3, which actually doesn't exist. However, there is MP3, which is often mistaken for the missing number 3, since they sound alike. Actually, this is the abbreviation used to denote a part of the audio specification in MPEG-1 and MPEG-2, which comes in three different flavors, called "layers." MP3 refers to layer 3 in MPEG-1/-2 audio. Layer 2 of MPEG audio, which you may find referenced as MP2, is used for digital television applications and digital audio broadcast (DAB). Expressed in simple words, MP2 is less complex than MP3 and does not compress as well. MP1 is based on a low-cost and low-complexity version of the MUSICAM algorithm, which is the core of MP2. This low complexity constraint reduces the coding efficiency for this codec. At the time MP1 was specified it was considered to be applicable for low end applications. Today, decoding of MP3 coded material does not represent any technological challenge for even small devices. Therefore, MP1 doesn't play a role in the market place and can be considered obsolete.

2.3.6. MPEG-7 Interface for Content Description

Up to MPEG-4, the main work item for MPEG was to find and standardize better compression technology for all sorts of digital audio-visual data. With the next step, MPEG-7, the focus has slightly changed. MPEG-7 is not about compressing 1.75 times better than MPEG-4, but about the description of multimedia content. This is sometimes loosely referred to as 'the bits about the bits.'

MPEG-7, formally named "Multimedia Content Description Interface," is a standard for describing the multimedia content data that support some degree of interpretation of the information's meaning. The information and the associated meaning can be passed on to a device or some form of machine. There is a vast list of applications people had in mind when thinking about MPEG-7. One of the driving visions was to make multimedia content searchable, just as you search for text on the Internet. But instead of searching by keywords, the user can specify his query by images, colors, sound examples, or even melodies (query by humming). See the MPEG Web site for more substantial facts.

2.3.7. MPEG-21 Multimedia Framework

MPEG-21 also does not address compression of audio-visual data as its main topic. Its aim is to define a normative open framework that supports multimedia delivery and consumption for use by all players included in the food chain of commerce with digital media data. Such a framework will open the field to content creators, producers, distributors, and service providers, with equal opportunities to participate in an open market of media assets. The end user will also benefit from MPEG-21 by providing access to an almost unlimited supply of media content in a seamless, secure, and interoperable manner.

The goal of MPEG-21 can thus be rephrased to the following: defining the technology needed to support users to exchange, access, consume, trade, and otherwise manipulate digital items in an efficient, transparent, and interoperable way.

MPEG-21 identifies and defines the mechanisms and elements needed to support the multimedia delivery chain as well as the various business relationships among the market participants and their interactions.

2.4. Why Use MPEG-4?

With the rise of the Internet and the introduction of streaming media over IP networks as a delivery mechanism, it appeared as if the era of standards was over, as more and more competing proprietary software solutions swept the market. However, in spite of a fierce marketing war about who will conquer the streaming market with superior technology, none of the proponents succeeded in developing a profitable business model or establishing the expected new mass market. Hardly anybody was asking for a standards-based solution, since for once there was no appropriate standard in existence and the common belief was that there was no further need for standardized media coding technology. The concept of downloadable software decoders gave the impression that everybody could offer his or her own codec as long as there was an Internet connection to download the software whenever needed.

Throughout the last decade, all those proprietary technologies or industry specifications were devised to address the range of applications of concern to one company or industry.

In contrast to this trend, the MPEG-4 technology has been developed, with wide participation of all industries involved, with the goal of creating a level playground for technology convergence to occur.

MPEG has a track record of high-performance and timely standards serving multiple industries, guaranteed by the efforts put forth by participating industries. The industry has invested a significant amount of money, time, and effort in the development of the MPEG-4 standard. MPEG-4 enables us to choose from a treasure trove of mature technology to either push existing media businesses to new revenue streams or to create new business opportunities based on entirely new user experiences originating from completely new applications. This process will continue to shape the standard by either defining new profiles based on existing tools or by picking up and adopting new technologies as they reach a certain level of maturity, to offer solutions to new requirements and visions.

Development and roll-out can start today, using very simple profiles (tool sets) and can be made to grow compatibly, and using more sophisticated profiles when technology enables them and the market so demands. There is no need to wait for the next holy grail.

There is an additional reason why MPEG-4 is ready to go and can be exploited by anybody: It is possible to download the reference software from the ISO Web site. ISO gives MPEG-4 users free license to the software and its modifications for use in products claiming conformance to MPEG-4.

2.5. Criticizing MPEG-4

When reading marketing brochures or articles about MPEG-4, the reader will sometimes notice a negative pitch to the story. The authors may be criticizing MPEG-4 for specifying a lot of technology that nobody is using or needing today. Here are a few words to try to set this straight.

Predicting the future is hard to do in the business world, unless your name is Dilbert. Consult Scott Adam's book [4] to pick up some useful techniques for safely predicting the future. It has been suggested that MPEG standardization is trying to anticipate the need for standardized technology in order to have a standard readily available at the time the need actually arises. This approach naturally leads to situations in which sometimes the standard is right and sometimes it is wrong. When the standard goes in a wrong direction, it may lead to dead technology. As long as the standard contains valuable technology, there is a good reason to use it. The standard is trying to satisfy the needs of many industries and many companies. It is natural that in hindsight one can detect technologies that nobody seems to need or want.

MPEG-2 already has dead parts. As MPEG-4 is much bigger than MPEG-2, one may expect a much bigger pile of dead, i.e., unused technology. The standard is worthwhile if some essential parts turn out to be successful and if a large number of applications have a choice of picking an appropriate standard.

The idea of interactive television, one of the inspirations for the development of MPEG-4, has not caught on to date. Neither has Video Telephony, which is an application idea that for decades has been serving as a major inspiration and motivation for developing a whole sequence of video coding standards such as the H.26x series. Video telephony has evolved in the past 15 years from an almost zero million dollar business to an almost zero billion dollar business.

Currently, we can see that businesses are concentrating on some essential parts of MPEG-4, i.e., video and audio coding for television or similar services. The portfolio of technology for interactive services or fancier applications, including true multimedia (where multi means more than two media types), is still waiting for its prime time. All this is not to diminish the leading role that MPEG takes in setting the pace for multimedia compression technology and standards.

2.6. Bibliography

Leonardo Chiariglione. Communication Standards: Götterdämmerung? in *Multimedia Systems, Standards and Networks*, A. Puri, T. Chen (Eds.). Marcel Dekker, Inc., 2000, pp. 1–22.

B. G. Haskell, A. Puri, A. N. Netravalli. Digital Video: An Introduction to MPEG-2. in *Digital Multimedia Standards Series*, Chapman and Hall, New York, 1997.

Rob Koenen. MPEG-4. Multimedia for our Time. IEEE Spectrum. Volume 36 Number 2, February 1999.

J. L. Mitchell, W. B. Pennebaker, C. E. Fogg, and D. J. LeGall. MPEG Video Compression Standard. in *Digital Multimedia Standards Series*, Chapman & Hall, New York, 1997.

MPEG Industry Forum. www.mpegif.org

2.7. References

[1] ISO Web site. www.iso.ch
[2] William Sweet. Chirariglione and the birth of MPEG. IEEE Spectrum. Volume 34 Number 9, September 1997.
[3] MPEG Web site. www.chiariglione.org/mpeg
[4] Scott Adams. *The Dilbert Future*. United Feature Syndicate, 1997.

CHAPTER 3
The Technology in the Standard

In this chapter, we provide an overview of the technology that has finally been standardized in MPEG-4. Let's start with a description of the underlying trends that have initiated and shaped the technical content of the standard. These trends have induced a number of new application scenarios and service proposals dictating technical requirements that were subsequently transformed into an overall technical framework for MPEG-4. We will discuss the resulting overall architecture on a conceptual level to highlight how it is fundamentally different from existing coding standards in terms of the basic approach. Subsequently, we will give a comprehensive description of the individual technical constituents of MPEG-4. Emphasis will be put on the application and the benefit of the individual technological item. For a more detailed exposition of the technology, such as what might be requested by a developer or a frantic technology aficionado, we recommend you pick up one of the more technically oriented books on MPEG-4, a list of which is given in the reference list for this chapter. Finally, we will comment on few points where MPEG has been criticized.

3.1. The Trends Behind MPEG-4

Throughout the 1990s, there were a few general technological trends that had a strong influence on the MPEG-4 standardization. Knowledge of these trends is essential to gain an understanding of why MPEG-4 has evolved into the standard as it is known today. In particular, one must know about these trends in order to evaluate the content of the various comments on MPEG-4, either critical or positive, which have been published in articles and uttered in talks and presentations.

3.1.1. Better Compression for Audio-Visual Data

Besides all sorts of trends that were shaping the course of MPEG-4, perhaps the most common request was to devise coding technology for audio and video that provides significantly improved compression performance than previously known standards or products. There appears to be a certain rate (once a year?) at which startup companies around the world are issuing breaking news, such as that a new algorithm has been found by some formerly unknown genius, which can compress video 100 times better than all previously known technologies. The news is spread across the business sections of magazines and newspapers. But ultimately, most of those breakthroughs turn out to be not so breathtaking after all. The point is how much publicity a bold enough statement in this direction is likely to get. This is an indication of the yet unquenched thirst for better compression and the enormous business expectations that arise from having access to better compression. And it's not just the startups; the established companies also are beating the drum of improved compression

As we will discuss in a later chapter, being able to pack digital media data more tightly is a fundamental capability that fuels a wide range of applications. A high level of compression provides significant cost savings and enables applications that would have been impossible before the compression technology was available. Take the impact that MP3 as a compressed audio file format had on the music business, since the advent of being able to download music over the Internet. The effect of increasing compression and increasing bandwidth is multiplying, strongly influencing the sheer number of new applications made possible by those technologies.

3.1.2. Object-Based Video Coding

For once, researchers in the field of video coding were intrigued by the idea of object-oriented video coding. This new approach promised to achieve better coding performance for video and image by segmenting video frames and images into meaningful objects, coding the individual objects more efficiently by overcoming the limitations of the more traditional approach of cutting an image into generic blocks of 8-by-8 pixels and coding those blocks. The video coding community had been attempting to overcome the limitations inherent in the more conventional approach by segmenting video frames and images generically into little square blocks and treating these blocks as the basic entity for coding. This traditional block-based approach had been employed in all the previous video and image coding standards, starting from H.261 all the way to MPEG-2 and also including JPEG. In contrast to the old block-based coding scheme, the new approach allowed for individual video objects that have an arbitrary shape, like the image you see when peeking through a key hole. In the decoding process, the video objects are decoded separately and glued back together to recreate the original video frames and images; that is, the scene shown in the image or video is recreated by composing the individual video objects to form the images and frames of the final presentation.

One of the more challenging research topics in this context is to actually find the meaningful objects in a video clip by means of segmentation. The segmentation problem has been and still is an active field of research. MPEG will not base a standard on technology that is not mature enough for prime-time applications. Since MPEG is not specifying the encoder, but only the decoder, solving the segmentation problem is of no major concern to MPEG. If in the coming years an ingenious researcher finds a smart algorithm with which to do video segmentation, i.e., to find the meaningful objects in a video automatically, there will already be a coding standard that can be used for building new products and services for transporting those objects to the consumers. In the meantime, it is possible to generate arbitrarily shaped video objects by means of blue-screen (or green-screen) production in the studios. As for the future of object-based video coding, the consumer's decoder may already be prepared to digest those new object-based applications.

3.1.3. Natural and Synthetic Video

Visual media objects can be captured by conventional recording devices such as an analog or digital camera or other similar gear producing digital video signals or images in terms of waveforms or pixels. This type of material is denoted by the term "natural" video or images. Besides using cameras to shoot a movie or to take a picture, computers are increasingly being used to create visual media objects. This includes the computer-based creation of entire animated movies and images using the latest computer graphics technology. The extension of the traditional concept of pixel-based videos and images, which are captured by cameras to more general visual information as conveyed by computer generated images and animations is the reason why the term video that was used in MPEG-1 and 2 and other traditional standards has been replaced by the term "visual" in MPEG-4. In other words, traditional pixel-based video is merely one specific type of visual media object along with other types of synthetic visual objects, the other alternatives being discussed in more detail in the coming sections.

3.1.4. Natural and Synthetic Audio

A similar computer-based approach is taken for creating synthesized or computer-generated audio signals for music, as well as for speech. This is a way of producing audio that is comparable to taking a microphone to record music or speech. Computer-generated audio objects are referred to as "synthetic" audio. A similar situation to video also holds for the coding of digital audio information. Using a general audio codec like MP3 for the compression of speech signals is overkill. Being able to code different types of audio information with the appropriate codecs has clear benefits in terms of added functionality and improved coding performance. In the music recording business, it is commonplace to use synthetically generated sounds to create audio content. Samplers and synthesizers are standard tools in every music recording studio. This is further exemplified by the extensive use of MIDI, which stands for Musical Instruments Digital Interface. MIDI and synthesizers constitute basic ingredients of a more general framework that is concerned with the production of music using synthesizing tools.

3.1.5. Mixed Media

Yet another trend came about from the increasing use of mixed media presentation, which consists of different media types being combined to form an entire presentation. The mix may include video and audio along with graphics and animation, as well as text overlays using naturally captured imagery as well as synthetically generated images and sound. A good example of a mixed media presentation can be seen daily when watching Bloomberg Television or CNN, where stock tickers are scrolling across the screen, video clips are shown, and other information is inserted.

In traditional TV broadcasting today, there is already a heavy use of mixed media presentations in the form of graphical inserts, for example, which are overlaid on top of the video material. One particular aspect of this concept deserves a few more words here. In the situation described before, the composition of text and graphics together with video happens on the transmitter side. That is, the content is produced in the studio and the final composition of the presentation is completed at the TV station. The presentation to be broadcast is then sent to the transmitter, which comprises an MPEG-2 video and audio encoder for the compression and subsequent play-out of the TV broadcast.

Many people have made the observation that the visual quality of graphics and text overlays in digital TV broadcasts suffers quite severely from compression that uses image and video coding tools such as JPEG or MPEG-2 codecs. In order to satisfy the expectations of TV broadcast quality, a higher data rate is needed for the video compression task to achieve a faithful representation of text and graphics in a digital TV feed. A better and more economical solution can be achieved if the text and graphics elements are treated as separate media objects. Those text and graphics elements can be compressed with a specialized encoder optimized to handle this particular type of data. The compressed data representing the text and graphics portion of the media are transmitted as a separate data stream to the decoder. The decoder will decode those separate streams to reconstruct the visual appearance of the text and graphics element, which will then be glued on top of the decoded video. In contrast to the traditional way, where the material is generated and finalized at the TV station, this compositing process takes place in the receiving device, that is, in the set-top box or TV set. This approach produces better visual quality for the entire presentation because the quality of graphics and text is not suffering from being compressed by a video codec, while the total amount of bits to be transmitted is substantially reduced.

An ever increasing amount of media content consists of a mixture of various types of natural and synthetic media objects. From its use in the movie production business, we are quite acquainted with mixing graphics elements and more traditional film footage. This is a trend that everyone who goes to the movies can experience and witness, and which will gradually move down the media content food chain, finally ending up at the graphics pipeline of the user's display device. Providing standardized ways to represent this mix in terms of units of audio, visual, or audio-visual content, called "media objects," was considered by MPEG to fit those needs and also reinforce the new approaches that researchers were working on.

Mixing naturally recorded audio signals with synthesized sounds is a standard way of doing things in the music production business. Considering audio content as being composed of various natural and synthetic audio objects also makes possible the compression of individual constituents and the rendering of the final audio scene after decoding the audio objects. This is similar to the example discussed earlier for handling text and graphics overlay in the TV broadcast feed, the result being to achieve better audio quality using smaller amounts of data.

3.1.6. Interaction With Multimedia Content

The notion of interactive television has been a topic of discussion for quite some time, originating from the world of interactive computer games. This type of interactivity spurred the desire to manipulate video content similar to the way graphics images can be created and manipulated via the computer. This functionality is now typically referred to as content-based interactivity. Within MPEG-4, the term "content-based interactivity" has been coined, with far-reaching implications giving rise to a number of interesting applications. The most direct interactive application is one that supports the clicking on video objects in a presentation to initiate actions such as changing channels, which enables the user to shop or to access additional information about the object being clicked on. As an example of such additional data, consider a user who desires more information about a running back in a televised football game. By clicking on the player, a window pops up, displaying additional information about the player such as career yards in rushing, and his college and previous teams. The concept of interactive television has been heavily debated, and a whole collection of innovative ideas for such services are continuously kicked around.

3.1.7. Universal Access and Mobile Communications

As modern society becomes increasingly mobile, there is more and more of a demand to have universal access to data in general, and media data in particular. By universal access, we mean the capability to access media content almost anywhere on a wide range of mobile or stationary playback devices, via heterogeneous network connections including the Internet and mobile and wireless channels.

3.1.7.1. Error Robustness

The vision of universal access necessitates the development of flexible schemes for representation of media data. But flexibility is not enough. If one thinks of the typical transmission characteristics associated with wireless transmission channels, it becomes clear that a data compression scheme must be rugged enough to protect against transmission errors. Even though channel coding techniques (error-correcting codes) that are part of the radio link can fix a substantial amount of transmission errors (that is, bit errors), a significant number of bit errors slip though undetected and uncorrected. The compression scheme that receives a compromised bit stream cannot decode the stream flawlessly and recreate the audio-visual presentation without impairments. However, the structure for representing the media objects and their composition can be designed in a way that the perceptible impairments are kept at a minimum, and the system can recover from corrupted data in a very short time frame. In other words, it is certainly not acceptable for a TV service to have the screen or parts of the screen go black for 30 seconds just because there have been some bit errors in the stream. However, if the failure to display the correct images and sound lasts for a split second and if the presentation is fine after that, then the service will be perceived as acceptable to consumers. Figure 3.1 shows an example of the difference error resilience tools can make in terms of visual appearance in case the bit stream carries transmission errors.

3.1.7.2. Scalability

The notion of scalability serves as another ingredient to support universal access. Some types of scalability have already been addressed in the course of MPEG-2, where the plan was to code and broadcast a high-definition TV signal in such a way that a standard-definition TV receiver can extract a standard-definition TV signal, while a high-definition receiver can utilize the entire

No Error Resilience   With Error Resilience

Figure 3.1 The effect of error resilience for digital video data [Source: Iraj Sodagar, Packet Video].

signal to produce higher quality images. This is referred to as spatial scalability (see Figure 3.2).

In addition to spatial scalability, there is the concept of SNR scalability (see Figure 3.3) in which the audio-visual signal is compressed in such a way that the receiver can decode parts of the stream in order to render images and sound at a quality level that varies with the transmission conditions. That is, if the transmission quality is bad, less bits of the presentation get delivered to the receiver. Instead of stopping, the receiver continues to play, though the quality is reduced. This type of operation is now fairly common when looking at videos that are streamed over the Internet. The abbreviation SNR stands for Signal-to-Noise Ratio and is a measure of the amount of noise or distortion in the signal in comparison to the undistorted signal. We will discuss such measures of quality in more detail in a later chapter.

In the context of MPEG-4, there has been discussion about a new form of scalability that is object- or content-based. This type of scalability is about adapting the content to the transmission channel and device capabilities by selecting the media elements or media objects that constitute the content deemed to be more important or more interesting to the user, and dropping the other

Increasing Bit Rate

Figure 3.2 Spatial scalability [Source: Touradj Ebrahimi, EPFL].

Increasing Bit Rate

Figure 3.3 SNR scalability [Source: Touradj Ebrahimi, EPFL].

elements from being transmitted altogether. This kind of scalability requires the object-based coding approach.

3.1.8. Convergence—Computers, Television, Telecommunications

The trends that fueled the MPEG-4 standardization process are based on concepts and notions that originated from three different industries and application domains—computers, television, and telecommunications. In the 1990s, this was commonly referred to as the convergence phenomenon. While the business models in these three domains may remain separate for a little longer, they already share much of their underlying technology. The convergence phenomenon can be understood as the combination of different technological approaches, which have evolved separately in the three domains and are now about to be fused to build a new technological basis for all three. Following this paragraph, you will find a partial list of concepts that the respective domains brought to the table, which are now combined in the MPEG-4 standard.

- *Computer Industry:* Computer games, Internet, interactivity, best-effort, download, software, IP protocols

- *Television Industry:* Entertainment, movies and television, consumer electronics, (Post-) production studios, broadcasting, satellite, terrestrial, cable, guaranteed QoS (quality of service), hardware
- *Telecommunications Industry:* Communications, wireless channels, bi-directional communication, back-channel, guaranteed QoS, universal access, mobility, ISDN, DSL, switched-circuit networks

3.2. Roles

The concepts underlying MPEG-4 also take into account the different roles one finds in the food chain of the digital media business—content authors, network service providers, and consumers. This section summarizes the various roles and their contribution to MPEG-4.

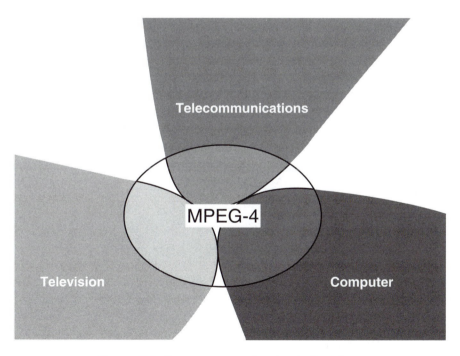

Figure 3.4 Convergence of major industries.

3.2.1. Content Authors

For content authors, it is commercially valuable to produce content that can be used more than once, i.e., it can be distributed several times via different digital transmission channels and consumed by end users on a wide range of different display devices ranging from set-top boxes via PCs all the way to mobile receivers. To this end, the digital content requires a representation that offers a level of flexibility that is not yet available today. Digital television, animated graphics, World Wide Web (WWW) pages and their extensions all use individual and non-interoperable technologies. The list of target display devices includes TV sets, computers, laptops, and portable media players, to name just a few alternatives. The content needs to be adapted specifically for each of these distribution channels and display devices. New exploitation channels, such as multimedia messaging services via wireless channels aiming at cell phones and PDAs, need yet another round of adaptation. Media produced for a traditional TV broadcast cannot be displayed on a handheld device without an appropriate modification or re-formatting of the content. The mobile transmission channel does not offer sufficient bandwidth to carry the broadband TV broadcast and, moreover, the mobile playback device is much too feeble in terms of its memory size and computational capabilities to render the full screen images in real time. Rendering low-resolution content on a TV screen is technically less challenging, but very disappointing from the user's perspective and thus unsatisfactory.

Authors who are searching for ways to exploit their creations in a cross-media approach need to create or re-create their content multiple times to adapt it for each of the various channels and playback devices. For such a cross-media approach, it is clearly beneficial for the content to be represented in a very flexible way that allows for an easy adaptation and conversion so the content will match the capabilities of the delivery mechanisms (transmission channels) and the playback device. If the content can be published in one generic format from which almost any type of exploitation scheme can be fed, then content management is made easier and longevity and cross-media exploitation of the content is also feasible. Furthermore, the longevity of a particular digital representation is also an important feature in order to justify the investment in creating a pool of digital media.

3.2.2. Network or Service Providers

The previous arguments also apply to the group of network service providers, where the need to maintain and manage a wide selection of differently formatted versions of a particular media content is a financial and organizational burden. Alternative to this, it is beneficial for the service provider to store and process only one generic source for the content, which can be sent out via its network after adapting the material appropriately for the delivery. If the content format allows for transparent hinting information to indicate which part of the media is more important for the presentation and which Quality of Service (QoS) parameters it requires, then this information can be interpreted and translated into the appropriate native signaling messages for each of the networks. Signaling of the desired media QoS end-to-end enables transport optimization in heterogeneous networks; the transmission mechanisms can be exploited and configured to keep the cost at a reasonable level for a certain type of service offering. If there are bits carrying media services, then they need to be transmitted and delivered to the customer. The transmission requires bandwidth, which costs money. Bringing more programs to the customers and delivering a better product in terms of image and audio quality at a given bandwidth, and hence for fixed costs, represent major objectives for service providers that have a strong influence on their profitability. Therefore, developing new compression technology to further improve coding efficiency or to increase the capabilities for compressing any type of media data is of prime importance to network service providers.

3.2.3. End Users—Consumers

It is not so hard to make a user or consumer of multimedia content happy, but the difficulty of turning him or her into a paying customer varies largely depending on the particular market segment. The value network for TV consumers is well known and has been handled for quite some time now. Let's have a look at what a media consumer may want in the current setting of the information age, bringing data networks and mobile communication infrastructure into multimedia delivery channels.

The role for the user is relatively easy to describe. Users appreciate a problem-free reception and the convenient, universal access to interesting and attractive media content that comes in high quality in combination with a wide range of choices. The appropriateness of the price tag that comes with consuming multimedia content is perceived differently, depending on the scenario. While many consumers, in particular the infamous couch potatoes, have no problem spending the money to have access to cable TV, for example, in the United States, it has been more difficult to establish the notion of paying for content when it comes to multimedia over the Internet. This aspect of different perceptions of value is beyond the scope of this book and may be covered elsewhere.

MPEG-4 brings brighter images and pictures to consumers, crystal-clear multi-channel sound, computer graphics and animations, or a mix of all these plus an entirely new interactive experience; that is, MPEG-4 enables the implementation of functionalities to achieve higher levels of interaction with the content. The quality and the amount of interaction offered to the user are designed by the author. This may range from no interaction at all up to full interaction, comparable to the experience of playing computer games. Even some new and innovative ways of interaction are anticipated and supported by MPEG-4. It also brings multimedia to new networks, including those employing relatively low bit rates, and mobile networks as well. For the end user, the type of underlying transport mechanism is not a concern since it is expected to be transparent. MPEG-4 allows the deployment of intelligent networks that include the capability to adapt the content to the target device in a smart way, which may be completely transparent to the end user. This means that a broadcast can be received simultaneously on totally different devices delivered via completely heterogeneous networks.

It is the task of content authors to design multimedia content that is considered to be interesting and attractive. In fact, it needs to be attractive enough to make people want to pay for it. In that sense, attractive content may include new functionalities and features, such as interactivity or various levels of personalization. It is the task of technologists to provide the tools, technologies, and products to create, format, and publish such content. Furthermore, the products in the hands of a consumer need make the access to and use of the potentially interactive and personalized content easy and seamless, while offering a premium product, in terms of the experienced visual and audio quality. However, there may be new applications that can get away with providing an inferior audio and video quality as long as the offered additional functionality is interesting. It is generally held that the overall service or product quality must offer added value to the end user in order to convince him to pay for the consumed content. In this sense, user satisfaction and added value are the ingredients that make new business models in the media world feasible and profitable. Better quality is one way of achieving added value, but there is certainly a limit for quality beyond which it doesn't make economic sense to push the envelope. Creating an entirely new user experience is a feasible alternative, at least from a technical point of view.

Improved convenience, ease of use, and attractive pricing are aspects that can be supported by standardized technology. In summary, for all those parties involved—that is, for authors, service providers, and consumers—MPEG-4 seeks to create a widely acceptable and open technological framework in order to avoid the existence of a multitude of proprietary, non-interworking formats and players. This also has a number of business-related benefits to reduce the risk of investing in technology. This is discussed in more detail in the chapter on business aspects of MPEG-4.

3.3. The Architecture of an MPEG-4 Terminal

As discussed in the previous section, the three major trends—audio-visual media over all networks to all displays, accounting for increased mobility of users, and a growing level of interactivity—have driven, and still drive, the development of the MPEG-4 standard. To address these identified trends in an integrated and comprehensive way, a media coding standard is needed that includes the means to efficiently represent all sorts of different media data types. The supported bit rates and the required visual quality levels necessitate a representation of visual data starting from very low bit rates and low video resolutions up to very high video quality and resolutions, to cover the range of videos to be watched on hand-held devices all the way to enjoying movies in a digital cinema. Music and speech data need to be represented for a very wide bit-rate range as well, supporting everything from transparent music (also known as CD-quality) down to very low bit rates for intelligible speech, the sound of which evokes memories of speaking robots in science fiction movies. In addition, the standard includes tools to deal with 3-D graphical objects and images as well as other specific visual objects such as human faces and bodies and their animation.

3.3.1. Coded Representation of Media Objects

The overall architecture of a complete MPEG-4 terminal is depicted in Figure 3.5. In the context of MPEG-4, audio-visual scenes are

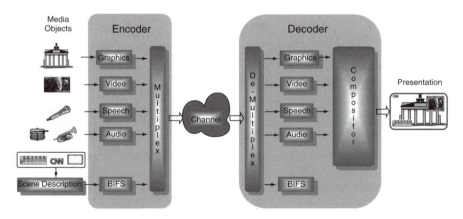

Figure 3.5 Overall architecture of MPEG-4.

considered to consist of a collection of several audio-visual objects, natural as well as synthetic, which are composited to form the final presentation. The objects are temporally and spatially placed in the scene. The individual audio-visual objects have a coded representation, where the underlying best possible coding approach is selected for the given object type. This approach achieves the best possible compression performance for the individual media objects.

MPEG-4 standardizes the coded representation for a number of such primitive media objects. In addition to more traditional audio-visual media objects, MPEG-4 also defines the coded representation of objects such as text and graphics, talking synthetic heads, and associated text used to synthesize the speech and animate the head, as well as synthetic sound.

A media object in its coded form consists of descriptive data elements that allow the handling of the object in an audio-visual scene. The object may also consist of associated streaming data. It is important to note that in its coded form, each media object can be represented independent of its surroundings or background.

The coded representation of media objects is as efficient as possible in terms of the number of bits needed, while taking into account further desired functionalities. Examples of such further functionalities are error robustness, easy extraction and editing of an object, or having an object available in a scalable form.

The various objects in the scene are represented independently, allowing independent access to the objects in order to enable their manipulation and re-use in a different context. Interaction and hyperlinking capabilities can be assigned to individual objects, as well as the capabilities to manage and protect intellectual property on audio-visual content and algorithms, such that only authorized users have access. The representation format is independent from the actual delivery media, so as to transparently cross the borders of different delivery environments. In other words, the principles for the coded representation of media objects are independent to the way the content is delivered. Prominent choices for the transmission media are satellite transmission, cable, terrestrial broadcast, IP networks (Internet), mobile communications, ISDN, WLAN, and the like.

3.3.2. Composition of Media Objects

Besides the data for the individual objects, which determine the players in a scene, additional information on how those objects are supposed to be composed is needed to render the final presentation. The composition of media objects (objects and frames) illustrates the way in which an audio-visual scene in MPEG-4 is made up of individual objects. The composition information forms a separate data entity, which must be created, compressed, and transmitted to the receiver. The receiver gets the data streams carrying the coded data for all the objects and for the composition information and builds the scene on the screen through a rendering process. Figure 3.6 shows a very simple example of a presentation that is composed of two video objects, a background image and a foreground object.

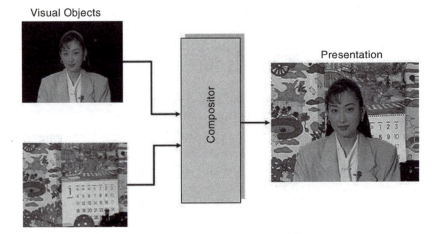

Figure 3.6 Composition of video objects to form a presentation.

The composition information is structured in a hierarchical fashion, which allows media objects to be constructed of smaller media objects in a recursive way. The hierarchical structure can be best depicted graphically as a tree. The leaves of the tree represent primitive media objects, such as a still image (for the fixed background in the scene), arbitrarily shaped video objects (e.g., showing a talking person without the background), and audio objects (e.g., for the voice associated with the person in the video object) or primitive graphical objects such as rectangles, square, or circles. While primitive media objects correspond to leaves in the descriptive tree, compound media objects encompass entire sub-trees. A sub-tree is a part of a tree structure that itself exhibits the properties of a tree. (See Figures 3.7 and 3.8.)

The scene description builds on several concepts from the Virtual Reality Modeling Language (VRML) in terms of both its structure and the functionality of object composition nodes, and extends it to fully enable the aforementioned features.

Figure 3.7 A scene composed of different media objects [Source: Carstin Herpel, Thomson Multimedia].

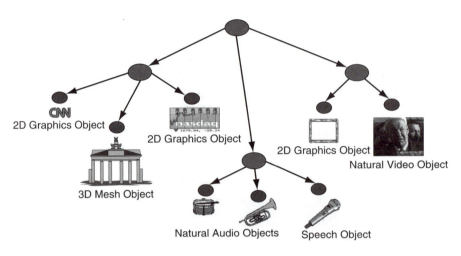

2D Graphics Object

2D Graphics Object

2D Graphics Object

Natural Video Object

3D Mesh Object

Natural Audio Objects   Speech Object

Figure 3.8 A graph representation for the scene in Figure 3.7 with the primitive media objects at the leaves of the scene tree. A very readable article on scene graphs can be found at [Source: A. E. Walsh, Dr. Dobb's Journal].

3.4. MPEG-4 Comes in Several Parts

The standard is divided into several parts. Each part covers a certain aspect of the whole specification. Figure 3.9 offers an overview of where the major technical parts of the MPEG-4 standard are located.

All parts have been designed and tested to work when taken together as components of a system. However, it is also possible to select individual parts of the specification in combination with other technologies for building products and systems. While the various MPEG-4 parts are rather independent and thus can be used by themselves, as well as combined with proprietary technologies, they were developed so that the maximum benefit results when they are used together.

3.4.1. ISO/IEC 14496-1—Systems

The systems portion of MPEG-4 (Part 1) contains the specification for the composition information for the scene, commonly referred

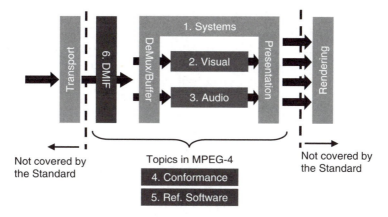

Figure 3.9 Overview of the parts of the MPEG-4 standard and their functional locations in a standard decoder.

to as the scene description. Part 1 also deals with multiplexing multiple data streams into one serial data stream carrying all necessary data for an audio-visual presentation. Furthermore, Part 1 also handles the synchronization of multiple data streams; for example, the video and the audio streams for a clip need to be aligned in time to achieve lip sync. The same applies in a multi-user scenario such as videoconferencing or multi-player gaming if there are multiple data streams coming in that have an influence on the actual look of an audio-visual presentation.

Buffer management is yet another topic, which comprises the task of managing the amount of data coming into a receiver device and the storage and handling of those streams in terms of available and necessary memory space. Running out of memory will lead to data loss and interrupted service. For content owners, it has become increasingly important to keep control over the media data and their usage. MPEG-4 Part 1 specifies tools for the management and the protection of intellectual property rights.

3.4.1.1. Object Composition—Scene Description

MPEG-4 Systems (or Part 1) provides the object composition technology referred to above. This is based on VRML but provides extensions to it by allowing the inclusion of streamed audio and video, natural objects, generalized URL, and composition updates. As VRML is a text-based language, it is easy to read and understand. However, the resulting amount of data for a complex 3D-graphics world can be overwhelming for streaming and online services. For this reason, MPEG has worked on a modification of VRML to achieve a binary version with very effective compression for VRML-type information. This modified version is called BIFS, which stands for Binary Format for Scene Description, and is a highly compressed format taking 10 to 15 times less data then a corresponding VRML-based scene description. The compression of scene description data, the capability to stream the scene descriptions and modify them dynamically, along with the addition of features that are useful for TV services and broadcast, are the main additions of MPEG BIFS that distinguish it from VRML.

The concept of streamability means that a scene being described can be used at the receiver side even before the entire scene description data has been downloaded. At the same time, MPEG has defined means to modify scene descriptions that already reside at the user's terminal. Thus it has become feasible to start offering live services or to implement remote interactivity via a backchannel (network gaming). For VRML worlds, the entire scene description needs to be downloaded completely before any interaction with the content can start. MPEG-4 BIFS contains a number of extra features that make it a binary superset of VRML. For example, VRML only addresses 3D worlds. MPEG-4 will be used in some applications where there is only a need for 2D graphics in combination with other natural video objects. Therefore, BIFS defines 2D nodes that are needed by 2D-only applications for reasons of higher efficiency and lower complexity. MPEG-4 also supports a powerful and flexible audio-processing sub-tree capable of generating from simple up to true 3D audio environments.

3.4.1.2. Interaction with Media Objects

In general, the user observes a scene that is composed according to the design of the scene's author. Depending on the degree of freedom designated by the author, however, the user may potentially interact with the scene. Operations a user may be allowed to perform include changing the viewing/listening point by navigation through a scene, or dragging objects in the scene to different positions, or triggering a cascade of events by clicking on a specific object, e.g., starting or stopping a video stream, or selecting the desired language when multiple language tracks are available. More complex kinds of behavior can also be triggered, e.g., a virtual phone rings, the user answers, and a communication link is established.

Interactivity is supported by the architecture of BIFS. Hierarchical groupings of objects allow for authors to construct complex scenes, and enable consumers to manipulate meaningful sets of objects. MPEG-4 BIFS provides a standardized way to describe a scene so that, for example, media objects can be dynamically placed and moved anywhere in a given coordinate system; transformations can be applied to change the geometrical or acoustical aspect of a media object; primitive media objects can be grouped in order to form compound media objects; streamed data can be applied to media objects in order to modify their attributes (e.g., a sound, a moving texture belonging to an object, animation parameters driving a synthetic face); and the user's viewing and listening points can interactively be changed anywhere in the scene.

3.4.1.3. eXtensible MPEG-4 Textual Format (XMT)

XMT is a framework for representing MPEG-4 scene descriptions using a textual syntax. In a way, this seems like a step backward from BIFS. It is true that XMT does not provide the same level of bit-efficient representation as BIFS. However, since BIFS is a binary format and highly compressed, it is very suitable for transmission and storage, but it is not easily accessible to human readers. For content authors, it is important to understand the intentions and the meanings of media objects and their interaction, especially if the design is to be shared and exchanged between several designers. This was one of the major motivations behind defining XMT. One could think of BIFS as a "compiled" version of XMT. With this image in mind, it is easy to understand the usefulness of XMT, since scientists in other disciplines, for example, exchange ideas

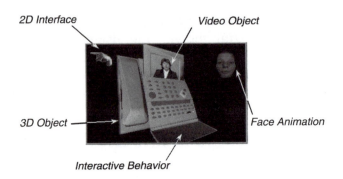

Figure 3.10 Interactive content [Source: Julien Signis, France Telecom].

and algorithms by means of looking at source code instead of trying to decipher compiled machine language code. XMT allows the content authors to exchange their content with other authors, tools, or service providers, and facilitates interoperability with both the Extensible 3D Format (X3D) being developed by the Web3D Consortium (the new name of the VRML Consortium), and the Synchronized Multimedia Integration Language (SMIL) from the W3C consortium. XMT builds on top of proven concepts and

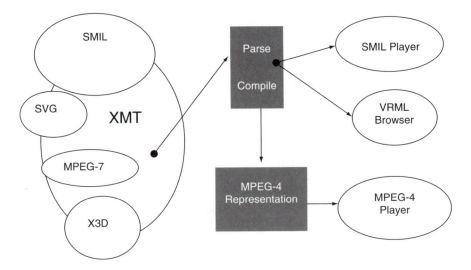

Figure 3.11 Schematic representation of XMT as a link between different formats for media data types [Source: MPEG-4 Overview].

architectures from XML (eXtensible Markup Language), which can be regarded as a sophisticated evolution of html.

3.4.1.4. Stream Synchronization

Precise synchronization of audio and video objects is an important feature that builds on features similar to MPEG-1 and MPEG-2. MPEG-4 Systems supports both push and pull delivery of content. MPEG-4 also supports Object Content Identification (OCI) so that searches in databases of MPEG-4 objects are possible. To accommodate the needs of content rights holders, each MPEG-4 audio, visual, and audio-visual object can be identified by a registration number similar to the well-established International Standard Recording Code (ISRC) of Compact Disc Audio. Synchronization of elementary streams is achieved through time stamping of individual distinct units within elementary streams. Distinct units of a bit stream, which are somewhat self-contained and can be directly accessed in an independent way, are called "access units." An individual frame in a conventional video clip can be considered as an access unit. The synchronization layer manages the identification of such access units and their time stamping. Independent of the media type, the synchronization layer allows identification of the type of access unit (e.g., video or audio frames, scene description commands) in elementary streams, recovery of the media object's or scene description's time base, and it enables synchronization among the various media objects and the corresponding scene description. The syntax of this layer is configurable in a large number of ways, allowing use in a broad spectrum of systems.

3.4.1.5. Digital Rights Management

Another important feature of the Systems part of MPEG-4 is the so-called Intellectual Property Management and Protection (IPMP). IPMP consists of a number of specified interfaces to an MPEG-4 system to support the possibility of plugging in proprietary technologies to manage and protect content. MPEG has refrained from specifying Digital Rights Management (DRM) systems or standardizing watermarking technology. It is commonly believed among MPEG delegates that content protection systems lie outside of the

MPEG standard. Such systems deploy encryption of the content and embedded IP (Intellectual Property) information.

However, it is necessary to provide hooks and interfaces and some elementary mechanisms that allow a service provider or content owner to select a state-of-the-art and potentially proprietary system for digital rights management offered by a third party to take care of protecting the content via watermarking or whatever. This way, MPEG-4 enables the use of DRM systems that manage and protect intellectual property, similar to conditional access systems used for pay-TV services.

It is vital to be able to identify intellectual property in MPEG-4 media objects. To that end, MPEG has worked with representatives of different creative industries in the definition of syntax and tools to support this. MPEG-4 incorporates identification of intellectual property by storing unique identifiers that are issued by international numbering systems (e.g., ISAN, ISRC, etc.[1]). These numbers can be applied to identify a current rights holder of a media object. Since not all content is identified by such a number, MPEG-4 enables intellectual property to be identified by a key-value pair. Also, MPEG-4 offers a standardized interface, which is integrated tightly into the Systems layer, for people who want to use systems that control access to intellectual property. With this interface, proprietary control systems can be easily amalgamated with the standardized part of the decoder.

3.4.1.6. MPEG-J

MPEG-J is a programmatic system that specifies application programming interfaces (APIs) for interoperation of MPEG-4 media players with Java code. The programmatic approach contrasts with the parametric approach offered by the rest of the MPEG-4 system. Using MPEG-J, it is possible to execute Java applets (MPEGlets) that add richer behavior to MPEG-4 content, and to provide interfaces to network and terminal resources. The term 'richer behavior'

---

[1] ISAN: International Audio-Visual Number; ISRC: International Standard Recording Code

is often meant that the terminal can support operations that are more complex and feature rich than simply pressing buttons for pausing, rewind, or continue. This approach is schematically depicted in Figure 3.12, where a decoder terminal is shown that receives MPEGlets, which can then be used to control resources in the decoder terminal. To accomplish this, a Java Virtual Machine and a Java Runtime Environment must be present.

3.4.1.7. ISO/IEC 14496-14—MP4 File Format

For the reliable exchange of complete files of MPEG-4 content, the file format "mp4" has been specified. The mp4 file format has been developed based on Apple's QuickTime file format, with its technical features extended. A file format that facilitates interchange, management, editing, and presentation of media information of an MPEG-4 scene in a flexible and extensible format is an important addition to the MPEG-4 Systems tools. This is provided by the mp4 file format. The presentation may be "local" to the system, or may be via a network or other stream delivery mechanism. The file format is independent of any particular delivery protocol, while enabling efficient support for delivery in general.

3.4.2. ISO/IEC 14496-2—Visual

Part 2, the visual part of MPEG-4, specifies the coded representation of natural and synthetic visual objects. In MPEG-1 and MPEG-2, the corresponding part used to be called "video." Since MPEG-4 has extended its scope far beyond the traditional notion of video to support a wide variety of types of visual information such as graphics or still images, the name of this part of the standard has been changed to "visual."

3.4.2.1. Compression of Natural Video

MPEG-4 Visual provides video coding algorithms for the compression of natural video that is capable of coding video at very low bit rates, starting from 5 kbit/s with a spatial resolution of QCIF

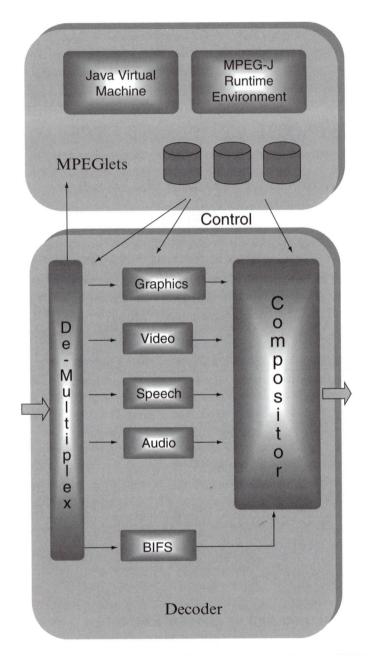

Figure 3.12 The marriage of MPEG and Java produces MPEG-J.

(144x176 pixels) up to bit rates of some Mbit/s for standard television resolution video (Recommendation ITU-R 601). On the upper end of the quality scale and bit rate range are coding tools combined in the Studio Profile, which supports bit rates of over 1 Gbit/s. In addition, MPEG-4 offers a Fine Granularity Scalability mode that allows for transmission of the same video content at different bit rates (SNR scalability). This wide range of bit rates and supported features is the result of specifying MPEG-4 Visual as a true box of video coding tools, according to the established principle—one functionality; one tool. The tools can be selected individually and combined to specify a terminal that satisfies the needs of a particular application domain. In order to prevent the possibility of too many incompatible terminals, MPEG includes a number of preset configurations of its video coding tools. Such a preset is called a "Profile." The concept of a profile is not restricted to the visual part of the standard, but applies to MPEG in general. The underlying principle for profiles will be discussed in a later chapter. Profiles were initially designed to match the requirements of prototypical application scenarios, which were conceivable by the time the specification was done.

One important feature of MPEG Visual is the ability to code not just a rectangular array of pixels, but also the video objects in a scene, where the object may have an arbitrary shape. An object can be a walking person or a running car or the ball on the foot of a soccer player.

3.4.2.2. ISO/IEC 14496-10—Advanced Video Coding (AVC)

Part 10 of MPEG-4, also known as H.264, is probably the most publicly discussed part of the standard these days, as it contains the latest addition of video coding tools that have been developed by the Joint Video Team (JVT). JVT consists of the joint forces of video coding experts from both the ITU and MPEG. The ITU experts developed the major part of the technology, which was later adopted and further integrated into the MPEG-4 standard. The corresponding ITU title for this excellent piece of technology is H.264.

How did this come about? Around the year 2000, the discussion in the world of video compression concerned the quest for better coding technology than the algorithms that had been standardized by MPEG-4 thus far. MPEG decided to issue a Call for Evidence. This call invited all parties to bring examples of their coding technology to the next MPEG meeting and to demonstrate their tools in an informal way to MPEG experts. At the next meeting, a number of interesting approaches were demonstrated very effectively.

Based on those demonstrations, MPEG decided to issue a formal Call for Proposals for new coding technology. The quality of new proposals was to be assessed by means of a round of subjective quality testing under controlled and fair-testing conditions. The results of the subjective tests were presented and discussed during the MPEG meeting in Sydney, Australia, in 2001. The proposal submitted by the ITU video coding experts, known under the project name H.26L, turned out to be the best technology among the candidates.

What followed was that the Joint Video Team (JVT) was formed, as described above, consisting of video coding experts from the ITU and MPEG. The mandate for the JVT was to create a new joint specification for MPEG and the ITU, based on the H.26L proposal, within a very short time frame. This activity on the ISO side led to the creation of Part-10 of MPEG-4, called "Advanced Video Coding," and on the ITU side, it led to the standard called "H.264." Technical features that were added to H.26L through the work of JVT include the support for interlaced video, which is still an important scanning format in the world of television. AVC/H.26L is currently limited to the coding of rectangular-shaped video objects. However, if the object-oriented video coding paradigm one day takes off, MPEG will be open enough to further extend AVC/H.264 to also support shaped video objects.

AVC contains a list of technical innovations that lead to improved coding performance. The fundamental concept of a hybrid codec based on motion-compensated prediction and transform coding using an integer-valued variant of the discrete cosine transform

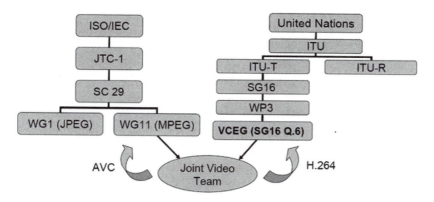

Figure 3.13 The genesis of the Joint Video Team (JVT) and its parents, ISO and ITU.

(DCT) still forms the backbone of the codec. This is conceptually the same signal processing ingredients as used in MPEG-1 and MPEG-2 and MPEG-4 Visual. So AVC/H.264 is not a revolution, but can be seen as another step in the evolution of video coding technology. In that sense, AVC represents a sustaining innovation, pushing forward products and services in an established value network.

As soon as the technical work was done, subjective quality tests were performed by the end of 2003 to assess the coding perform-ance of AVC/H.264 in comparison with previously specified MPEG standards such as MPEG-2 and the previous versions of MPEG-4 Visual. The bottom line coming out of those tests was that AVC/H.264 offers coding performance gains against previous standards that lie typically around a factor of 2 and sometimes more. Besides the improvement in terms of compression perform-ance, the implementation complexity for AVC/H.264 is also higher than for previous coding standards. As microelectronics technology is advancing, this higher complexity tends not to be a problem for the industry in the long run. However, it is a dimension that needs to be investigated thoroughly when choosing a video coding tech-nology to be integrated into a new application. The question may be to determine if the improved coding is worth the additional imple-mentation cost. In some cases it will be and in others it won't.

When it comes to coding video, this improvement is dramatic. It is relatively easy to see the next logical step, that a compression-based business model benefits from such an improvement in compression technology. We'll cover that aspect in more detail in a later chapter.

3.4.2.3. Still-Image Compression—Texture Coding

Besides coding arbitrarily shaped video objects, that is, moving pictures, MPEG-4 Visual also addresses the coding of still images (textures), which also may exhibit an arbitrary shape. An important ingredient for generating synthetic visual objects is the projection of the texture onto a synthetic 3D object, which comes as a 3D mesh, and which defines the geometry of the object in 3D space. This process is commonly referred to as "texture mapping." Still images may also be used as a static background texture for a 2D video scene.

MPEG-4 Visual employs an algorithm for coding still textures that uses wavelets' transformations. The wavelet transformation has a number of favorable technical features for achieving high-compression factors, while offering very elegant scalability properties. However, it is worth noting that the MPEG algorithm for compressing still images is different from the wavelet-based coding algorithm adopted in JPEG2000. The MPEG tool for still-image compression is inferior in terms of coding efficiency when compared to the JPEG2000 algorithm. A valid question is then, why has MPEG adopted an inferior algorithm if there is ISO's JPEG 2000 standard, issued by MPEG's sibling working group WG 1. The reason is that the schedules for the two standards, MPEG-4 and JPEG2000, were not aligned. While MPEG-4 had progressed to a certain level of maturity, JPEG2000 was still in an early stage and lagging behind MPEG-4. In 1996, MPEG realized the urgent need for a still-image coding tool as an important ingredient to make synthetic video fly. MPEG experts inspected the schedule of the JPEG2000 standardization project and discovered that the sibling standard was too much behind MPEG's time line. Even though MPEG members were in favor of adopting an algorithm from JPEG, MPEG could not afford to wait for JPEG2000 to provide a solution without sacrificing its own delivery deadline. As sticking to dead-

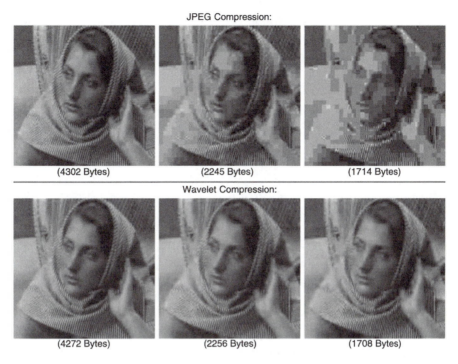

Figure 3.14 Still-texture coding in MPEG-4.

lines is one of the basic principles in MPEG standardization, the decision was made to develop a still-image codec within MPEG.

3.4.2.4. 2D Animated Meshes

This is a technology to turn still images into animated video clips or to modify (edit) the motion associated with a given video object. A 2D mesh is placed on top of a still image, for example. A visualization of this looks a bit like a rendition of a "Spiderman look." The nodes of the mesh can then be displaced according to motion information taken from elsewhere or according to some interactive action. The pixels around the displaced nodes are moved around accordingly. The resulting effect then looks like the pixels are moving, as determined by the externally imprinted motion information. For an example, think of a photograph of a person's face onto which the typical motion of a cloth flapping in the wind can be applied to generate an animation effect that looks like the image of the face being printed on a flag. Another simple example is to apply the motion pattern of a winking eye to the image of Mona Lisa, thus bringing her to life. Yet another idea might be to use 2D mesh animation for lip sync in order to convincingly dub foreign language movies by changing the movements of the lips to match the dubbed language. While European customers are used to the mismatch between lip movement and actual speech, U.S. customers tend to be annoyed at the technique of dubbing. However, reading subtitles is not that thrilling, either. 2D mesh animation is a tool that allows interactive manipulation of pixel-based visual objects and is still waiting to reach its prime time.

3.4.2.5. Sprite Coding

A sprite is a term that was first used in computer graphics or computer gaming, where a sprite is a relatively small piece of graphic or texture that can be used as an atom to build animated

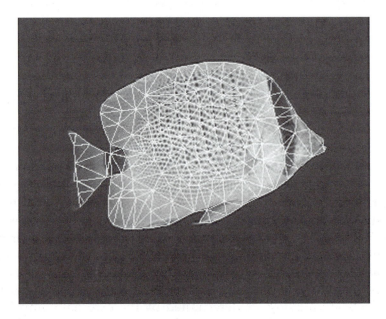

Figure 3.15 A 2D mesh overlay over a fishy object [Source: MPEG-4 Overview].

graphics in interactive computer games, such as jump-and-run games like "Super Mario Land" or similar. In MPEG-4, the term is used to mean something slightly different. In this context, a sprite is a kind of large still image that can be used as the backdrop of a scene into which other visual objects can be placed for interactive applications. In the context of interactive TV applications, Sprite Coding is a powerful tool to achieve high compression at the same time as interactivity. Sprite coding comes in a number of flavors, which differ mainly in terms of the technical details, for example, different levels of acceptable delay or the capability to generate sprites online. As sprite coding is a powerful but expensive tool, it is not yet included in the mainstream of MPEG-4-based product announcements. However, it is definitely a hot piece of technology, which may be considered for inclusion into video surveillance products of the future. A sprite can be generated, for example, for a surveillance camera that is panning back and forth collecting information about the scene. In such a case, it may be beneficial to build up a background sprite of a parking

Figure 3.16 An example of Sprite Coding. The background image is coded as a sprite. The figure of the tennis player is glued onto the background and coded as a separate video object with arbitrary shape. For interactivity, the user may exchange Wimbledon center court for Roland Garros [Source: MPEG-4 Overview].

lot and only transmit the cars and people moving in and out as separate video objects.

3.4.2.6. Interlaced Coding Tools

Nobody in the video coding community is in favor of video sources that have been scanned in an interlaced way. Within MPEG-4, this topic has been excluded from serious consideration since MPEG-4 was initially aiming at very low bit rate coding for communications applications, a realm of digital video where interlacing is not a topic. As soon as the new coding technologies became intriguing for entertainment-type video content, that is, when television-oriented companies started to have an eye on the emerging technology, interlacing became an active subject in standardization circles. The reason for this is the enormous amount of legacy video material stored in the cellars of TV stations and elsewhere. In order to be able to (re-)use this stock of existing audio-visual content, interlacing is a sad fact of life. MPEG-4 has addressed this aspect by specifying video-coding tools that are able to natively deal with interlaced video sources. The result of using these tools is better coding performance for interlaced video material when compared to coding such material while ignoring its interlaced nature. In other words, for TV-centric applications, interlaced coding tools are beneficial. For showing pictures only on computer screens or handheld devices, you can save the money by not including interlaced coding tools.

3.4.2.7. Alpha Shape Coding

For applications where image quality when dealing with arbitrarily shaped video objects is the ultimate criterion of merit, Alpha Shape Coding tools have been developed and standardized. Alpha shape coding allows the shape of a video object to be described with gray-level values. The alternative is to use only a two-valued data, i.e., zeros and ones, to denote if a pixel belongs to an object or not. Those binary-valued object shapes tend to create somewhat artificial-looking compositions that are of unacceptable quality, for example, in studio applications. This is why alpha shape coding tools were introduced. However, it should be noted that alpha shape coding comes with a price tag of increased implementation complexity as well as higher bit rate requirements. So if your anticipated application needs are simple and your requirements are for a low-transmission bandwidth, then you don't want alpha shape coding. If, however, you are planning to create video material with Hollywood quality, then you will need it.

3.4.2.8. Synthetic Video

A unique asset of MPEG-4 Visual is that its objects need not be natural images, that is, the images can be synthetically generated. To this end, MPEG-4 Visual supports 2D and 3D meshes that may model the geometry of complete generic 2D/3D objects. The 2D/3D meshes, and hence the geometry of the object, can be modified in time in order to create a computer-generated video sequence of animated characters. 2D/3D meshes are an established tool in the bag of tricks of computer graphics. They are commonly used in Hollywood and elsewhere to generate artificial characters such as the dinosaurs in the motion picture *Jurassic Park* (3D meshes), or to modify the appearance of real images in a spectacular way, such as in the motion picture *Terminator 2*.

Since MPEG is mainly concerned with the bit-efficient representation of media objects, its main contribution to the field of 3D mesh-based computer graphics is to devise methods and standardize an algorithm to compress those 3D meshes. Thus, a 3D mesh

Figure 3.17 3D mesh object [Source: Gabriel Taubin, IBM].

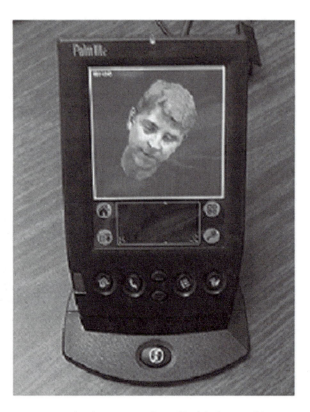

Figure 3.18 3D mesh object on a handheld device [Source: Gabriel
Taubin, IBM].

becomes yet another visual object type that is tightly integrated into
the media standard. In this context, the kick comes from making
these sophisticated media objects streamable over band-limited
channels. Figure 3.18 depicts an example in which simple 3D
graphics can be used on a handheld device for a media-based
application.

Within the domain of synthetic video, a special emphasis is given
to dealing with synthetic human faces and bodies (Avatars), which
may be represented by predefined 2D or 3D meshes, where certain
feature points are specified. The meshes can be designed to look
like "real" faces by either shading the surfaces of the mesh or
mapping texture onto the mesh. For this we need still-image

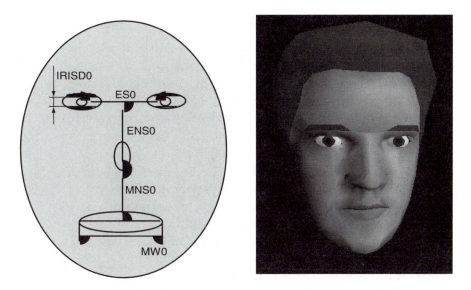

Figure 3.19 Example of a face animation object [Source: MPEG-4 Overview].

textures (see above). The feature points of the mesh describing faces or bodies may be animated by means of moving them around. The displaced feature points influence the appearance of the textures, which in turn creates the impression that the face or the bodies are moving, making it possible to create face or body animation (Avatars). The necessary amount of bits to be transmitted to perform a face animation, for example, is very low—in the range of a few kilobits per second. Face animation in combination with Text-to-Speech synthesis is a very bit efficient way to use talking heads in a multimedia application.

3.4.3. ISO/IEC 14496-3—Audio

Part 3 specifies the coded representation of natural and synthetic audio objects. Even though for Part 3 the conventional notion of audio has been extended to support more general types of audible information, the people in the audio group did not wish to change the name to the more general term, "aural." (Admittedly, "aural" sounds funny in this context if you utter it aloud.)

3.4.3.1. Audio Compression

MPEG-4 Audio provides a complete coverage of the bit rate range, starting as low as 2 kbit/s and going up as high as 64 kbit/s. Good speech quality is obtained already at 2 kbit/s, and transparent quality of monophonic music (sampled at 48 kHz at 16 bits per sample) is obtained at 64 kbit/s. Three classes of algorithms are used in the standard.

The first class covers the low bit rate range and has been designed to encode speech. For speech signals, separate codecs are part of the MPEG-4 toolbox. Speech codecs allow operation at 2 to 24 kb/s. The second class can be used in the midrange bit rate to encode both speech and music at an acceptable quality for music. The third class can be used in the high bit rate range and is targeted to be used for high-quality music. For audio signals at the highest quality level, MPEG-4 includes the advanced audio coding (AAC) algorithm. The algorithm provides CD-quality audio at considerably lower bit rates than the mp3 audio format.

Examples of additional functionality are speed control and pitch change for speech signals. The speed control functionality allows the playback of an audio signal to be slowed down or sped up without altering the pitch during this process. This can, for example, be used to implement a "fast forward" function (database search) or to adapt the length of an audio sequence to a given video sequence. For a music student who needs to practice his or her piano playing along with a combo or orchestra, it is a helpful feature if it is possible to choose a slower playback speed for the combo or orchestra without a change in the pitch. The pitch change functionality allows a change of pitch without altering the speed during the recording or playback process. This can be used, for example, for voice alteration or Karaoke-type applications. This technique only applies to parametric and structured audio coding methods.

Audio Effects provide the ability to process decoded audio signals with complete timing accuracy to achieve functions for mixing, reverberation, and spatialization. By the term "spatialization" we mean that the freedom of individually coded objects entails the need to tell the decoder where to position audio and visual objects in a scene. This is a functionality that must be provided to the author of a scene and is the MPEG-4 equivalent of the role of a movie director who instructs the scene setter to put a table here and a chair there, and asks an actor to enter a room through a door and speak a line, and another to stop talking and walk away. A human observer expects the direction of sound to coincide with the position of the corresponding visual object creating the sound.

3.4.3.2. Synthetic Audio

In the area of synthetic audio, two important technologies have been standardized. The first is a Text-to-Speech (TTS) interface, i.e., a standard way to represent prosodic parameters, such as pitch contour, phoneme duration, and so on. Typically, these can be used in a proprietary TTS system to improve the synthesized speech quality and to create, with the synthetic face (face animation visual object), a complete audio-visual talking face. The TTS can also be synchronized with the facial expressions of an animated talking head. TTS coders live in the bit rate range from 200 bit/s to 1.2 kbit/s, which allows a text or a text with prosodic parameters as its inputs to generate intelligible synthetic speech. TTS includes the following functionalities:

- Speech synthesis using the prosody of the original speech
- Lip synchronization control with phoneme information
- Trick mode functionality: pause, resume, jump forward/backward
- International language and dialect support for text (i.e., it can be signaled in the bit stream which language and dialect should be used)
- International symbol support for phonemes
- Support for specifying age, gender, speech rate of the speaker
- Support for conveying facial animation parameter (FAP) bookmarks

As a completely new ingredient, MPEG-4 supports "Structured Audio." This is a method for creating synthetic audio that operates on extremely low bit rates. Structured audio is a format for describing methods of audio synthesis algorithms. MPEG-4's standard for it can accommodate any current or future synthesis method. Structured audio is in essence a musical score-driven synthesis method.

Using newly developed formats to specify synthesis algorithms and their control, any current or future sound-synthesis technique can be considered to create and process sound in MPEG-4. The sound quality is guaranteed to be exactly the same on every MPEG-4 decoder.

One nice application of structured audio is that a hobby musician can have the opportunity of playing along with an orchestra where the hobby musician's instrument is left out of the playback. This kind of object-based scalability allows specific objects to be de-selected from the presentation. As an additional benefit, the orchestra can play a piece much slower, in order for the hobbyist to be able to follow, without experiencing a pitch shift.

3.4.4. ISO/IEC 14496-4—Conformance Testing

Part 4 defines conformance conditions for bit streams and devices. This part is used to test the compliance of MPEG-4 implementations. Conformance is an important step toward interoperability, one of the major motivations of standardization. The standard offers bit streams that contain audio-visual presentations corresponding to the specified profiles. These bit streams are then decoded by a newly developed device, which has to produce an output (i.e., a presentation that stays within specified bounds from the reference), as laid down in MPEG-4 Part 4. If a device passes the conformance test, it is judged as conforming to the standard. The conformance test is a kind of self-certification procedure.

Even if a device can rightfully claim to conform to the MPEG-4 standard, it is not automatically guaranteed that the device is fully interoperable with other devices in the market. Achieving true interoperability takes extra effort. The MPEG Industry Forum has been very active in establishing programs and activities that are aimed at achieving full interoperability between as many vendors as possible. For more details, the reader may want to check the corresponding Web site as cited in the references.

3.4.5. ISO/IEC 14496-5—Reference Software

Part 5 comprises software corresponding to most parts of MPEG-4. The software includes normative and non-normative tools, which means decoder as well as encoder software. The software comes as source code, which can be used freely for implementing products that claim compliance with the standard. For those cases, ISO waives the copyright of the code. Furthermore, the software is now also a normative part of the standard (Part 5). This means that there are actually two equivalent descriptions of the standardized technology. First, the textual description for the visual specifications as written down (e.g., in Part 2 of the standard). Second, there is the equivalent description of the technology as implemented by the reference software, which is Part 5 of the standard. If there is a discrepancy between the two descriptions, a more complete review of the situation is necessary in order to decide which description is correct and which needs to be fixed. This is a rather new policy brought forward by MPEG. The purpose is in part to facilitate the adoption of the standard by providing a reference implementation, which can also be used to get products to the marketplace within a short period of time. DivX, as one of the most prominent implementations of MPEG-4 Visual, is largely derived from this open-source software. The reference code for the visual part of MPEG-4 has been donated to MPEG by two independent sources. One version of the software comes from a European project in the ACTS program (5th framework), which is called MoMuSys. The other implementation has been donated by Microsoft! You can imagine the amount of effort it takes to keep both reference software implementations, plus the textual description for the Visual part, aligned.

3.4.6. ISO/IEC 14496-6—Delivery Multimedia Integration Framework (DMIF)

Much of what goes on technically during a multimedia presentation such as streaming media over the Internet or cable television takes place beneath the surface. If it is done well, then a lot of those technical processes stay completely invisible to the consumers. These essential but largely invisible aspects of an MPEG-4 terminal are covered in Part 6 of the standard. The technology covered in Parts 1, 2, and 3 of MPEG-4 are designed to be independent of the underlying delivery mechanism. That means that those parts are independent to the transmission mechanism for the audio-visual content. Candidate transmission protocols are the Internet, satellite or cable broadcast, or point-to-point communication links such as those used in telephony, as well as packeted media such as DVD or the like. One aspect of DMIF is also the ability to mix content coming from different channels in a way that is transparent to the user. As an example, think of an interactive game, where some parts of the game come from a CD-ROM and other parts come through a network connection. It is left to Part 6, the Delivery Multimedia Integration Framework (DMIF), to deal with the various technical details associated with the underlying delivery layers. It defines a session protocol for the management of multimedia streaming over generic delivery technologies. DMIF provides three types of abstraction.

The first is abstraction from the transport protocol, which can be any one of a number of Internet protocols, such as RTP/UDP/IP or MPEG-2 Transport Stream or others with the ability to identify delivery systems with different quality of service (QoS) levels. QoS level can be specified for a single object in a scene.

The second is the abstraction of the application from the delivery type—interactive (client-server), local, or broadcast delivery is seen through a single interface.

The third abstraction is from the signaling mechanisms of the delivery system. DMIF provides a practical solution to achieve one dream of content creators: "Create once; play everywhere from anywhere."

The synchronized delivery of streaming information from source to destination, exploiting different Quality of Service parameters as made available by the network is specified in terms of the synchronization layer and a delivery layer containing a two-layer multiplexer.

3.4.7. Further MPEG Tool Sets

MPEG-4 is a standard that keeps evolving in order to meet new technical challenges and to include new solutions and approaches as they become available. Beyond the parts that have already been specified and approved, there are a few more extensions for MPEG-4 in the making. In this section, we want to give a quick overview of what else is out there on the horizon. In addition to the documents being lifted to the status of international standard, there is still the option to publish a new part of MPEG as a Technical Report. Such a report is not normative but is classified as informative. It typically contains supplementary technical information that is helpful for implementing the standard.

- *ISO/IEC 14496-7—Optimized Software:* Part 7 is not a normative part of the MPEG-4 standard. This document has the status of a Technical Report (TR), which is classified as being informative only. However, Part 7 provides optimized software implementation for a couple of video coding tools. In particular, the optimized software contains fast software tools for motion estimation, global motion estimation, and fast sprite generation.
- *ISO/IEC 14496-8—MPEG 4 on IP (MPEG-4 Contents over IP Networks):* As the title already indicates, Part 8 of MPEG-4 describes how media content represented with MPEG-4 tools can be transported over IP networks. The document indicates how the MPEG-4 content is to be mapped into several IP protocols.

- *ISO/IEC 14496-9—Reference Hardware:* Part 9 is another Technical Report that describes MPEG-4 tools in terms of a hardware description language (VHDL). The information is considered helpful for speeding up hardware implementations of MPEG-4 technology.
- *Animation Framework eXtension (AFX):* AFX—pronounced "effects"—will provide users with enhanced visual experiences in synthetic MPEG-4 environments. The framework will define a collection of interoperable tool categories that collaborate to produce a reusable architecture for interactive animated contents.

3.5. Toward Interoperable Terminals

3.5.1. Profiles

MPEG-4 covers an enormous amount of technology. It is simply impossible to envision a device or a product that comprises the entire MPEG-4 specification. Such an endeavor is not commercially viable and probably not even possible. Implementing the entire standard certainly is overkill for any one particular application. Building a product and being forced by a standard to include costly technical features and capabilities that are of no particular interest to a targeted market basically loads a major cost burden onto the product. MPEG mitigates this obvious danger of overloading products with its concept of "Profiling." A profile in MPEG refers to the collection of specified tools that form a subset of the complete specification. A profile puts qualitative restrictions on the permissible syntactic elements to be used in a bit stream. The syntactic elements in a bit stream typically have their counterpart in the functionalities being implemented in the decoder. A profile thus describes which syntactic elements are allowed in a bit stream such that a decoder will not be stalled by a request to perform a function it has not implemented. In other words, profiling implies a restriction on the coding tools to be implemented to cap complexity and hence implementation cost. This way, MPEG terminals can be shaped to match the requirements of applications and market needs.

The range of requirements and application-specific needs is vast. For example, a mobile receiver has technical limitations and capabilities that are quite different from the capabilities of a broadcast set-top box. The applications for each device also look quite different. It would be inappropriate to equip both devices with the same set of functionalities and features.

It is up to the individual markets and players to pick an existing profile or to request from MPEG the definition of a new profile to make their products and services fly. Each application domain or industry may request from MPEG an appropriate toolset to satisfy its needs for bit-efficient representation and control of audio-visual content. In this way, the market in fact decides which parts of MPEG-4 will be successful and which will not.

3.5.2. Levels

The profiling concept is complemented by a second area, in which so-called "Levels" are defined. For each profile, a number of levels are defined. These levels put quantitative restrictions on parameters, which determine the implementation complexity in terms of required computational capabilities and memory requirements. The two dimensions, computational capability and memory size, are the dominant factors for determining the cost of an MPEG decoder. The levels are specified by putting quantitative limits on, for example, the maximum permissible bit rate, or maximum number of objects in a scene, the maximum macro blocks per second, maximum sampling frequency and channels, or the maximum number of pixels in the vertical and horizontal direction. All these parameters have an immediate influence on the implementation complexity for a terminal. The level determines the maximum or worst-case requirements a terminal has to be able to handle in real time in order to achieve compliance with the standard. The terminal is always allowed to offer more resources than necessary if the manufacturer thinks this is useful, but it shall never offer fewer capabilities than specified by the respective level.

To offer an example, let's say that there is an industry consortium putting together the technologies and standards on which the participants want to base their future systems and products. As the technical experts of this consortium are scanning the MPEG profiles in order to find an appropriate candidate, they find out that none of the profiles will satisfy their needs at an acceptable level. In such a situation, representatives of the consortium then address MPEG with the request to specify a new profile that contains all tools the consortium think is necessary for its field. If there is in fact a good technical reason why none of the existing profiles can be used, or if the consortium simply represents a major business opportunity for MPEG technology, then MPEG may issue another profile for the consortium.

Just to be clear on the meaning of the limits set by the various levels. For the sake of explanation, let us consider a level definition for a certain visual profile specifying that the bit stream, in order to be compliant, must not exceed a bit rate of, say, 128 kbit/sec. A decoder, in order to be compliant to this specification, has to be able to digest at least 128 kbit/sec. It may well be able to accept 500 kbit/sec, or even higher if this is desired by the product designer. In other words, for the decoder, the limits given by the level definition are interpreted as lower limits, while for the bit streams and the encoder, those definitions are interpreted as upper limits.

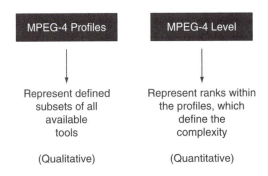

Figure 3.20 Conceptual difference between Profiles and Levels.

3.5.3. Conformance Points

The two concepts, profile and level, are intimately related. Pairing up one profile and one level is meant to define a so-called conformance point. Devices can be tested as to whether they fulfill the specifications of a particular conformance point. A Profile@Level combination allows a codec builder to implement only the subset of the standard he needs, while establishing a basis for achieving interoperability between MPEG-4 devices built to the same specification, and checking whether MPEG-4 devices comply with the standard (conformance testing).

Profiles and levels are a normative part of the standard, i.e., an implementation of MPEG-4 must conform to a Profile@Level combination if it claims to be compliant with the standard. Thus, each Profile@Level combination determines a conformance point.

The ultimate purpose of developing the concepts of profiles and levels is to achieve interoperability between devices within one profile and level definition. Furthermore, the definition of profiles and levels is done in a way to maximize interoperability between devices adhering to different profiles. Complete interoperability in the latter sense cannot be achieved because one profile may be "richer" than another in terms of the number and type of functionalities or tools.

Profiles exist for various types of media content (audio, visual, and graphics) as well as for scene descriptions. MPEG does not prescribe or advise combinations of these profiles, but care has been taken that good matches exist between the different areas.

Not unlike its predecessors, MPEG-4 would have a reduced impact if an MPEG-4 decoder would have to be able to decode all of the MPEG-4 tools. Furthermore, following the traditional approach of keeping the individual parts of the standard (Audio, Video, Systems, and DMIF) separate, profiles are only defined for the individual parts and *not* for Audio, Video, Systems, and DMIF combinations. This means that an application developer can just choose the parts of the standard he or she needs, and for each part, the profile that best suits his or her application.

Finally, the approach to specify conformance and interoperability originates from domains where devices have a more or less fixed set of capabilities and where it is expected for the device to guarantee the quality of service. This can be termed a "guaranteed quality" concept. The alternative approach can be called "best effort," where the quality of a service is not guaranteed, but the devices are doing the best they can. As examples for both conceptual frameworks, think of TV services, where it is expected that the broadcast will be displayed in real time and an acceptable image and audio quality, irrespective of the channel you have chosen and whether the content is a news cast or a feature movie. A "best effort" approach is more commonplace in the computer world, where a consumer has to learn that her last year's (and hence obsolete) computer is currently unable to perform a certain computer game unless the consumer buys herself a software update or a new graphics card or a new computer altogether. Even if the computer can execute the computer game, it may be that the game is slowed down, as the rendering speed of the machine only permits play at "slow-motion" speed.

3.5.4. Profiles and Levels in the MPEG-2 Standard

A prominent example of the effectiveness of the profiling approach is MPEG-2 Video. At the time of development, some industries requested the standard to be scalable (i.e., capable of extracting a subset of the stream and still obtain a usable picture). Other industries were not interested in this feature and opposed its introduction because of the increased decoder complexity that they would have had to bear. The profile approach provided the solution of defining a non-scalable profile (called Main Profile) and a set of scalable profiles. A scalable profile decoder can decode a Main Profile bit stream. Eventually, all implementations came to be based on the Main Profile. For standard-resolution (SD) television services, the size of the images is restricted to 576×720 pels coming in a rate of 25 frames per second (PAL) or 480×720 pels at a rate of approximately 30 frames per second. The SD television service application is supported by a decoder compliant with the Main Profile@Main Level. Main Level has been specified to allow picture sizes up to 576×720 pels at a maximum frequency of 30 frames per second, and the total bit rate for the coded video is limited to 15 Mbit/sec.

As high-definition television (HDTV) becomes more prevalent, a decoder is needed that supports larger images (1080×1920) and that can digest a high bit rate for the coded bit stream at the input. The video coding tools offered by the Main Profile are considered to be sufficient (and in fact they are). This is why HDTV services only need a level definition that exceeds the Main Level definition to satisfy the higher demands. The corresponding level in MPEG-2 is called "High Level," supporting HDTV image sizes (see above) and bit rates of up to 80 Mbits/sec. An overview of the profiles and levels defined in MPEG-2 is shown in Figure 3.21. Note the circle that indicates the Main Profile@Main Level conformance point, which comprises over 90% of all MPEG-2 implementations.

This type of solution has been very effective in promoting adoption of the standard. The first consumer electronics products were based on MPEG-1 Audio Layer 1 because of limited complexity and battery life. Immediately after that, Layer 2 was used in digital

	Simple Profile	Main Profile	SNR Scalable Profile	Spatially Scalable Profile		High Profile		4:2:2 Profile	MVP Profile
High Level		1920 H 1152 V 60 Hz				1920 H 1152 V 60 Hz	720 H 576 V 30 Hz		
High-1440		1440 H 1152 V 60 Hz		1440 H 1152 V 60 Hz	720 H 576 V 30 Hz	1440 H 1152 V 60 Hz	720 H 576 V 30 Hz		
Main Level	720 H 576 V 30 Hz	720 H 576 V 30 Hz	720 H 576 V 30 Hz			720 H 576 V 30 Hz	352 H 288 V 30 Hz	720 H 512/608 V 30 Hz	720 H 576 V 30 Hz
Low Level		352 H 288 V 30 Hz	352 H 288 V 30 Hz						

Figure 3.21 Table of Profiles and Levels in MPEG-2 Video

television set-top boxes where battery life was not a concern. The constant progress of number-crunching capabilities of personal computers has made software Layer 3 decoders possible on PCs. From the service provider and consumer point of view, this is a very positive situation because content produced in the first phases of the technology can still be played back on the newer decoders.

3.6. Overview of Profiles in MPEG-4

An MPEG-4 terminal may be composed of different independently chosen components. The choice of the components included depends on the application. It is also possible to combine MPEG tools with other non-MPEG tools. This is done with success in the DVD player market, where MPEG-2 Video is used for coding video and Dolby Digital is used for coding of audio signals. Outside of the United States, MPEG-2 Audio was originally used. By now, most consumer DVD players support both formats. In Figure 3.22, the concept is shown graphically, in which different profiles as part

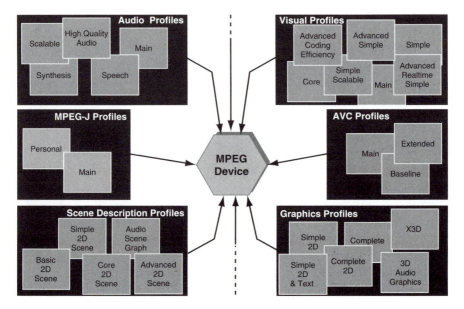

Figure 3.22 Combining profiles for terminals.

of the MPEG-4 standard may be combined. A more detailed description of the profiles and their basic capabilities is given in the following paragraphs.

3.6.1. Visual Profiles

When considering the visual part of MPEG-4, one needs to abandon the idea of a single-purposed video coding standard addressing the needs of one dominant industry. MPEG-4 is much more a toolbox standard offering a wealth of technology to enable and foster a wide range of products and services all dealing with interactive multimedia. This is the reason such a large number of profiles have been defined to choose from. There has been a considerable amount of discussion about whether it is sensible to define such an excessive number of visual profiles. As it stands, the developers of new applications can choose the most appropriate profile that satisfies their needs best and that provides a reasonable basis for deploying interoperable terminals. This way the market actually determines which profiles will be implemented and will stand the test of time. It is to be expected that quite a few of the profiles mentioned in the sequel will never be implemented commercially.

Let's have a quick overview of the visual profiles.

3.6.1.1. Simple Visual Profile

The Simple Visual Profile (SP) provides efficient, error-resilient coding of rectangular video objects, suitable for applications on mobile networks. The profile has a strong similarity to the coding technology included in ITU's H.263 standard. The Simple Visual Profile is targeted toward low-complexity decoders and small displays. A prominent example is wireless channels and mobile receiving devices. Simple Profile has been adopted initially by the 3GPP consortium for the roll-out of 3rd-generation mobile receivers to enable multimedia applications on cell phones. Simple Profile is also attractive if real-time encoding in software on desktop platforms is a requested feature. Simple Profile sacrifices some compression performance to support low-delay coding, which is a common requirement in bi-directional communication applications such as videophone or teleconferencing. Simple Profile is also usable for applications that employ streaming video on the Internet. In spite of public dismay at the inferior visual quality offered by this profile, it still is able to deploy reasonably good video services at relatively low implementation cost. It is not the latest, hottest, and coolest video codec, but it is better than its reputation implies. Note that the Simple Profile does not support the native treatment of interlaced video sources. Simple Profile is not seriously considered as a profile to be used for TV services, or more generally, for video services asking for large images and premium image quality.

3.6.1.2. The Advanced Simple Profile

The Advanced Simple Profile (ASP) adds a few coding tools (B-frames, 1/4-pel motion compensation, extra quantization tables and global motion compensation, interlaced video coding tools) to the Simple Visual Profile in order to achieve better compression performance (i.e., 25 to 30% better compression than Simple Profile) at the price of a slightly higher implementation complexity. This has been considered an interesting visual profile for building streaming applications on the Web or for TV applications (as a replacement for MPEG-2). Advanced Simple is the profile for all applications where improved coding efficiency for rectangular-shaped video is of primary importance. The supported bit rates of up to 8 Mbit/sec and image formats reaching CCIR-601 or 4CIF (TV screen size) resolution, together with the support for interlaced video, makes MPEG-4 ASP an attractive technology platform for broadcasting services. Advanced Simple Profile has been selected by ISMA (Internet Streaming Media Alliance) to be used for streaming media applications over the Internet. MPEG-4 ASP is also an attractive candidate for building streaming services supporting a wide range of transmission bandwidths between narrowband modem connections (56 kbit/s), from DSL bit rates (300–750 kbit/sec) up to broadband streaming in the range of 1–2 Mbit/sec. Until AVC/H.264 was adopted by MPEG, ASP codecs were considered the flagship codecs of MPEG-4, offering the best video coding performance, outperforming MPEG-2 codecs in the

TV-relevant bit rate domain of 1–4 Mbit/sec. ASP also includes support for interlaced video, making it a contender for future TV services. In particular for its use in digital video security systems (CCTV), the "Global Motion Compensation" tool promises to excel at video content where panning and zooming cameras are dominant. The benefit for ASP is that there are already a number of well-performing codecs in existence for this profile. One more comment regarding ASP: During the early days of the ASP decoder, a product brochure was published in which a company announced that it offered decoder chips targeted at the set-top box market that were implementing the Advanced Simple Profile. The brochure came with a little footnote that stated that the chips do not support 1/4-pel and global motion compensation. Looking back at the original meaning of Profile definitions, it becomes clear that this offering did not represent a compliant ASP decoder implementation, since in a decoder, all specified coding tools are mandatory for compliance. In other words, this was a cheap marketing trick to jump on the bandwagon.

3.6.1.3. The Fine Granularity Scalability Profile

The Fine Granularity Scalability Profile comes in combination with either the Simple or Advanced Simple profile. The profile offers a scalable coding mode where the so-called "base layer" is designed to deliver a basic quality video service. An additional bit stream, the "enhancement layer," is sent along. The bits coming with the enhancement layer allow gradual improvement of the received video as more bandwidth is available. It allows the truncation of the enhancement layer bit stream at any bit position so that delivery quality can easily adapt to transmission and decoding circumstances. The main point of this profile is that video quality follows the variations of the transmission bandwidth in fine granular steps so as to mimic the graceful degradation behavior of analog video reception. This feature may be attractive for situations where the transmission bandwidth is subject to significant temporal variations. Proprietary video codecs, such as Real Networks' or Microsoft's offerings, also implement related approaches to overcome the bandwidth variations experienced in Internet streaming applications. As is often the case with scalable video coding, this coding approach suffers from losses in compression efficiency in order to achieve the scalability functionality. MPEG is about to produce more technology under the title "scalable video coding" (SVC) to fulfill this desire for scalability *and* efficiency.

3.6.1.4. The Simple Studio Profile

The Simple Studio Profile is a profile that has been designed by companies interested in video post-production applications. It offers very high visual quality for use in studio editing applications. It is an I-frame-only codec so frame-exact editing and random access is easily achieved. The profile includes the tools to code arbitrarily shaped video objects and multiple alpha channels. Shaped video objects are made possible in television production studios by means of chroma-keying techniques (blue-screen). Furthermore, blending and mixing of objects are commonplace operations in studio applications. The range of bit rates supported by this profile goes up to almost 2 Gigabits per second. The profile is of interest for the development of studio equipment that can deal with compressed video data while still enabling ease of editing and uncompromised video quality. Sony has a strong position when it comes to shaping the Studio Profile to be used in HD editing systems, similar to MPEG-IMX in the SD domain.

3.6.1.5. The Core Studio Profile

The Core Studio Profile adds P-frames to the Simple Studio Profile; that is, the video compression is more efficient, but the implementation is more complex.

3.6.1.6. The Advanced Real-Time Simple (ARTS) Profile

The Advanced Real-Time Simple (ARTS) Profile includes advanced error-resilient coding techniques for rectangular video objects using a back channel. For real-time communications applications such as the videophone, teleconferencing (over IP networks), and remote observation, the design has been tuned to offer improved temporal resolution stability and low buffering delay.

3.6.1.7. The Simple Scalable Visual Profile

The Simple Scalable Visual Profile is based on the Simple Visual Profile and adds support for coding of temporally and spatially scalable objects. It is designed to be useful for applications that provide services at more than one level of quality due to bit-rate or decoder resource limitations, such as Internet use and software decoding.

3.6.1.8. The Core Visual Profile

The *Core Visual Profile* is based on the Simple Visual Profile and adds support for coding of arbitrarily shaped and temporally scalable objects. It is designed to be useful for applications that provide relatively simple levels of interactivity (such as Internet multimedia applications).

3.6.1.9. The Main Visual Profile

The Main Visual Profile is based on the Core Visual Profile and adds support for coding of interlaced video objects, semi-transparent objects (alpha channel), and sprite objects. It is designed to be useful for interactive and entertainment-quality broadcast and DVD applications. So far, the profile has often been considered to be too heavy for implementation in actual applications, but if truly interactive TV services make it to center stage, this profile may be reconsidered for its interactive features.

3.6.1.10. The N-Bit Visual Profile

The N-Bit Visual Profile takes the Core Visual Profile and adds support for coding video objects with pixel depths ranging from 4 to 12 bits. It has been designed for use in surveillance applications where the infrared cameras produce gray-value images (no color information needed) with a high dynamic range for which the commonly used 8 bits of dynamic range are considered insufficient. This is clearly a very special profile for which it may be difficult to find a mass market, but the 12-bit feature certainly has interesting potential for surveillance video.

3.6.1.11. The Core Scalable Profile

The Core Scalable Profile starts with the Core Visual Profile and adds tools for coding of temporally and spatially scalable, arbitrarily shaped video objects. Note that the Core Visual Profile already includes simplified mechanisms for enabling temporal scalability. This profile offers a more complete set of tools for supporting fully scalable functionalities such as object-based SNR and full spatial/temporal scalability for regions or objects of interest. It is yet another profile that may turn out to be useful for applications such as the Internet, mobile, and broadcast services.

3.6.1.12. The Advanced Core Profile

The Advanced Core Profile combines tools and features from two less advanced profiles. It takes the ability to decode arbitrarily shaped video objects from the Core Visual Profile and combines this with the ability to decode arbitrarily shaped scalable still-image objects from the Advanced Scalable Texture Profile. This profile is meant to be suitable for various content-rich multimedia applications such as interactive multimedia streaming over the Internet.

3.6.1.13. The Advanced Coding Efficiency (ACE) Profile

The Advanced Coding Efficiency (ACE) Profile is an extension of the Advanced Simple Visual Profile. ACE inherits all the coding efficiency tools from ASP and adds further tools to compress arbitrarily shaped video objects. It is suitable for applications such as mobile broadcast reception, the acquisition of image sequences (e.g., from camcorders), and other applications where high coding efficiency is desired for rectangular and arbitrarily shaped video objects, and a small footprint is not the prime concern. ACE has been specified as an alternative to the Main Visual Profile that can achieve maximum compression while not having to support sprite coding, which is considered heavy in terms of implementation complexity.

3.6.1.14. The Simple Facial Animation Visual Profile

The Simple Facial Animation Visual Profile offers a simple means to animate a face model. The technology is meant to be suitable for applications such as audio/video presentation for the hearing impaired and online kiosks.

3.6.1.15. The Scalable Texture Visual Profile

The Scalable Texture Visual Profile provides spatially scalable coding of still images (aka texture objects). It is useful for applications that require multiple scalability levels, such as mapping texture onto 3D mesh objects in interactive games, and as a storage format used in high-resolution digital still cameras.

3.6.1.16. The Basic Animated 2D Texture Visual Profile

The Basic Animated 2D Texture Visual Profile provides spatial scalability, SNR scalability, and mesh-based animation for still-image (textures) objects as well as simple face-object animation. No real application of this profile is known to the authors.

3.6.1.17. The Advanced Scalable Texture Profile

The Advanced Scalable Texture Profile supports decoding of arbitrarily shaped texture and still images including scalable shape coding, wavelet tiling, and error resilience. It is useful for applications that require fast random access as well as multiple scalability levels and arbitrarily shaped coding of still objects. Examples are fast content-based still-image browsing on the Internet, multimedia-enabled PDAs, and Internet-ready high-resolution digital still cameras.

3.6.1.18. The Simple Face and Body Animation Profile

The Simple Face and Body Animation Profile is a superset of the Simple Face Animation Profile, which has added body animation.

3.6.1.19. The Hybrid Visual Profile

The Hybrid Visual Profile combines the ability to decode arbitrarily shaped and temporally scalable natural video objects (as in the Core Visual Profile) with the ability to decode several synthetic and hybrid objects, including simple-face and animated still-image objects. It appears to be suitable for various content-rich multi-media applications. More concrete examples of its use are not known to the authors.

3.6.2. Profiles for H.264/AVC

AVC contains a rich set of video coding tools that mainly address improved compression and improved error robustness. Object orientation and coding of shaped video objects has not been addressed in this context to date. The profiles defined for AVC try to address the dominant needs for better video compression for the industries that are expected to benefit the most from the progress in video coding technology, notably broadcasting, Internet streaming, and mobile communications.

A decoder may choose to implement one of the following three profiles, which are currently defined:

3.6.2.1. The AVC Baseline Profile

The AVC Baseline Profile includes basic video coding tools (I-slices, P-slices, error-resilience tools, and context-adaptive variable-length coding [CAVLC]), and leaves out some of the constructs that are more costly to implement. This profile does not contain B, SP, and SI-slices; interlace coding, and context-adaptive binary-arithmetic

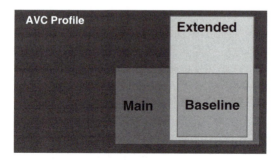

Figure 3.23 AVC Profiles

coding [CABAC] tools. It was designed with those applications in mind that run on platforms with low processing power and in hostile transmission environments with large packet losses or a high probability of transmission errors. A typical example is mobile communication and wireless services. Among the three AVC profiles, it has the least coding efficiency and is probably the cheapest to implement.

3.6.2.2. The AVC Extended Profile

The AVC Extended Profile is a superset of the Baseline profile and includes the heavier coding tools that mainly provide additional coding efficiency (B, SP, and SI-slices, and interlace coding tools); that is, the extended profiles adds those tools to the set already included in the Baseline Profile. The inclusion of interlaced coding tools is an indication that the Extended Profile may be used for broadcasting applications. It is more complex than Baseline and provides better coding efficiency. Streaming media is another application area that might pick the Extended Profile as its basis for video coding.

3.6.2.3. The AVC Main Profile

The AVC Main Profile includes all the fancy video coding tools (I, P, and B-slices; interlace coding; CAVLC; and CABAC). In particular, CABAC is considered to give an extra boost to compression, but it is slightly more complex to build. CABAC also implies some subtle changes in the coding schemes, which may be challenging to combine with tasks such as simple scrambling of video content. Since the profile can be considered as "fat," it is certainly beyond the capabilities of a mobile or wireless terminal. Main Profile does not include error-resilience tools, as it is anticipated to be used in environments where the error rate caused by the transmission channel is relatively low. On the other hand, it has been designed to provide the highest possible coding efficiency. High-definition DVDs are an example where high coding efficiency meets the almost error-free transmission channel. By now you probably get the picture.

3.6.3. Audio Profiles

For the Audio part of the standard, a number of profiles have been specified and discussed. We will now try to provide some insights into these profiles.

3.6.3.1. The Speech Profile

The Speech Profile provides a very low bit rate parametric speech coder, a narrowband/wideband speech coder, and a Text-to-Speech interface.

3.6.3.2. The Synthesis Profile

The Synthesis Profile provides score-driven audio synthesis and wave-tables synthesis as well as a Text-to-Speech Interface to generate sound and speech at very low bit rates.

3.6.3.3. The Scalable Profile

The Scalable Profile is a superset of the Speech Profile. It is designed for scalable coding of speech and music for networks, such as the Internet and narrow-band audio digital broadcasting (NADIB). The supported bit rates range from 6 kbit/s to 24 kbit/s, with audio bandwidths between 3.5 and 9 kHz.

3.6.3.4. The Main Profile

The Main Profile is a rich superset of all the other profiles, also containing coding tools supporting natural and synthetic audio.

3.6.3.5. The High Quality Audio Profile

The High Quality Audio Profile contains a speech coder and the Low Complexity AAC coder (Advanced Audio Coding, the successor of MP3). A new error-resilient (ER) bit stream syntax is also offered.

3.6.3.6. The Low Delay Audio Profile

The Low Delay Audio Profile contains multiple options for speech coders, the low-delay AAC coder, and the Text-to-Speech interface (TTSI). Low delay is always an important feature for bi-directional communication applications.

3.6.3.7. The Natural Audio Profile

The Natural Audio Profile contains all the natural audio coding tools available in MPEG-4, but not the synthetic ones.

3.6.3.8. The Mobile Audio Internetworking Profile

The Mobile Audio Internetworking Profile (MAUI) contains the low-delay and the scalable AAC. This profile is intended to extend communication applications using non-MPEG speech coding algorithms with high-quality audio coding capabilities.

3.7. Graphics Profiles

Graphics Profiles define which graphical and textual elements can be used in a scene. The graphics profiles are defined in the Systems part of the standard.

3.7.1.1. The Simple 2D Graphics Profile

The Simple 2D Graphics Profile provides for only those graphics elements of the BIFS tool that are necessary to place one or more visual objects in a two-dimensional scene.

3.7.1.2. The Complete 2D Graphics Profile

The Complete 2D Graphics Profile provides the full set of two-dimensional graphics functionalities and supports features such as arbitrary two-dimensional graphical elements and text, possibly in conjunction with other visual objects such as video.

3.7.1.3. The Complete Graphics Profile

The Complete Graphics Profile comprises advanced graphical elements such as elevation grids and extrusions and allows the creation of content with sophisticated lighting effects. The profile enables applications such as complex virtual worlds that exhibit a high degree of realism.

3.7.1.4. The 3D Audio Graphics Profile

The 3D Audio Graphics Profile does not propose visual rendering, but it does provide graphics tools to support the rendering of the acoustical properties of a scene (geometry, acoustics absorption, diffusion, transparency of the material). This profile may be used for applications that perform environmental spatialization of audio signals such as tele-presence applications.

3.7.1.5. The Simple 2D + Text Profile

The Simple 2D + Text Profile looks much like the Simple 2D Graphics Profile, with the added means to display moving text on screen, which can be colored or transparent. Like Simple 2D, this is a useful profile for low-complexity audio-visual devices.

3.7.1.6. The Core 2D Profile

The Core 2D Profile supports fairly simple 2D graphics and text. Meant for set-top boxes and similar devices, it can do such things as picture-in-picture, video warping for animated advertisements, logos, and so on.

3.7.1.7. The Advanced 2D Profile

The Advanced 2D Profile contains tools for advanced 2D graphics. Using it, one can implement cartoons, games, advanced graphical user interfaces, and complex streamed-graphics animations.

3.7.1.8. The X3D Core Profile

The X3D Core Profile is a 3D profile that is compatible with Web3D's X3D core profile. It provides a rich environment for games, virtual worlds, and other 3D applications.

3.8. Scene Graph Profiles

Scene Graph Profiles, defined in the Systems part of the standard, allow audio-visual scenes with audio-only, two-dimensional, three-dimensional, or mixed 2D/3D content.

3.8.1.1. The Audio Scene Graph Profile

The Audio Scene Graph Profile provides for a set of scene graph elements for use in audio-only applications. The profile supports applications like broadcast radio.

3.8.1.2. The Simple 2D Scene Graph Profile

The Simple 2D Scene Graph Profile utilizes only those BIFS scene-graph elements that are necessary to place one or more audio-visual objects in a scene. The Simple 2D Scene Graph Profile allows the creation of presentations of audio-visual content with potential update of the complete scene but no interaction capabilities. The Simple 2D Scene Graph Profile supports applications like broadcast television.

3.8.1.3. The Complete 2D Scene Graph Profile

The Complete 2D Scene Graph Profile includes all the 2D scene-description elements from the BIFS toolbox. It supports features such as 2D transformations and alpha blending. This profile enables 2D applications that require extensive and customized interactivity.

3.8.1.4. The Complete Scene Graph Profile

The Complete Scene Graph Profile unites the complete set of all scene-graph elements (2D and 3D) from the BIFS toolbox. This profile enables applications like the dynamic virtual 3D world and games.

3.8.1.5. The 3D Audio Scene Graph Profile

The 3D Audio Scene Graph Profile specifies the tools for three-dimensional sound positioning in relation either to acoustic parameters of the scene or its perceptual attributes. The user can interact with the scene by changing the position of the sound source, by changing the room effect, or moving the listening point. This profile is intended for use in audio-only applications.

3.8.1.6. The Basic 2D Profile

The Basic 2D Profile combines 2D composition for very simple scenes with audio-only and visual elements. Only basic 2D composition and audio and video nodes interfaces are included. These nodes are required to put an audio or video object in the scene.

3.8.1.7. The Core 2D Profile

The Core 2D Profile has tools for creating scenes with visual and audio objects using basic 2D composition tools. This includes quantization tools, local animation and interaction, 2D texturing, scenetree updates, and the inclusion of subscenes through Web links.

3.8.1.8. The Advanced 2D Profile

The Advanced 2D Profile forms a full superset of the Basic 2D and Core 2D profiles. It adds scripting and means for streamed animation, local interaction, and local 2D composition, as well as advanced audio.

3.8.1.9. The Main 2D Profile

The Main 2D Profile adds the FlexTime model to Core 2D, as well as Layer2D and WorldInfo nodes and all input sensors. This profile was designed to be an interoperability point with SMIL. It provides a very rich set of tools for highly interactive applications on, for example, the World Wide Web.

3.8.1.10. The X3D Core Profile

The X3D Core Profile was designed to be a common interworking point with the Web3D specifications (Web3D) and the MPEG-4 standard. The same profile will be in a Web3D specification. It includes the nodes for implementation of 3D applications on a low-footprint engine, taking into account the limitations of software renderers.

3.8.2. MPEG-J Profiles

For MPEG-J, which is included in the Systems part of the standard, two profiles have been specified.

3.8.2.1. The Personal Profile

The Personal Profile—This is a lightweight package that targets personal devices. The profile addresses a range of constrained devices including mobile and portable devices such as cell video phones, PDAs, and personal gaming devices. This profile includes the Network Scene Resource API.

3.8.2.2. The Main Profile

The Main Profile—This includes all the MPEG-J APIs. The Main profile addresses a range of consumer devices including entertainment devices such as set-top boxes, computer-based multimedia systems, etc. It is a superset of the Personal Profile. In addition to the packages in the Personal Profile, this profile includes Decoder API, the Decoder Functionality Section Filter API, and the Service Information API.

3.9. Testing in MPEG-4

Progress in any engineering discipline needs to be assessable and measurable. Of course, this is also true for many other scientific fields, but here we will limit our scope to the engineering aspect. The process of measuring, counting, and weighing is intimately related to a consensus on the figures of merit that are used to assess progress. However, assessing the quality of products and services, the quality of a coding technology, or even the quality of a standard can turn out to be a scientific discipline in itself, or at least the subject of interesting philosophical ramifications.

In the context of MPEG, various types of test procedures exist that serve to measure the quality of work and to assess progress. The individual test procedures differ in the methodology applied and in the motivation for testing. In this section, we will briefly describe the nature of the tests done in MPEG. Other aspects of the subject of testing will be presented in a later chapter.

3.9.1. Verification Tests

At the end of a standardization activity, MPEG carries out so-called "verification tests." It is the purpose of such tests to check whether the newly specified standard delivers technology that fulfills the requirements that were set up at the beginning of the project. To this end, MPEG performs formal tests, the results of which are an important step in the standardization process since they prove that MPEG standards are not paper standards, but that the standard is implemented and its feasibility and feature set are verified. This level of verification gives the markets the necessary confidence to venture into building products based on the standard.

Verification includes tests that measure the performance of the audio and video coding technology by comparing the new tools with older standards or carefully selected reference codecs. A relative statement of coding performance is helpful, as it is a clear message to the markets that the new codec X is x-times better than the previously available codecs Y and Z.

Besides the testing of the coding performance, it is necessary to test other features that come with the new standard, for example, testing for error robustness.

Verification tests are focused on small sets of coding tools that are appropriate in one application arena, and hence can be effectively compared. Since compression is a critical capability in MPEG, the verification tests, for the most part, compare coding tools operating at similar bit rates. The results of these tests are then presented in a range from high to low bit rates.

A list of reports about previous verification tests done in MPEG can be found at the MPEG Web site and can be downloaded for free.

3.9.2. Conformance Testing

An entirely different type of information is compiled when testing for conformance. Conformance testing is done by a company to check if its product is compliant with a target profile and level combination relevant for its business. That is, the engineers in the company will have built chips or programmed software according to the book. After they are done, the result will need to be tested for conformance. To this end, MPEG offers Part 4 of the standard, which describes in detail how the tests need to be done, what figures need to be measured, and what the results should look like in order to successfully verify the compliance with the standard. Furthermore, part 4 of the MPEG standard also contains bit streams that have been verified in the course of the standardization work to be legal MPEG bit streams. The engineers in the company can now take those bit streams and decode them with the newly implemented decoder tool. If the deviation of the decoded material from the specification is below a certain threshold, then the decoder is considered to be compliant. The result of conformance testing is a black and white answer to the question of whether a product is compliant with a conformance point in the standard. Hence, conformance testing is a self-certification process for a company, as there is no legal entity to officially distribute certificates of conformance.

The question that we have jumped over is how to verify that the bit streams are legal in the first place. This is done by bit stream exchange in the course of the standardization work. Several MPEG member companies develop independent implementations for encoding and decoding tools. They then produce encoded bit streams that are exchanged among those companies. Each company tries to decode the other companies' bit streams. The results are communicated and deviations are documented and discussed until all involved parties converge to verify the correctness of the streams.

3.9.3. Interoperability Tests

Even though conformance testing is an essential ingredient for achieving interoperability, it is not enough. A conformance point in MPEG is defined for profile and level combination, which is valid only for a part of the standard, for example, the Visual part. However, in general, a product includes coding tools to deal with audio, video, graphics, and other technologies. Conformance can be tested individually for each of these constituents. However, the conformance of the parts of product A does not guarantee the full interoperability with product B, the parts of which are also assumed to be conformant. Each product may have chosen different tools to use.

In order to harmonize the tools used for products in a specific market segment, other organizations are established to perform so-called interoperability tests to verify the seamless exchange of coded media data between products coming from different vendors. For example, the Internet Streaming Media Alliance (ISMA) comprises many companies that want to start streaming businesses using MPEG-4 technology. These companies specify the tools they want to adopt from MPEG-4 in order to agree on a common technological basis. ISMA also tests for interoperability of the products. Further interoperability tests were done by the MPEG Industry Forum. Yet another industry consortium is the 3rd-Generation Partner Program (3GPP), which deals with multimedia on 3rd-generation hand phones (cell phones). Yet another candidate organization to adopt MPEG-4 in a similar fashion is the Digital Video Broadcasting (DVB) project. It is the intention of all the companies within one domain of business to have products that truly interoperate.

Again, interoperability testing results in making binary entries in a matrix to indicate if the product of company A is able to play back the content generated by company B. Check the Web sites of ISMA [1], MPEGIF [2], DVB [3], 3GPP [4], or others for corresponding press releases and reports about the results of interoperability tests in the individual consortia.

3.10. MPEG-4 Keeps Adding Tools

A standard is a living body, no different from a company product. While companies and consortia are getting ready for a new wave of interoperable products, the MPEG group is adding more features to the standard in a compatible way, i.e., without disrupting any installed basis that an industry or a company may have already deployed. Let us emphasize, there will be no obligation on the part of industrial users to add these new features to their products.

3.11. Bibliography

B. G. Haskell, A. Puri, & A. N. Netravalli. Digital Video: An Introduction to MPEG-2. In *Digital Multimedia Standards Series.* New York: Chapman & Hall, 1997.

ISO/IEC JTC1 SC29/WG11 N4400

R. Koenen. MPEG-4: Multimedia for our Time. *IEEE Spectrum*, Vol. 36, No. 2, February 1999, pp. 26–33.

R. Koenen (Ed.). *Overview of the MPEG-4 Standard.* www.chiariglione.org/mpeg. March, 2002.

H. Martens, & M. Martens. *Multivariate Analysis of Quality.* New York: Wiley, 2001.

The Media Standard. *MPEG Industry Forum White Paper. 2002.* Download from www.mpegif.org

J. L. Mitchell, W. B. Pennebaker, C. E. Fogg, & D. J. LeGall. MPEG Video Compression Standard. In *Digital Multimedia Standards Series.* New York: Chapman & Hall, 1997.

MPEG Web site. www.chiariglione.org/mpeg

F. Pereira, T. Ebrahimi. *The MPEG-4 Book.* Upper Saddle River, NJ: Prentice Hall, 2002.

R. Pirsig. *Zen and the Art of Motorcycle Maintenance: An Inquiry Into Values.* New York: Vintage, 1974.

A. Puri, T. Chen. *Advances in Multimedia, Standards and Networks.* New York: Marcel Dekker, 2000.

R. Schäfer, T. Wiegand, & H. Schwarz. The emerging AVC/H.264 standard. *EBU Technical Review*, January 2003.

A. Walsh, & M. Bourges-Sevenier. *MPEG-4 Jump Start.* Upper Saddle River, NJ: Prentice Hall, 2001.

A.E. Walsh. Understanding Scene Graphs. *Dr. Dobb's Journal.* July 2002.

3.12. References

[1] ISMA Web site. www.isma.tv.
[2] MPEG Industry Forum. www.mpegif.org
[3] DVB Web site. www.dvb.org/
[4] 3GPP Web Site. www.3gpp.org

CHAPTER 4
Technology Beyond the Standard

In order to better understand the implications of some of the items in the standard, this chapter will provide a bit of additional technical background. The material presented here cannot be considered to be complete, however. The selection of topics is based on many discussions and conversations about MPEG-4 with business-oriented professionals throughout recent years.

4.1. Why Do We Need Compression to Begin With?

Digitizing analog video signals expands physical bandwidth requirements. Physical transmission bandwidth or storage capacity is a natural resource that is scarce and thus expensive. This is where compression of digital data comes into play—to make transmission and storage of digital data economically feasible (Watkinson, 2000a [1], 2000b [2]).

Compression techniques have already been used during the age of analog audio and video as a way to achieve bandwidth reduction and to save cost and natural resources. For example, it takes about 10 times as much data for the digital representation of a linear-light progressive scan RGB (Red-Green-Blue) picture, when compared to the representation of the same visual impression as a gamma-corrected interlaced composite video. This fact can also be expressed in that a linear-light progressive scan RGB picture can be represented by the gamma-coded interlaced composite video with a compression factor of 10:1. While the first format is delivered natively by a camera during the course of a movie production, the second is used in television and other forms of entertainment video.

Composite video systems such as the analog domain TV standards PAL, NTSC, and SECAM are all (analog) compression schemes that embed a subcarrier signal, modulated with the color information, in a luminance signal such that color pictures are available in the same bandwidth as monochrome images. Already in the early days of television engineering, it was found that human vision is less sensitive to seeing very fine structures in color signals, i.e., we can see details best in a gray-scale image. This is one reason why color video is represented by color difference signals (YPbPr) instead of plain RGB (Red-Green-Blue). The effect is that the PbPr color difference signals can be presented with a reduced resolution (downsampled), which lowers bandwidth requirements. Furthermore, the representation of video signals in terms of a gray-level channel (called luma Y) and two color difference signals (called chroma and denoted by PbPr) enabled a backward-compatible migration from black-and-white television to color television in 1953 (NTSC), while preserving the existing channel allocation in the physical frequency spectrum for the TV signals. Thus, consumers could still use their "old" black-and-white TV sets and upgrade to color TV whenever the wanted to. This is a good example of an upgrade policy that treats consumers responsibly.

Gamma correction (non-linear relationship between signal voltage and image brightness) is yet another analog technique to adjust the video signal and the physical characteristics of CRT screens and computer monitors—to better match the characteristics of the human visual perception.

Interlace scan is a widely used technique for signal compression in the analog domain (e.g., NTSC, VHS, etc.). There is a huge amount of legacy video material that is available in this format. The idea of interlacing is to display only one half of an image in one instant of time. This is achieved by showing the odd and the even lines of video images in an alternating sequence. If this alternating display of half images is done quickly enough, human perception is not negatively affected. In fact, interlacing helps to reduce the annoying flicker perception using a higher temporal resolution, while bandwidth is saved. However, in the world of digital video there are more effective ways to compress the video signals. Therefore, interlacing is not really needed any longer as a means for bandwidth reduction or compression. In addition to its being outmoded, dealing with interlaced video generally makes the lives of video engineers more difficult. Most MPEGers would like to get rid of interlaced video material, as do many people dealing with computer graphics and animation. However, there is a massive stock of television and movie content that is stored as interlaced video material, which represents an enormous amount of capital and investment. Thus, interlaced material has become a legacy problem for digital video when the broadcasting industry is the field of application. Today's TV sets are still dominantly interlaced displays. If the application scenario is either computer-centric, targeting mobile, or handheld terminals, the displays are not interlaced, but are purely "progressive." (By progressive scan we mean that all lines of one video image are shown at one instance in time.) However, the source material still may be interlaced.

There are several reasons why compression techniques for digital data are popular:

- Compression extends the playing time of media content when stored on a given storage device. Take music playback from MP3 players or the storage of movies on CDs or DVDs. Better compression provides longer playback time.
- Compression allows miniaturization. With fewer data to store, the same playing time is obtained with smaller hardware.
- Demands on physical tolerances for building hardware devices can be relaxed. With fewer data to record, storage density can be reduced, and equipment can be more resistant to adverse environments and require less maintenance.
- In transmission systems, compression allows a reduction in transmission bandwidth requirements, which will generally result in a reduction of cost. For example, satellite transponders are rented or sold by the booked physical transmission

bandwidth, which is measured as a frequency in Mega Hertz (MHz).

- If a given bandwidth is available for an uncompressed signal, compression allows faster than real-time transmission in the same bandwidth. This is of interest to professional services like digital news gathering, or for exchanging audio-visual contributions between TV stations or news agencies.
- If a given bandwidth is available, compression provides a better-quality signal in the same bandwidth.

When it comes to compression of audio-visual data, be aware that there are different perceptions of what constitutes a compressed or an uncompressed signal. The attitude toward this question depends on the actual technical environment. A movie producer dealing with Hollywood-quality material filmed on 35mm film or working with high-quality digital production considers a signal that comes in a YCbCr format, using 4:2:0 chroma sampling at a resolution that, according to ITU-T Rec. 601, is a highly compressed signal (never mind the abbreviations). This is in contrast to the point of view of a video-coding expert at MPEG, who calls the very same signal "uncompressed." A similar point can be made about audio signals. For audio-coding experts, a music signal that comes in stereo with a sample rate of 44.1 kHz with a resolution of 16 linearly quantized bits per sample can be considered an uncompressed signal. This opinion is in direct contrast to the thinking of a professional music recording engineer working in a mastering studio about the very same signal. This difference in the use of terms can lead to some confusion at times.

Let us finish this section with a comment on compression for medical applications. Medical doctors tend to be very critical when it comes to compressing videos and images. They are not willing to accept useful image and video compression technology because there is a chance for the decoded images (images after being compressed and subsequently being decompressed) to slightly deviate from the original images. If the compression technique is applied in an appropriate way, those deviations will not be visible to a human. This is true in particular if the compression is not too hefty. The fact that there may be a mathematical deviation between original and decompressed image is denoted as a lossy compression technology. In contrast to this, a lossless compression technology guarantees the mathematically identical reconstruction of the original image after decompression. In cases where there is a visible deviation between the original image and the decompressed version then those visible deviations are called "coding artifacts." A lossless coding technology cannot produce artifacts. However, lossy image compression achieves more compression. We will talk about this in more detail later. No physician wants to be sued by some lawyer because he operated on a patient based on a coding artifact introduced by a lossy compression technology. So for medical applications, only lossless compression technology is acceptable, regardless of how lousy the imaging process is that produces the "original" images.

4.1.1. Numerology of Digital Audio-Video Data

Bits and Bytes: Sometimes the use of bits and Bytes can be confusing, especially when actual numbers are at stake. Both terms are commonly used in the context of digital technology. A few remarks on the use of these terms are in order to avoid unnecessary confusion.

The size of a file in the computer world is typically measured in terms of Bytes, where a Byte today is taken to be 8 bits. This is not a globally valid definition for a Byte, but it is the interpretation that most people have come to implicitly agree on. When data is transferred in a computer, for example, from a disk to an external device, the transfer rate is typically measured in Bytes per second.

In a communications environment, engineers measure the number of bits that need to be transmitted from A to B. Therefore, bit rates for transmission are measured in terms of bits per second. As indicated above, there is a factor of 8 between 'bits per second' and 'Bytes per second', which seems simple enough. Unfortunately, the situation is slightly more complicated. A kilobyte (KB) denotes $2^{10} = 1024$ Bytes $= 1024*8$ bits, whereas a kilobit (kbit) $= 1000$ bits.

Similarly, 1 Megabyte (MB) denotes $1024*1024 = 2^{20}$ Bytes, and a Megabit (Mbit) is $1000*1000 = 10^6$ bits.

When bit rates for compressed or uncompressed media data are quoted, then the usual measure used is bits/second (bps). Sometimes, in particular when bit rates for video streams over the Internet are quoted, one may read data rates expressed in terms of Bytes per second.

As a general recommendation, we advise reading the quoted numbers carefully with the different meanings in the back of one's mind.

Image formats and bit rates: The notion of image formats in our context describes the size of the images and the frequency with which the images are displayed as a sequence to generate the impression of moving images. Note that the images are not actually moving. It is a feature of our brain to fuse the fast display of images in order to create the perception of motion in video. Nothing is really moving; it is only pixels that change their brightness and color over time. In that sense, our technical language is somewhat sloppy in referring to moving images, motion estimation, motion in video, and so on. However, it is a useful language that helps to simplify the discussion.

The main impact that actual image formats have in the course of this discussion has to do with the amount of data that the images are creating. In various markets, different image formats are used as input to the video and image encoders. We will cover the more dominant aspects of this topic in order to more easily calculate bit rates even before we start compressing. Table 4.1 lists a number of image formats. The formats differ in the size of the images, starting from the two formats for HDTV, which are the largest, all the way down to QCIF images, which are about 1/8 the size of a regular TV screen. The smaller formats may be used for mobile multimedia.

HDTV typically comes in two sizes. While the United States most commonly relies on the HDTV format with 720x1280 pixels and a frame rate of 60 fps, Europe seems to be more interested in the

Table 4.1 Video formats and raw data rates

Format	Rows	Cols	Bits/ sample	Frame Rate	Pixel/sec	kBits/ frame	Bit Rate [kbit/sec]
HDTV 4:4:4	720	1280	24	60	55.296	22.118	1,327.104
HDTV 4.2.2	720	1280	16	60	55.296	14.746	884.736
HDTV 4.2.0	720	1280	12	60	55.296	11.059	663.552
HDTV 4:4:4	1080	1920	24	30	62.208	49.766	1,492.992
HDTV 4:2:2	1080	1920	16	30	62.208	33.178	995.328
HDTV 4:2:0	1080	1920	12	30	62.208	24.883	746.496
Rec. 601 [625] 4:2:0	576	720	12	25	10.368	4.977	124.416
Rec. 601 [525] 4:2:0	480	720	12	30	10.368	4.147	124.416
Rec. 601 [625] 4:2:2	576	720	16	25	10.368	6.636	165.888
Rec. 601 [525] 4:2:2	480	720	16	30	10.368	5.530	165.888
CIF [625]	288	352	12	25	2.534	1.217	30.413
CIF [525]	240	352	12	30	2.534	1.014	30.413
QCIF [625]	144	176	12	12,5	317	304	3.802
QCIF [525]	120	176	12	15	317	253	3.802

1080x1920 format. The formats, according to ITU-T Recommendation 601, come in two versions; one is the 625 version, which corresponds mostly with European PAL systems, and the other is the 525 version, which is associated with the North American NTSC format.

Table 4.2 shows how long video clips can be in order to be storable on either a standard CD-ROM or a standard DVD. (For the purpose of the example, we have assumed that either an HDTV video or a standard definition video clip is being stored.) That is, without compression, it is possible to store 43 seconds of a standard-resolution video on a 650MB CD-ROM. That is a very short movie. Compressing the video using an MPEG-2 video codec at a bit rate of 9 Mbit/sec, we can store a full-resolution video of about 25 minutes in length on a 650MB CD-ROM, and a video of about 74 minutes in length on a 4.7GB DVD. For this example, we have assumed a compression factor of about 13. Typical compression factors for broadcast TV are in the range of 35 or higher. For squeezing the video through an ISDN connection with 64 kbit/sec bandwidth, we require a compression factor in excess of 1900. Clearly, compression is both helpful and necessary.

Audio resolutions and bit rates: As with video, the main impact that audio formats have concerns the amount of audio data before a compressor starts its work.

Looking at Table 4.3, one can calculate that a 650MB CD-ROM can store 64 minutes of uncompressed music (consumer CD), while a 64MB flash memory card can only hold stereo music of about 6 minutes in length. An MP3 player with a storage capacity of 64 MB can hold about 69 minutes of music if the material is

Table 4.2 Storage of video on disks

	DVD (4,7 GB)	CD-ROM (650 MB)
HDTV 4.2.0	1.01 minutes	8.22 seconds
Rec. 601 [625] 4:2:0	5.41 minutes	43.83 seconds

Table 4.3 Audio formats and uncompressed bit rates

Application	Channels	Sample Rate [kHz]	Bits/ sample	Bit Rate [kbit/sec]
Telephony				
Speech	1	8	16	128
Digital Radio	2	35	16	1.120,00
Consumer CD	2	44,1	16	1.411,20
Studio CD, DAT	2	48	16	1.536,00
Studio CD, DAT	2	48	20	1.920,00
High-End Stereo	2	96	24	4.608,00
Studio Surround	6	48	16	4.608,00
High-End				
Surround	6	96	24	13.824,00

compressed at a bit rate of 128 kbit/sec. Looking at the fanciest audio format in the table, it is easy to see that audio bit rates are dwarfed by the bit rates necessary for video, which may be one reason audio compression is often underestimated. However, the tremendous success of MP3 makes it clear that high-quality audio compression has a tremendous impact on the music business and the consumer electronics markets.

4.2. What Actually Is Compression for Audio-Visual Data?

It is the goal of any type of compression to reduce or minimize the amount of data necessary to represent digitally coded information. Even though the layperson tends to interchange the notions of information and data, a clear distinction is made between the concepts when it comes to compression. Compression is reducing the *amount* of data while preserving somewhat the information *contained* in the data.

The data rate of a data source is reduced by the compressor or encoder. The compressed data are then passed through a communication channel or stored on a storage device and returned to the original rate by the decompressor or decoder. The ratio between the source data rate and the channel data rate is called the compression factor. The term "coding gain" is also used. The tandem of an encoder and a decoder is called a codec. Where the encoder is more complex than the decoder, the system is said to be asymmetrical.

Compression of digital data is divided into two major categories—lossless and lossy compression.

4.2.1. Lossless Compression

Lossless compression features a bit-exact reconstruction of data after decompression, i.e., when data is compressed and decompressed, the original data is restored exactly, bit for bit. This implies that there is no loss of information throughout the compression process, which is what a user expects when, for example, he compresses a text file using a ZIP program. After extraction of the corresponding .zip file, the original text file is restored.

The actual compression is achieved by a process that eliminates the redundancy inherent in a given data set. The information content (or entropy) of a sample is a function of how different it is from the value that can be predicted by knowing the value of other samples. Most signals have some degree of predictability. A sine wave is highly predictable, because all cycles look the same. According to Shannon's theory, any signal that is totally predictable carries no information. In the case of the sine wave, this is clear because it represents a single frequency and so has no bandwidth, and all its values can be safely predicted. The amount of information increases with the unpredictability of an event. The message that the New York Yankees have won the World Series certainly carries less information than the message that the Boston Red Socks finally got rid of the 'spell of the Babe.' The second event is clearly harder to predict and may even make bigger headlines. Newspapers have a tendency to measure the amount of information by the size of the printed headlines. An alternative example is the headline "dog bites man" which represents a more predicable or more probable event than "man bites dog." Therefore, the amount of information carried by the second news item is higher.

At the opposite extreme, a signal such as noise is completely unpredictable and as a result, all codecs find noise difficult or even impossible to compress. The difference between the information rate and the overall bit rate is known as the redundancy. Compression systems are designed to eliminate as much of that redundancy as is practical or perhaps affordable.

The performance of a lossless compression system is measured in terms of compression speed, or computational complexity, for encoding and decoding and the achievable compression factor (calculated as the quotient of the uncompressed file size and the compressed file size) when applied to a set of representative data sets.

Coding performance for lossless compression techniques applied to audio-visual data is typically restricted to compression factors of between 2:1 and 3:1. Lossless compression applied to other types of data, such as text, can lead to significantly higher compression factors. The interested reader may perform some experiments by applying a ZIP program (e.g., WinZIP) to various files sitting on the hard disk. Take for example a Word file, which only contains text, and compress it. Then take a PowerPoint file, which contains text and additional graphical elements or images, and compress this. There should be quite a significant difference in the achieved compression factor.

4.2.2. Lossy Compression

The main difference between lossy and lossless compression is that lossy compression does not allow for a bit-exact reconstruction of the original data after decompression, i.e., the decompressed data deviates from the original data. Therefore, lossy compression is not suitable for compressing computer data such as text files or .exe files.

Lossy codecs are used in situations where the end receiver of the data is a human being. In such a situation, the errors after decoding, that is, the deviation of the decompressed data from the original data, have the property that a human viewer or listener finds them subjectively difficult or even impossible to detect. In other words, the person watching images and listening to audio can not distinguish between the original and the decompressed data. Of course, this statement is conditional to the individual sensory abilities of the person involved. Some people see and hear more than others.

An example of a lossy compression application from everyday life will help to clarify the underlying concepts. For this discussion, consider the illustration in Figure 4.1. Orange Juice is to be produced. Oranges are picked in Florida and squeezed at a factory. If this "freshly squeezed" orange juice is supposed to be shipped around the world, it weighs a lot and the transport would be costly. The producers therefore would want to remove constituents of the juice that are redundant, that is, constituents that are not unique to orange juice from Florida. For example, water is redundant. The formula for pure water is fairly well known around the world (in contrast to the formula for Coca-Cola, for example). Therefore, water can be extracted from the orange juice. This process leaves

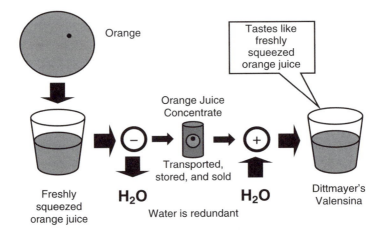

Figure 4.1 Schematic representation of the concept of lossy compression.

us with orange juice concentrate, which weighs much less and takes less storage space, and is much easier to package and ship around the world. Once the orange juice arrives at its destination, water can be brought back in to recreate "fresh-squeezed" orange juice. Of course, the orange juice recreated from the concentrate is not identical to the original juice. However, if the process of extracting water, that is, the compression, is done in a faithful way, the recreated juice is hardly distinguishable from the freshly squeezed orange juice. The error is not perceptible, at least for the majority of people. (There will always be some French chefs who can clearly tell the difference.)

It's the same situation with compressing video or audio data. There are always experts with those golden eyes or golden ears who can tell the difference between original and coded data. But the average person will not be able to detect the difference. Lossy compression aims to reduce or eliminate information that is irrelevant to the receiver. If we, as the final receiver of the audio-visual information, cannot hear or see the difference, then it is certainly irrelevant to us.

For a system to eliminate irrelevant information, a good understanding of the psycho-acoustic and the psycho-visual perception process is necessary. Compression systems based on such models or perception are often referred to as perceptive coders. Perceptive coders can be forced to operate at a fixed compression factor. However, in such a situation, the subjective quality of images and audio can vary with the "difficulty" of the corresponding input material.

The performance of a lossy compression technique is measured in terms of the complexity of encoders and decoders as well by assessing the tradeoff between compression factor and quality of the decoded images or audio. Measuring the quality of audio and video compression is a critical and difficult task, which we will discuss in more detail in a later chapter.

Compression factors achieved by lossy compression techniques applied to audio-visual data are generally much higher than the compression achieved by lossless methods, and lies sometimes in the range of 100:1, depending on the application.

In summary, a data-compression system consists of three major building blocks, which are shown in Figure 4.2. The first box contains algorithms to predict the signal values that are about to be processed. If the system can make good predictions, it understands the signal well and there is not much that needs to be memorized or transmitted in order to recreate the signal. Whatever portion of the signal the predictor cannot predict or anticipate must be unanticipated and hence new information, which will be fed to the second box. In the second box, a mathematical model is included that helps determine which information is supposed to be irrelevant to the receiver. This is the part of the process where data may be lost and the final quality of the audio or video is determined. Finally, whatever is left as relevant information will be further analyzed for inherent redundancies, which can be exploited by a lossless compression algorithm. Thus, the elimination of redundancy in the data sets is also a topic for lossy compression systems.

Of course, a pertaining decoder must invert those processing steps in order to recreate the audio or visual data. However, the information lost in the second block cannot be regained. The lost and (hopefully) irrelevant information is responsible for any type of mathematical deviation between the original signal and the decompressed one. If the model for distinction between relevant and irrelevant information is accurate and precise, a better compression performance can be achieved. This is actually the case with audio coding à la MP3, where a mathematical model is used to determine the parts of the audio signal which are not perceivable by a human

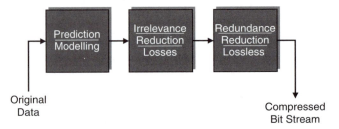

Figure 4.2 Main building blocks of a lossy compression system for audio-visual data sets.

listener, and hence, can be discarded for achieving better compression. The various MP3 encoders in the market mainly differ in the quality of this model for the human hearing system.

In the field of lossy compression, there is no overall theory that helps to precisely predict the achievable compression results of the next-generation lossy compression schemes. The proof of the pudding comes after implementing a coding strategy and assessing the achieved performance by means of subjective tests.

4.2.3. Some Video Coding Terminology

An essential part of MPEG video coding is based on exploiting the similarity of subsequent frames in a video sequence. For a video sequence to make sense for a human the pixels should not change arbitrarily from to frame. If this were the case our brain would not be able to fuse the individual pictures into a continuous flow of moving pictures and the illusion of motion would be lost.

This effect can be used for compression. Subsequent frames of a video sequence have a lot of pixels in common. The pixels are either identical from frame to frame in which case nothing really happens throughout the video. This applies to the background of a scene or if still images are shown. If a picture has been already transmitted and is therefore known to the decoder it is sufficient to only transmitt the pixels that have changed since then in order to update the image. This helps to save bits. If it is not the background then a lot of pixels from the previous frame are still visible in the current frame, but slightly displaced at a different location. This displacement of pixels may be due to moving objects in the sequence. It is not necessary to transmitt all the changed pixels, but it is sufficient to tell the decoder where the pixels have moved in the meantime. This information is conveyed by means of so-called motion vectors, which need to be estimated in the encoder by means of a costly estimation process, the motion estimation.

Based on this concept of only sending information that has changed a compression is achieved for video. In this context three types of images are used, called I-frames, P-frames, and B-frames, which will be introduced in the following.

4.2.3.1. I-Frames

An I-frame is a single frame in a video clip that is compressed without making reference to any previous or subsequent frame in the sequence. This frame is compressed using techniques that are similar to still image compression techniques, such as those employed in the JPEG compression standard. For professional video editing systems that use compression as a means to extend hard disk capacities or required transmission bandwidth, so-called 'I-frame only' video codecs are used. This way, a frame-accurate editing of a video clip is still possible. However, using 'I-frame only' codecs for video compression is by all means a luxury as such codecs are inferior in compression efficiency as compared to a codec that uses B-frames or P-frames (to be explained in the next sections). For television systems, an I-frame is sent typically every half second in order to enable channel surfing. I-frames are the only frames in a video data stream that can be decoded by its own (i.e., without needing any other frames as reference).

4.2.3.2. P-Frames

P-frames have their name from being predicted from a previous reference frame. That means that if a particular P-frame needs to be decoded, a reference frame is needed which is a frame that appears at an earlier time instant in the sequence (see Figure 4.3).

Even though P-frames are based on predictions coming from previous reference frames, a P-frame can again serve as a reference frame for predicting later P-frames. P-frames are an effective video coding tool to improve coding efficiency as compared to a pure image encoder, which compresses each frame individually without making reference to any other frame. All coding schemes offering premium coding performance have a P-frame mechanism employed. However, using P-frames for coding requires the encoder and in the decoder to store the reference frame. A price to be paid for using P-frames is that frame exact editing in the coded bit

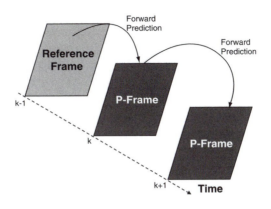

Figure 4.3 Concept of a P-frame.

stream is no longer possible. In order to reconstruct a P-frame the pertaining reference frame is needed. If it is gone due to cutting the video material during editing, the P-frame is gone as well.

4.2.3.3. B-Frames

B-frames have their name from being bi-directionally predicted from at least two reference frames. That means for decoding a particular B-frame a reference frame that appears earlier in the sequence (reference frame 1) and one other reference frame that appears later in the sequence (reference frame 2) are needed (see Figure 4.4).

Even though B-frames are based on predictions coming from two neighboring frames, a B-frame is not itself used as a reference frame for predicting other frames. This would lead to an aggregation of coding errors, which kills coding efficiency or image quality. B-frames are an effective video coding tool to improve coding efficiency. All coding schemes offering premium coding performance have a B-frame mechanism employed. However, using B-frames for coding requires more memory in the encoder and in the decoder as an extra frame (reference frame 2) needs to be stored during the decoding process. Furthermore, B-frames introduce extra delay, which is unacceptable for example in conversational applications. There, no B-frames are used. This holds for H.263 and

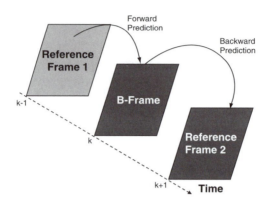

Figure 4.4 Concept of a B-frame.

its precursors as well as for MPEG-4 Simple Profile. For television services based on MPEG-2, there are typically 2 successive B-frames between two reference frames to further increase coding efficiency. Another price to be paid by B-frames is that frame exact editing in the coded bit stream is no longer possible. In order to reconstruct the red coloured B-frame in Figure 4.4, both reference frames are needed. If either one of them is gone due to cutting the video material, the B-frame is gone as well.

4.2.4. Constant Bit-Rate Coding (CBR) vs. Variable Bit-Rate Coding (VBR)

CBR coding and VBR coding are two principles that are often mentioned in the context of video coding products. In this section, we give a brief explanation of those modes of operation for a video encoder. For the decoder, both modes are the same as long as the parameters and limitations set by the profiles and level definition are not breached.

Variable bit-rate coding: A compression system as shown in Figure 4.2 produces at its output a bit stream that has a variable bit rate. This variable bit rate is part of the principles employed as a compression algorithm in the encoder. The bit rate variations correspond to the difficulty of the signal to be compressed. In other words, the bit rate increases if the signal carries more relevant information, and it drops if there is very little relevant information in the signal. Hence the name, variable bit rate coding, or VBR for short. The variation in the bit rate is not controlled by any mechanism, and the image or audio quality stays more or less constant, corresponding to "quantization parameter Q," a coding parameter in the irrelevance reduction block in Figure 4.5, which controls the amount of information that is considered relevant. Therefore, this particular variable bit rate coding mode is more correctly called "constant Q mode." The bit rate of such an encoder is not predetermined, which is the reason why this mode is hardly ever used in real applications. But for research and development purposes, such as standardization work, this is the regular mode for encoding. One reason why 'constant Q' mode is used dominantly during the standardization work is that rate control is a component of the encoding process, which is not the main focus of MPEG standardization. Yet another reason is that in real products, the rate control algorithm is the part that makes the difference in quality between the products of different vendors. This is also the part of the encoder which contains the models for the human perception, to distinguish between relevant and irrelevant information. Thus, rate control is a major aspect of competition. Of course, no serious vendor of MPEG technology is willing to share her own approach or solution for rate control with the competitors during standardization.

Constant bit-rate coding: An alternative mode of operation, and one that is more standard for an encoder in the market, is to introduce a mechanism to control the bit rate at the output of the encoder. The fullness of a buffer is measured, and according to the level of fullness, a parameter in the irrelevance reduction block is modified in order to influence the production of bits at the output. It is the purpose of the buffer to average out over time the fluctuation of the bit rate. The bit stream is read from the buffer at a constant rate, while it is filled at a variable rate. This works fine as long as the average filling rate is equal to the constant emptying rate. The corresponding encoder structure is shown in Figure 4.5. The result is that the encoder produces a bit stream at its output that has a constant bit rate. Hence the name, constant bit rate or CBR coding.

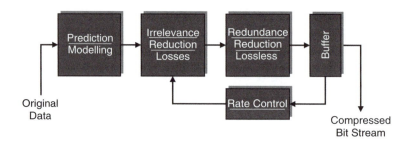

Figure 4.5 Rate control for lossy compression system.

CBR coding is used when TV channels are distributed over satellite channels, for example. A fixed bandwidth or bit rate is assigned to a TV channel, say 6 Mbit/sec, and charged accordingly. CBR coding is also important when streaming video over the Internet, especially if the users are using connections with a fixed maximum bit rate, like ISDN or dial-up connections. The video needs to be compressed such that the best possible video quality is delivered. To this end, the encoder makes use of the maximum available bit rate. But the maximum coded bit rate must not exceed the transmission capacity, otherwise information may get lost and the video stops or goes black.

Variable bit-rate coding revisited: Let's come back to variable bit-rate coding for a minute. As mentioned before, a variable bit rate is created by running an encoder with no rate control. But there is another way of creating a bit stream with a variable bit rate. This is done by controlling the bit rate as in the CBR coding scenario (Figure 4.5), but the rate control mechanism tries to adjust the bit rate to achieve a pre-specified average while not exceeding a pre-specified maximum bit rate. This may be seen as the true variable bit-rate coding setup. The benefit over the previously described VBR coding scheme is that the variation of the bit rate is not happening in a random and thus unpredictable way, but under the regime of a rate control algorithm. If the variation in the bit rate is controlled and therefore known, this can be used constructively by broadcasters, for example, to employ statistical multiplexing. Statistical multiplexing is a technique that enables multiple independent TV channels to be transmitted over a satellite link sharing a bulk of bandwidth. Each channel may come as a variable bit-rate stream, and the multiplexer assigns his bandwidth budgets dynamically to the individual channels. This allows savings on bandwidth and cost, somewhere in the range of 20%. However, it may be difficult to guarantee a specific quality of service for the individual channels. From a business point of view, this may make it challenging for the satellite service provider issuing the invoices.

4.3. Do We Still Need Compression in the Future?

Ubiquitous broadband access in the future: As has been widely discussed in press articles, there is a bright future ahead of us, where more and more bandwidth is available for delivering any sort of media data over a variety of transmission channels to any consumer, wherever she is. The list of transmission media includes the Internet (IP networks) and more traditional broadcast channels such as satellite, cable, or terrestrial distribution channels. Various flavors of DSL or cable networks also offer increasing transmission capacities contributing their share to this enjoyable future. Furthermore, wireless technologies such as WLAN, GPRS, or UMTS show the promise of adding further broadband capabilities to the bag of tricks. Regardless of which technology you choose, it is clear that, in the foreseeable future, broadband access will be ubiquitous and affordable for everyone.

Compression technology—dinosaur technology? Imagine a lively discussion between a compression technologist and technology-savvy business person about the long-term value of compression technology. In the course of the discussion, the compression technologist may be faced with the question of why we continue to bother to compress audio-visual data if there is enough bandwidth around to stream or broadcast or exchange any sort of media material. Isn't media compression about to become the dinosaur of information technology, bound to be extinct once ubiquitous broadband access has arrived?

We could pull out many facts to prove the opposite, to make a strong statement in favor of the longevity of compression technology and to establish it as one of the crown jewels of information technology. Rather than giving such a formal explanation, we'll draw on a simple story to make the point.

Electrical power generation and consumption 100 years ago: Consider the situation with electrical power at the beginning of the 20th century. While it was technologically possible at that time to produce electrical power, building a large-scale power plant was a technological challenge and not economically feasible. At that time, production and consumption of electrical energy was in its infancy, and the volumes were rather low compared to today. Imagine that there was an entrepreneur who wanted to build a large and modern factory utilizing the latest technology. The factory would contain a large number of machines, all powered by electrical energy. Asking a power production company around 1900 to provide an outlet to offer a couple of hundred Megawatt hours of electrical energy would have represented a major technological challenge and an insurmountable economic obstacle.

Today it still pays to save on electrical power: Today, providing the necessary amount of electrical energy for such a factory no longer poses any real technical or economic challenge. The power company would only ask how much energy is needed and when it should start delivering. In addition, the company would negotiate a price and ask a few questions concerning finances. This last bit of information is still required, as power doesn't come for free. Today, energy consumption is of course much higher than what people used 100 years ago. But there is also far more electrical power available, and as the price for power drops, more and more appliances are being used that consume electrical power. Power outlets are ubiquitous and electrical power is always available (except for California and some developing countries). However, since energy still costs money, it usually pays to save energy, for example, by using energy-saving light bulbs or dishwashers with an economy mode, and so on. Companies often advise their employees to switch off electrical devices at the end of the day in order to save energy.

Even ubiquitous bandwidth will not be free: Compare this picture of power consumption today to the situation concerning broadband access today and tomorrow. If broadband access is widely available, getting high-speed data connections will no longer be an issue of technological feasibility. Also, as more and more bandwidth becomes available at lower and lower prices, we will be using more and more bandwidth. As a consequence, there will be more and more appliances in use, which will rely on seamless access to broadband data pipes. Finally, transmission or storage bandwidth will become cheaper as time progresses. However, bandwidth will not be completely free, and hence it will still pay to save on bandwidth for the simple reason of cutting cost. Compression is the technology to save bandwidth and thus to save cost. Saving money never seems to be out of fashion.

Ride the wave with largest growth: As a last comment on this topic, observe that the performance of compression is largely dependent on the available computation power. This also means that there is a connection between achievable compression and Moore's law, which governs the speed by which computing power is increased. Typically, processor performance grows faster than transmission bandwidth. Therefore, it will be more economical to apply compression to digital data as a means to reduce the amount of data than waiting for the next generation of broadband access offering more bandwidth and/or lower prices. To this end, you will need to compare the cost of compression technology with the cost of transmission/storage media.

4.4. Measuring Coding Performance—Science, Marketing, or a Black Art?

Assessing the performance of audio-visual compression technology is done by calculating compression factors and comparing the resulting figures. Also, you may read press releases of companies who make bold statements that their most recent coding product is 10% better than the best previously known codec. While this sounds like a fair enough statement, it is quite difficult to come up with such a conclusion, as it is very difficult to actually quantify such improvements. It is often not clear what aspect of the codec has been improved by those 10%, and what are the conditions under which this claim needs to be seen. That's all part of marketing and some level of murky statements helps to sell. Therefore, in this section we try to elaborate a bit more on how the quality or performance of audio-visual codecs can be thoroughly assessed. This process may appear to be straightforward at the outset, but the job of testing can involve a number of pitfalls.

4.4.1. Questions on Coding Performance

First of all, for lossy compression of audio-visual data, there is no theory that gives you a formula to determine the coding performance. The performance needs to be evaluated based on coding experiments that are designed to give answers to questions, such as the following.

- **How does the latest coding technology compare to previously known coding technologies?** This question needs some clarification. By coding technology we mean the coding tools and options offered by a standard like MPEG-4. More specifically, the question is currently phrased as "How much better is MPEG-4 than MPEG-2?" or "How does MPEG-4 compare to H.263?" Within one standard, the question might be phrased, "How much better is the coding performance of Advanced Simple Visual Profile when compared with Simple Visual Profile?" The difficulty in answering this question properly is to exclude the influence of the encoder as far as possible. Various encoders may exploit the features of a coding technology very differently, with very different compression quality, and still produce coded bits streams within the same coding technology. That is where competition comes into the picture.
- **How does the current status of a codec implementation compare to previous versions?** This is a question that developers of codecs need to ask regularly to assess the progress of their work. By that time, the choice of a certain compression

technology, e.g., MPEG-4, has already been made. The encoder is continuously optimized for coding performance and the developers need to monitor and document the progress of their work. To this end, the visual quality of the current iteration needs to be compared with the performance of the previous version.

- **How does encoder A compare to encoder B (for the same standard)?** This is basically the same situation as for the previous question. The difference lies in the fact that the two encoders may be originating from different vendors, and you have to make a choice of which one to buy. For this scenario, it is assumed that the decoder is considered fixed, that is, a broadcaster is about to buy new encoding equipment for his already existing MPEG-2-based TV services.
- **How does a video coding product from company A based on coding technology X compare to the product of company B that uses technology Y?** This is the most generic question, and therefore may be the most involved to answer correctly. Comparing codecs which are based on different coding technologies requires performing thoroughly designed subjective quality tests. Different coding technologies tend to produce different types of coding artifacts, which tend to make comparisons more difficult. Also, if fundamentally different codecs are supposed to be compared there are numerous criteria which can be compared. Examples are the encoding and decoding complexity and cost, encoding speed, and delay. Furthermore, various products may employ some proprietary pre- and post-processing tools, which again make a faithful comparison difficult. Usually, a report on comparing codecs in such a context requires a report of several pages. It is all doable, but beware for oversimplified conclusions.

Besides these questions, there are others that are frequently discussed in public mailing lists, press articles, conferences and the like, the meaning of which sometimes is a bit difficult to understand. Here are some examples.

- **Which offers the better compression—MPEG-4 or Windows Media?** This question sounds a lot like the previous one and looks legitimate at first sight, but is it really meaningful? It is similar to asking, Is this race car faster than a V6 cylinder motor? To compare a motor with a car is meaningless. The motor would need to at least have a competitive chassis, right? This is similar to comparing a coding standard like MPEG-4 with a product like Windows Media. MPEG-4 is not a product; it takes more the role of the motor without the chassis. For such a comparison, it is certainly a valid approach to pick a video coding product from company C on the market that is based on MPEG-4 coding technology and do a fair test against Microsoft Windows Media codec. This test will answer who has the better product, but the meaning of the original question still remains murky. After all, a ranking of coding products according to their coding performance is only a temporary thing, as new updates and improvements are issued that mix up the order on a regular basis.

4.4.2. Calculating a Compression Factor

Out of the many figures of merit, the compression factor achieved by any compression technology is certainly the most interesting single factor to express the performance of a scheme, reminiscent of the use of the clock cycles for expressing the speed of a microprocessor. It is not wrong to state that a computer with double the clock frequency offers more speed and performance than a computer with a lower clock frequency. But experience tells you that the actual performance of a computer system depends on more parameters and characteristics than clock frequency alone.

Compression factor is an easy-to-calculate quantity and a feature that is even easier to sell. So it runs the risk of sometimes being oversold. To calculate the compression, determine the file size or bit rate of the uncompressed material. Next, determine the file size or bit rate of the data *after* compression. Calculate the quotient of uncompressed and compressed file sizes and—voila—you are done! When comparing the compression performance of two competing systems or schemes, we may face the question of what happens if video parameters are very different and the compression ratios are hard to compare. As we mentioned earlier, there may be different points of view when it comes to the notion of uncompressed material. Starting from HDTV (720p, 60fps) material and compressing it to QCIF resolution at 10fps yields a different compression factor than compressing an NTSC resolution video to CIF resolution at 30fps. In order to compare coding systems operating on entirely different video material, it is helpful to calculate the bit rate in terms of bits/pixels to get a rough idea of coding efficiency, bit rates, and quality.

Let's look at a small example. We take two video sequences denoted by S_1 and S_2, which have different technical parameters and playing time. The parameters for both sequences are listed in Table 4.4.

To continue with the same example, we have two codecs denoted by Codec A and Codec B. Sequence S_1 will be encoded with Codec A, and S_2 will be encoded using Codec B. The resulting file sizes for the compressed video sequences are given in Table 4.5 below. Calculating the compression factor based on those file sizes gives the impression that Codec B compresses better than Codec A since

Table 4.4 Parameters for the two different test sequences

Sequence	Codec	Duration [seconds]	Frame Rate [fps]	Horizontal Size [pixel]	Vertical Size [pixel]	Bits/ pixel	File Size [byte] uncompressed
S_1	A	10	30	176	144	12	11,404,800
S_2	B	12	25	720	576	20	311,040,000

Table 4.5 Parameters for the two different test sequences

Codec	File Size [byte] compressed	Compression Factor	Bits/pixel (compressed)
A	133,056	85.7	0.14
B	2,177,280	142.9	0.14

it results in a higher compression factor. It needs to be noticed that the two examples S_1 and S_2 are very different in terms of image size and frame rate, for example. In order to take those differences into account it is easy to calculate the average number of bits per pixel. Then it becomes apparent that Codec A and Codec B actually give the same coding performance.

Table 4.6 shows three examples for bit rates that may be used for video services. HDTV television services may operate using bit rates somewhere around 19 Mbit/sec. For standard television services, 3.5 Mbit/sec is not uncommon. Finally, for services over DSL lines, a bit rate of 800 kbit/sec is reasonable. For each of these services, the image size has been reduced to make the video fit the size of the transmission pipes. The bit/pixel calculation for the compressed bit streams for the three services mentioned here show that the compression factor a video codec must provide is in the range of 35.

Note that the calculation so far implicitly assumes that the visual quality generated by the codecs to be compared is the same. This is generally very difficult to achieve and even more difficult to guarantee. When lossy compression is used, we need to take into account the visual impairments in the compressed video.

This approach of calculating compression factors works well as long as lossless compression is employed exclusively. But if the compression introduces losses, then the compression factors are

Table 4.6 Compression factors for three reference applications

Format	Rows	Cols	Frame Rate [fps]	Bit Rate [kbit/ sec]	Bits/pixel (compressed)	Compression Factor
HDTV						
4.2.0	720	1280	60	19.0	0.344	35
Rec.601						
[625] 4:2:0	576	720	25	3.50	0.338	35
CIF [625]	288	352	25	800	0.316	38

contingent on the distortion (amount of losses) the audio-visual has endured. There are two basic approaches to doing this.

1) Adjust the parameters of the codecs to be compared such that they all produce the same visual quality. Then read off the resulting bit rate for each codec when compressing a set of chosen test sequences and take the one with the smallest file size as the winner.
2) Take a set of target bit rates (or compression factors) for compressing a set of test sequences. Adjust the coding parameters for each codec such that they all produce the specified target compression. The winner is the codec that produces the best quality.

Approach 1 is the most appealing from a marketing and sales perspective since the final message is easy to quantify and easy to communicate to people. If one particular codec produces 10% better compression, for example, this is easy to communicate and business benefits based on this improvement are easy to calculate. The difficulty with this approach lies in the task of adjusting the parameters for equal visual quality. What does equal visual quality mean and how do you measure it, not to mention shoot for a certain level of quality? In short, this may be a highly desirable way of comparing codecs, but practically speaking, it will not work. If you try to convince a video coding expert to do this type of test, you will immediately see an unhappy face.

Approach 2 is technically the only feasible and sound approach. The difficult part is still the measurement of visual quality, but this can be taken care of by the methodology that is used to design the experiments to be done and the type of measurements to be taken. We will further discuss the quality measurement issue in the section that follows.

4.4.3. Measuring Quality

As mentioned in the previous section, measuring the quality of the compressed video or audio is an essential part of determining the compression performance of a codec. In this section, we will elaborate a bit more on how to measure quality.

All the following explanations are based on the assumption that Approach 2 from the previous section is used. This means that test material is selected (audio or video examples), coding conditions are set, and target bit rates are specified for each test sequence. The encoders compress the test material to produce coded representations of the video or audio samples. Subsequently, the coded bit streams are decoded to create the decompressed video or audio, the quality of which needs to be determined. Quality in this context can be measured fundamentally by two different methods.

1) Calculating measurable quantities—objective measurements
2) Performing viewing tests—subjective testing

Objective measurements: As a unit of quality measurement, the root mean square error is calculated (RMS). The original audio/video signals are taken and the decoded versions are subtracted from them. The result is either an error image or an error sound. All error image pixel values are squared and summed up. The lower the RMS, the better the quality. Engineers often prefer to deal with logarithmic quantities for pure convenience, and therefore the RMS value is transformed into a logarithmic value, which is called PSNR (Peak Signal-to-Noise Ratio). A higher value for the PSNR implies a better quality image. If a quality measure is required for the entire sequence, then the PSNR values for all the frames in the sequence are averaged to produce one single number. The same procedure is applied in principle for audio signals. Interestingly, it has become common for sequence quality measurements to be calculated using the mean value over the PSNR values for all frames, which is mathematically different than calculating the average of the RMS values and then transforming the resulting mean RMS into PSNR. (The second way is the mathematically correct way of doing it.)

This a simple calculation and leads to consistent results. However, the PSNR values do not necessarily correspond very well with the visual quality that is perceived when people are actually looking at the images or listening to the audio. It often happens that in spite of a higher PSNR value, a sequence is visually judged to be inferior. Similarly, it just as often happens that a video sequence shows a lower PSNR value while still being judged to be superior. The same observation holds for assessing audio quality. PSNR is a mathematical tool that does not reflect human visual or audio perception very well, but which is often used due to its simplicity.

Using PSNR values to evaluate visual quality is a reasonable way of answering the second question that was formulated in the previous section. That is, during development of encoders, the progress can be efficiently measured using PSNR.

Unfortunately, in situations where comparisons are to be made between fundamentally different coding techniques, PSNR values become almost useless. This is because if coding techniques are fundamentally different, then they are likely to produce different types of artifacts and the distortions will look or sound very different. In such situations, PSNR does not tell you very much and what it tells you is usually inaccurate. One important method of assessing coding performance involves producing a so-called "rate-distortion curve." Video codecs typically have a parameter, mentioned earlier, which is called quantization parameter Q. This parameter determines the amount of losses or distortion that a codec produces. Parameter Q has a certain range of permissible values, typically in the range of 1 to 32. In order to determine the rate-distortion curve, a video sequence is coded with all codecs that need to be compared. For each encoding run, a new fixed value for quantization parameter Q is set. This is called "constant Q" coding mode. After the encoding is done, the mean PSNR value for the coded sequence is determined along with the average bit rate (file size divided by length of sequence). Both values are entered in a chart the plots the PSNR values as a function of the average bit rate. An example of such a rate-distortion plot is shown in Figure 4.6.

This is a reasonably sound approach for assessing the coding performance of codecs that are not too different in terms of coding techniques. The rate-distortion curve depicted in Figure 4.6 suggests that Codec 3 has only half the coding performance of Codec 2, (i.e., Codec 3 needs about twice the amount of data compared to

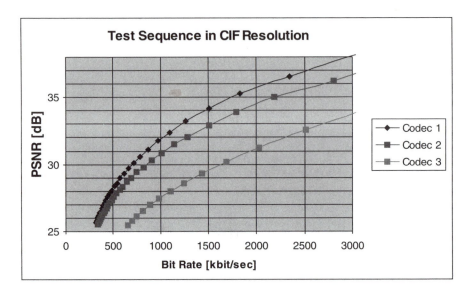

Figure 4.6 Rate-distortion curve for three different video codecs using constant Q coding mode and measuring PSNR as a measure of quality.

Codec 2 to achieve the same level of quality). Codec 2 has a PSNR-measured quality of 31 dB at a bit rate of 1 Mbit/sec. Codec 3 requires a bit rate of 2 Mbit/sec to reach the 31 dB point. This observation indicates a 2:1 performance ratio.

Of course, when the rate-distortion curves of many sequences have been determined, then all the corresponding curves can be averaged again to come up with a summarized rate-distortion curve. All of the calculated numbers are easy to plot out and to publish. However, care must be taken not to draw the wrong conclusions from these curves, as they only loosely correspond to subjectively perceived video and audio quality.

Note that there is a lot of averaging going on here. That means that the actual benefits for one codec or another may differ significantly depending on the test material chosen.

Subjective testing: Since measuring compression performance is difficult and it is apparently much easier to issue bold performance claims for any given technology or product, we would like to discuss the subjective assessment of coding quality and performance in some depth. In essence, a thorough performance assessment requires that a subjective evaluation procedure be performed. To do this, people are put in front of a monitor where they watch images and listen to audio and are then asked to vote on what they saw and heard in a kind of blindfolded test. This way, the test subjects rank the codecs based on their subjective quality perception.

There are standards and recommendations for how the experimental setup is supposed to look—what type of monitor, the amount and type of ambient light, the color on the walls of the laboratory environment, the view distance, the voting procedure, and so on. The idea is to be able to create reproducible test conditions in any laboratory around the world and to minimize the influence of the laboratory setup. Another necessary step to ensure the success of the test is to measure the people's visual acuity to exclude blind or nearly blind test persons. Finally, the choice of tools and techniques for doing the statistical analysis on the voting data is another important task. Detection and removal of outliers and other undesirable trends, as well as the validation of the results, are time-consuming jobs that require experienced and skillful engineers.

All this subjective testing is made necessary by the lossy nature of audio-visual compression technology, and it is the reason why the quality assessment of coding performance for lossy compression systems is a very difficult and costly procedure. Clearly, doing an objective measurement instead would be much easier.

The machinery is available to do such subjective meaningful measurements automatically without the inclusion of test persons, based on the concept of "just noticeable differences" (JND). However, those "objective measurements" are not yet able to provide the full truth—so far the coding experts only rely on real eyeballs if a final conclusion on coding quality is needed.

Figure 4.7 is an example of plotted data as it comes out of a subjective test. In this particular test, three codecs (MPEG-4

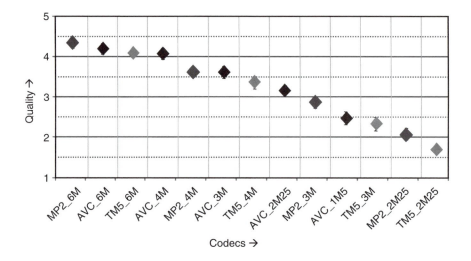

Figure 4.7 Example of a result from subjective testing of three different codecs (MPEG-4 AVC, MPEG-2 TM5, and MPEG-2 High Quality) on standard-definition resolution video material ("Football" sequence).

AVC/H.264, MPEG-2 TM5, and MPEG-2 High Quality) have been tested to compress a sequence called "Football." The sequence had standard-definition resolution (SD) and was coded with five different bit rates (6, 4, 3, 2.25, and 1 Mbit/sec). The dots in the plot represent the average score the test persons gave, and an error bar is given to indicate the variation of the answers of the test persons. The value 5 represents excellent quality, whereas a value of 1 represents poor quality. A simple but reliable reading of this plot is based on the rule that if the error bars belonging to measurement points have an overlap, then the difference between the average scores are not statistically significant. This particular plot tells us that in this test, AVC at 4 Mbit/sec performed as well as the MPEG-2 High Quality codec at 6 Mbit/sec. Alternatively, one may interpret that AVC at 1 Mbit/sec is visually equivalent to MPEG-2 TM5 at 3 Mbit/sec. Now you can calculate the difference in coding performance and be sure that this is a sound result. However, this result is only valid for the one test sequence. For a more general statement a variety of test sequences need to be coded and voted on.

In Figure 4.8, another example is shown of a plot from a subjective test. In this particular test, two codecs (MPEG-4 AVC/H.264 and MPEG-4 Advanced Simple Profile) have been tested to compress a sequence called "Mobile and Calendar." The sequence had a CIF resolution and was coded with four different bit rates (96, 192, 384, and 768 kbit/sec). The dots in the plot represent the average score the test persons gave and an error bar is given to indicate the variation of the test persons' answers. This plot tells us that in this test, AVC at 192 kbit/sec performs as well as the MPEG-4 ASP codec at 768 kbit/sec. Now you can calculate the difference in coding performance for this case. When the tests are performed using any other set of test sequences, the differences between AVC/H.264 and ASP need not be as pronounced, but will be still significant.

In Figure 4.9, test results are shown for coding a high-definition sequence with an MPEG-4 AVC/H.264 codec, an MPEG-2 High Quality codec, and the MPEG-2 TM4 reference implementation.

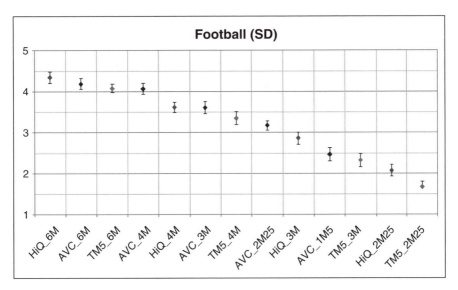

Figure 4.8 Example of a result from subjective testing of two different codecs (MPEG-4 AVC and MPEG-4 Advanced Simple Profile) on CIF resolution video material.

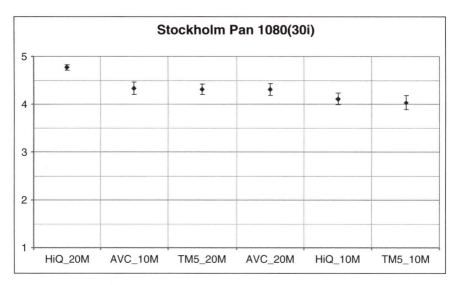

Figure 4.9 Example of a result from subjective testing of three different codecs (MPEG-4 AVC, MPEG-2 TM5, and MPEG-2 High Quality) on HD resolution video material at two bit rate s (10 and 20 Mbit/sec). The interested reader is invited to surf the official MPEG Web site (www. chiariglione.org/mpeg), where a number of results on formal tests for earlier standards activities can be found and downloaded.

This plot doesn't make any clear statement about the benefits of coding technologies. One conclusion could be that there is no clearly superior coding technology for this particular example. Another interpretation is that the test material was not sufficiently difficult to encode so that 10 Mbit/sec turned out to be a high enough bit rate to achieve excellent results for all tested codecs.

The choice of test sequences is certainly another important dimension for creating meaningful test results.

4.4.4. Some Notes on Test Material

Testing coding performance is dependent on the availability of good test material. During the development of coding technology, test material must also be produced. It is not always easy to determine what constitutes a good test sequence. Throughout the years, a couple of test sequences have been established as good test material, and these are regularly used. One of the problems with these test sequences is that they are used for development *and* for testing. This runs the risk of codecs being developed to match the characteristics of the test material used during the development phase. If the same sequences are used for testing and evaluating coding performance, one can expect that the codecs will do fairly well. In principle, the test set should be completely different from the development set. However, there is not much choice for commonly shared and accepted test material.

Another issue with test material has to do with copyright problems. A video has copyrights, and sometimes the sequences cannot be cleared of copyright issues, either because the copyright holder does not agree to grant licenses or because the copyright owner is unknown. Both scenarios lead to a situation of legal uncertainty for all companies involved in standardization. This legal uncertainty prevents the development of a generally accessible and freely usable suite of test sequences that can serve as a common test set for all parties involved in standardization related areas. A number of commercial entities have recently attempted to mend this situation (see Videatis GmbH at www.videatis.com [3] and Video Quality Experts Group [VQEG] at www.vqeg.org [4]).

As we have seen in Figure 4.9, sequences may not be sufficiently appropriate to make a clear distinction between a good codec and a worse codec, i.e., the material is such that all codecs either can handle the video content equally well or equally bad. This makes it difficult to make a decision between good and better codecs. In Figure 4.10, test sequences are differentiated as being too easy, or too difficult, or too steep. The figure also shows how the ideal test sequence might look. The curves show the subjective quality perception as a function of bit rate. If the test material is too easy, then there is no clear distinction between different bit rates and it is difficult to assess quality differences. The same holds if the material is too difficult. Then the bit rates are never enough to achieve a good coding result. Too easy and too difficult sequences can also be seen as the upper or lower part of a curve that is too steep. The ideal

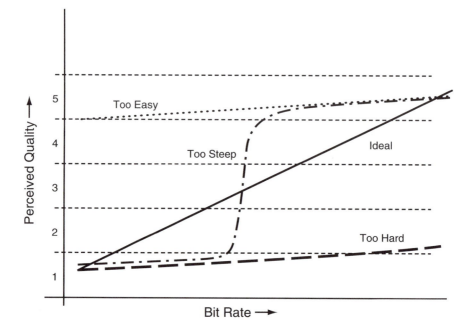

Figure 4.10 Classification of test material.

curve shows a linear relation between bit rate and perceived quality. It is hard to say from looking at a sequence if it is appropriate for testing. Only testing will reveal that. That is why test sequences that have been found over time to fulfill the requirement of creating a smooth transition curve, as shown in Figure 4.10, are kept in the commonly used test set.

4.5. Different Value Networks for Compression

When talking about compression systems for audio-visual data, there are two major topics of discussion. One is about the perceptual quality of the compressed video and audio data, the question of which codec offers better quality. The other line of discussion is about the achieved compression factor, that is, the bit rate that can be achieved by a given codec. These two topics represent two sides of the same coin. Which topic is discussed mainly depends on the application environment where the discussion takes place. The application environment determines the set of values, which leads to two different viewpoints regarding the evaluation of compression technology.

4.5.1. Narrowband Scenario

In a narrowband scenario, bandwidth is the scarce resource that represents the limiting factor for any type of service using audio-visual data. Examples of this scenario are video streaming over the Internet or streaming to mobile or portable devices. In such a case, dial-up modems, ISDN connections, or so-called broadband connections (DSL, cable modems) are used, which offer a transmission bandwidth of 28 kbit/sec up to 1 Mbit/sec. In those situations, the offered bandwidth will be exploited to the maximum. Note also that the available transmission bandwidth is often subject to temporal variations. Here, the quest is for the best achievable perceived quality for a given transmission bandwidth; i.e., the audio-visual quality achieved is the main factor for competition between different codecs.

4.5.2. Broadband Scenario

In a broadband scenario, bandwidth is not unlimited, but it is also not a limiting factor in order to offer a particular audio-visual service. Typical examples are digital television over cable or satellite and DVDs. The available transmission bandwidth is in excess of 1 Mbit/sec, sometimes exceeding 10 Mbit/sec. In those cases, a minimum quality of service in terms of audio and video quality is required for the offered service to be feasible. This minimum quality can easily be achieved by using the available bandwidth to the full extent. However, from a business point of view, it is important to control the costs for the used transmission/storage bandwidth per program. The goal is to minimize the cost per channel while satisfying the minimum quality requirements. Hence, the quest is for the lowest achievable bit rate that still offers a given subjective quality level for video and audio.

4.5.3. Further Criteria

Comparing compression performance is of course the primary figure of merit for performance evaluation and competition for coding products. In this section, we will discuss a few additional criteria that must be taken into account to arrive at a final verdict about a coding product or technology. Implementing a coding system has associated costs, and there is a trade-off between coding performance and implementation cost. A simplified formula is that the ideal coding system for audio-visual data has high coding performance, causes a low delay between input and output, and it can be implemented at a low cost. If the system offers high coding performance, then it may need to include more video frames to base its coding decision on. This leads to extra processing delay. If the codec is supposed to be cheap and have low delay, coding performance will be compromised. Coding performance may be fixed even for low-delay codecs, but this is not cheap. The options are pair wise contradictory, such that the problem is that you can only choose two options at a time.

Every market or application domain where audio-visual data are used comes with its own particular network of values. The value networks pertaining to different applications put an emphasis on different aspects of a compression technology. While one aspect is important to one market, it may be rather unimportant in another market. In this section, we present a few of the prevailing criteria for evaluating compression technologies and products.

Real-time decoding: Such decoding is a minimum requirement for any compression technology. Today's microprocessors offer enough horse power to enable real-time decoding of video and audio. However, to decode HDTV material in real time may still require dedicated hardware. But this frontier is moving fast, and more advanced technology is being developed all the time.

While decoding in real time is a must, real-time encoding is a highly desirable feature that is not requested for all application situations. Take for example the DVD as an application domain. The quality of the encoded material is of prime importance. Since the coded representation of a movie to be sold on DVD or CD is only encoded once, it may take hours or even days to produce the optimum result. Thus, real-time encoding is not critical.

The same holds true for movie material to be distributed to customers via TV channels or the Internet. If real-time processing is not critical for those applications, it is possible to let the video encoder go several times (at least twice) through the video material. This is called "multi-pass encoding." The first run collects statistical information about the video material, which can then be used in the second run to optimize the coded video quality. In professional video encoding products, you'll find two or more encoding chips, which can accomplish a kind of multi-pass encoding by virtue of tandem encoding in real time. The first encoder encodes the material in real time and passes on the statistical information to the second real-time encoder for optimized performance. This is not exactly cheap, but it works fairly well. For broadcasting applications in combination with statistical multiplexing and variable bit-rate coding, this is very useful.

Video editing tools and multimedia authoring software can survive easily without real-time encoding if the achieved quality is flawless and the processing time is not too outrageous.

In application scenarios like live broadcast or bi-directional communications (e.g., video conferencing), surveillance video real-time encoding is absolutely indispensable for the applications to be meaningful.

But also note that real time is not always as critical as it may sound. For example, take a weather station on TV that shows satellite imagery of weather changes. Typically, satellite images are delivered to the TV station on a frequency of one image every 15 minutes. That gives the real-time encoder quite a bit of time to encode a frame! Real time for regular TV means that one video frame needs to be encoded every 33 milliseconds (ms) (30fps frame rate). In Europe, the encoders can be a bit slower; they need to be done with encoding of one frame within 40 ms (frame rate 25 fps).

Low-delay encoding: For some applications, real-time encoding is not enough. Additional constraints may come from the requirement that the encoding process is not supposed to experience delays beyond a certain value. This is true for all sorts of bi-directional communications applications like video conferencing and video telephony, but also for broadcast applications where the program contains live interviews between someone who is present and someone who is located remotely. If there is a bi-directional communication going on, the perceived quality of the service is largely dependent on the so-called round-trip delay of the signals. If the delay is beyond, say, 50 ms, then the communication is about to break down. That means that the communication between people is suffering from those round-trip delays so badly that the conversation will be experienced as being very annoying or will be even ended. It is like doing transatlantic telephone conversations over bad phone lines, where you can hear the echoes of your own voice coming back quite loud. This is a very unpleasant experience since you tend to start stuttering quite badly.

Surveillance also demands low delay. Security personnel require immediate notification about any strange or suspicious happenings, with as little delay as possible.

Much of broadcast television services and many streaming services are not very sensitive to delay. For example, consider the tradition of delaying the broadcast of MTV shows like the MTV Awards for about 60 seconds in order for the producer of the live event to "beep" out any unwanted four-letter words that a person on stage may choose to use. The whole live experience of the show is not jeopardized, since none of the customers at their home TVs has an absolute point of temporal reference to gauge the delay.

The constraint of low-delay coding reduces the achievable compression performance of a codec. Improving the exploitation of the similarities between temporally neighboring pixels, frames or sound samples in videos in order to improve compression requires the encoder to collect and store a couple of frames to work on, that is, to keep a few fractions of a second's worth of video or audio data. This produces additional delay commensurate with the number of frames being stored for this purpose. If you look at the definition of the visual profiles, you may see the term "B-frame." The use of this type of frame implies improved compression performance but also increased memory requirements and additional coding delay. The more B-frames are used, the more pronounced this effect is.

Within MPEG-4, profiles have been defined to address such aspects like encoding with low delay. For example, the Simple Visual Profile has been designed with low-delay encoding applications in mind.

Low-complexity decoders: It is always beneficial to have low-cost decoding. However, for audio-visual services over wireless channels that will be received by handheld devices, low decoder complexity is more important. High computational requirements for decoding audio and images drain any battery within a very short period of time. Having to recharge the battery every couple of hours defeats the purpose. The same applies to some surveillance topics. However, for television, low complexity is not that critical, even though it is always beneficial from a cost point of view if a set-top box can function with less demanding components. If PCs are the receiving device, decoder complexity is also not a main concern, since the resources of a state-of-the-art PC certainly exceed the requirements for real-time decoding of video up to standard definition resolution. Most PCs with a DVD drive can decode MPEG-2 DVDs while the user is typing in a word-processing program.

Complexity for decoders is measured in terms of the required computational resources such as arithmetic operations, memory requirements, and memory bandwidth.

Again, several profiles have been specified in MPEG-4 to allow the implementation of low-cost decoding devices while still giving a satisfactory level of compression performance. The same is true for audio coding profiles, which have been defined to specifically address the requirements for low complexity.

AVC/H.264 is not necessarily categorized as a low-complexity codec. The AVC/H.264 video coding technology has been developed without considering complexity constraints. The goal was to find a new algorithm that can provide the best video compression performance possible. The question is still open as to whether it is possible to implement AVC/H.264 while keeping up premium compression performance.

Low-complexity encoders: MPEG is by definition an asymmetric compression scheme. By asymmetric we mean that the encoder is much more complex than the pertaining decoder. A symmetric coding scheme provides encoders and decoders with about the same level of complexity. In essence, this means that an MPEG-4 encoder is always much more complex than the decoder. Therefore, we can talk only about an encoder that is of relatively low complexity. Whenever the encoders must do their job in real time and when they need to be deployed very often, the complexity of the encoder becomes a subject of concern. For example, in video conferencing, each device contains an encoder and maybe multiple decoders. Therefore, for video conferencing it is beneficial to use a low-complexity encoder. The same would be true if plans to have video encoders included in hand-held devices come to fruition.

For broadcasting services or for video-on-demand type of applications, compression performance is the primary concern, rather than the complexity of the encoder. Since there are only a few encoders operated by the service provider, the cost for an individual encoder is not critical. Therefore, encoders for broadcast applications can be more complex and hence more expensive without jeopardizing the pertaining business models.

In the encoding process, the designer or implementer has a relatively high degree of flexibility. The encoder doesn't need to include all coding tools specified in a profile; the implementer can choose to utilize only a subset of the possible tools to reduce implementation complexity for the encoder. If the implementer thinks that using B-frames or 1/4-pel motion compensation will render the encoder too expensive and complex, the feature can simply be dropped from the encoder. The bit stream that is generated is still fully compliant with, say, the Advanced Simple Visual Profile. As was discussed earlier, the encoder can always do less than is specified, whereas the decoder can always do *more* than is specified.

One problem that arises in the industry is that a company may advertise its video encoding product as implementing the AVC/ H.264 standard. This does not necessarily mean that the product has implemented all the fancy coding tools. The customer may end up surprised to get a compression performance that is much lower than expected, because the company may not necessarily have advertised that the encoder has dropped, i.e., not implemented, some of the tools that are responsible for high performance.

Random-access stream editing: Random access in our context means that it is possible to start decoding a bit stream somewhere in the middle and still be able to decode the remaining part of the stream correctly. This is a typical situation for broadcasting or live streaming events. If you have missed the beginning of your favorite show, you may still want to tune in at a later point in time. In order to be able to do this, essential data for decoding needs to be retransmitted at a certain frequency. Also, care has to be taken to provide regular entry points (synchronization) at which a decoder can tune into the ongoing data stream. The entry points necessitate to retransmit configuration data characterizing the multimedia content, such that the decoder can be synchronized. The more granular the random access is, the more regularly the retransmission is necessary causing an additional data overhead. Therefore, the need to allow random access leads to a loss in compression efficiency due to this overhead. In broadcasting application, the rule of thumb says that there should be re-entry or random-access point in the stream every half a second. This number originates from the expectation of consumers concerning how fast a channel can be changed when channel surfing with the remote. In the United States, this results in a digital video stream that carries an I-frame every 15 frames (30 fps frame rate); an I-frame in European television occurs every 12 frames (frame rate of 25 fps). An I-frame is a coded frame that does not need any information from previous frames in order to be decodable. Since I-frames require the most bits in a coded bit stream, having a high frequency of I-frames reduces the compression efficiency.

In contrast to the broadcasting scenario that requires re-entry points, there are the communications applications, where random access is not an issue. The communication session is started at some point in time and the session is kept alive as long as necessary. There is less of a requirement to be able to jump into a stream, and the streams are initiated at the time the communication session starts. The participating parties stay in the session as long as it takes. Consider making phone calls as an example. If the line is dropped for some reason, you can initiate a new call, conveying all the necessary information at the beginning of the new call, and then continue. In other words, there is no urgent need to send synchronization overhead and extra I-frames for random access. This is beneficial for compression.

An extreme form of random access occurs in video editing applications such as those used in post-production studios, where the video material must be edited so that it is frame-accurate. In other words, it must be possible to cut a video scene at any arbitrary frame. This is not possible in the standard MPEG bit stream, since for decoding P-frames or B-frames, the preceding frames are needed. If those preceding frames are gone, due to some cut in the stream, they can no longer be decoded. The decoding can restart only after the next I-frame has been found in the stream. MPEG-4 Studio Profile addresses this requirement by coding a sequence in an I-frame-only mode. Of course, the compression performance is much reduced in comparison to using P- and B-frames, but this functionality is essential for video editing.

Further criteria: Functional aspects have not been considered in this chapter, as we are concentrating on assessing the compression performance of codecs. However, as mentioned in an earlier chapter, MPEG-4 offers additional features that are not necessarily tied to compression performance. There are scalability features, error robustness, and object-oriented functionalities. It is difficult to test these features, as their value depends strongly on the anticipated application. During the MPEG standardization process, verification tests were performed to evaluate the performance of both the object-based coding and the error-resilience tools. A report of the findings from those tests can be found on the MPEG Web site.

MPEG-4 has specified various audio and visual profiles to cover these additional functional requirements, such as the ARTS profile, which has been briefly introduced in the previous chapter.

4.6. Technology Landscape

The world is full of technology for dealing with multimedia data in various forms. MPEG is not an island, but it is surrounded by a wide range of alternative technologies, products, and concepts. Some of the more prominent contenders will be discussed in this section.

4.6.1. The Role of Proprietary Compression Technology

The search for the ultimate compression technology can be compared to the search for the holy grail. Compression technology is considered a basic enabling technology that can make its developers a pile of money. Therefore, numerous companies and research institutions are venturing into developing new compression schemes and testing new ideas in search of the holy grail of compression.

Compression of audio-visual data is a complicated subject. Even if a group of engineers or an individual has a great new idea for compressing video or audio, it takes a large amount of resources to actually implement a competitive system. For the system to be competitive, it is not enough to have a good idea that applies to a single part of the codec. The entire codec needs to be designed in a balanced and highly optimized way. This process takes time and runs the risk that a single start-up company that tries to develop new and proprietary coding technology will fall behind the current state-of-the-art quite quickly. This is mainly because, in the world of compression standards, there is an enormous drive to pick up new ideas and bring together the best minds to push the boundaries of technology. Each contributor in the standards world of MPEG or the ITU can concentrate on the stuff he does best and bring forward the most recent and innovative ideas and proposals, while being able to benefit from the technical progress that is achieved for other parts in the compression system. New ideas will be scrutinized by many experts in the field. If the idea is good, it has a chance of making it into the standard. If it is not good, then it is best to know this early on and start thinking of something else.

It is good advice for investors who are betting on compression-oriented start-up companies to push them to go to the standards to find out if their ideas are worthwhile. This is particularly true if the new ideas have an impact on the decoder. It's vital to make sure that the new idea is good and is supported by the next generation of a standardized decoder.

The encoder is the domain where proprietary technologies and ideas can live and bloom. As stated earlier, the encoder is not specified by the standard as long as it produces standards-compliant bit streams. In that sense, finding better ways to encode video and audio is always a worthwhile endeavor.

The reader may want to check out the history of media compression technology to find products or companies that have achieved and sustained success while staying entirely proprietary—a difficult position to maintain, even for big companies.

Microsoft's Windows Media: Windows Media is often considered the major competition for MPEG-4 when it comes to coding products for audio and video. Microsoft definitely has an impressive team of video and audio coding experts on their payroll, and the Windows Media products are among the best tools available. As a product line for building products and services, Windows Media is a very efficient implementation and quite a complete offering, which also includes a system for Digital Rights Management—a topic that is becoming increasingly important as more and more media content is offered in digital formats.

So far the formats and the algorithms in Windows Media have not been made publicly available. This produces a single-source vendor situation for service and content providers who decide to use Windows Media. The members of the EBU (European Broadcasting Union), who are the European public service broadcasters, typically find this situation difficult to accept in spite of the good products. As a business person, one must decide how important it is to be the master of one's own destiny, and whether it is more beneficial to rely entirely on the willingness of a single vendor to provide long-term support. This is particularly true if the business is outside the mainstream and the package offered by Microsoft does not match 100%, or if Windows does not offer the control over the coding and decoding process needed for niche products. All in all, this topic demands a lot of political and strategic thinking.

More recently, Microsoft has shown willingness to submit its coding technology to SMPTE (Society of Motion Picture and Television Engineers) for standardization. This step may dramatically change the argument concerning the lack of publication of the bit stream syntax and the decoder semantics.

Whatever Microsoft is doing with Windows Media, one thing is clear: The coding technology is not fundamentally different from the technology used in MPEG-4. It is a very good implementation and the encoder certainly includes a number of very smart techniques. But if Microsoft would wholeheartedly support MPEG-4 and make Windows Media a 100% MPEG-4-compliant codec, we dare say that the resulting coding product would be among the best MPEG-4 solutions available in the marketplace, maybe even the best around. A lot of people would spend serious money to buy such an encoding and decoding product, which would also save them from being trapped in a single-vendor monopoly situation.

Such a step would also bring the discussion around streaming media to an end, which is dominated by questions around technological aspects of video coding. This technology-focused discussion lets streaming appear as an technically immature business proposition, which often causes confusion, uncertainty, and doubt among business strategists as well as end consumers. This move could potentially help to open up the market for streaming media, and maybe also for mobile multimedia. The ongoing discussion about the technology to be used for streaming hurts the market. Imagine a situation in which people would have to buy different TV sets in order to watch ABC or NBC programs, since each TV network has chosen a different video format. Or consider a telecommunications market where you cannot call your friend with your cell phone because she happens to own a Nokia phone while you have a Motorola product. This is similar to the situation with video formats for streaming. A content provider currently has to offer his video material in multiple formats—a Real stream, a Windows Media stream, and a QuickTime stream. This is clearly a less-than-ideal situation.

More recently, chip manufacturers have started moving in the direction of Windows Media to include those codecs as an additional option in their product portfolio. This seems to be a concession to the uncertainty chip manufacturers experience from their customers who may be afraid to place their bet on the wrong horse.

Real Networks: A lot of the statements that apply to Windows Media also apply to Real Networks' video and audio coding products. However, Real Networks (RN) has recently started to embrace MPEG-4 as the basis for its audio and video coding. At the same time, Real Networks is still developing their own coding products. One of the main advantages of Real Networks' products is that the server software is also available for the Linux operating system. The coding performance of RN's products is excellent, but they are adding to the format confusion just as much as Microsoft. Ultimately, it is up to the marketplace to decide which products and technologies will be successful.

4.6.2. Other Standards and Technologies for Multimedia—W3C Recommendations

The World Wide Web Consortium (W3C; see www.w3.org) develops interoperable technologies (specifications, guidelines, software, and tools) for the Web [5]. It provides specifications for

(X)HTML, XML, and PNG. The approach chosen by W3C to specify a multimedia description format is quite different from the approach of MPEG. While MPEG specifies the 2D and 3D primitives as well as the timing and the animation information in the same part of the standard (BIFS), W3C splits the recommendations in several pieces, taking advantage of the possibility offered by XML and the concepts of modularization and profiling.

SMIL: SMIL, Synchronized Multimedia Integration Language, defines an XML-based language that authors can use to create interactive multimedia presentations. Using SMIL, content authors can describe the temporal behavior of a multimedia presentation in terms of synchronization of the different media objects. The author can also associate hyper links with media objects and describe the layout of the presentation on a screen. Authors are able to create presentations that will adapt to the settings in the receiver selected by the user. SMIL does not include the description or compression of the media objects themselves. The media objects can be audio, video, still pictures, still text, text stream, and animations. SMIL benefits from all the technologies designed for XML (scripting, style sheets, linking, compression) and is seeing a lot of success in the Web community because of its integration in Microsoft Internet Explorer and RealNetworks' RealPlayer.

The SMIL format is not stream-oriented, which means that a presentation cannot be updated since no update mechanism exists. SMIL does not define how the different types of media fit in its architecture, and thus it is not a complete multimedia description format. For using formatted text based on SMIL, the SMIL+XHTML specification is needed. For inclusion of 2D graphics, a SMIL+SVG specification is needed. If 3D content is to be used in a presentation, a specification is needed that describes how to use a 3D XML language like X3D in conjunction with SMIL. This need for integrating several separate specifications at a time can lead to interoperability problems in cases where rich content consists of mixes of 2D/3D graphics, text, and video. SMIL does offer mechanisms to perform synchronization of media objects, such as for a video track and an audio track, each being played back by referencing an external player. No model is specified by

SMIL that describes the decoding of the media objects. Therefore, SMIL does not provide a fine synchronization mechanism. Finally, it does not offer any means of compression nor of encryption of the scene description.

SVG: SVG, Scalable Vector Graphics, defines an XML-based language for describing two-dimensional vector graphics and mixed vector/raster graphics. SVG comprises three types of graphical objects: vector graphic shapes, e.g., paths consisting of straight lines and curves (Bézier or elliptical arcs); images; and text. In addition, graphical objects can be grouped, styled, transformed, and composited into previously rendered objects. SVG drawings can be made interactive (simple interaction based on pointing devices) and dynamic (using deterministic animations). Animations can be defined and triggered by embedding SVG animation elements in SVG content or via scripting. In both cases, the animation is entirely contained in the SVG document. SVG lacks mechanisms for updating a presentation dynamically as well as means for adapting the content to streaming. W3C has proposed a recommendation annex that explains how to use a lossless general-purpose tool (e.g., gzip) to compress description files. But such compression tools are not appropriate to support streaming of media content. More recently, SVG is specifying some profiles targeted to mobile terminals.

The main drawback of SVG is that it has not been designed to fully support streaming applications. Vector graphics and scene description will become increasingly important for authoring Rich Media presentations. The initial delay that occurs when downloading an entire presentation or all its graphics will be an obstacle for the adoption of this type of media. Therefore, such scenes require a streaming mechanism to enable a convenient way of viewing. It is rather inconvenient for a user to have to wait 5 minutes until a download is completed before he or she can start to watch a cartoon. This is even more of an issue if the presentation itself only plays for that long. Alternatively, the presentation can be streamed and viewed at the same time, that is, the presentation of the multimedia content can start before the download of the entire file is completed.

Proprietary solutions: Of course, many proprietary multimedia description formats exist. Each of them uses its own method of describing a multimedia presentation, resulting in little interoperability between the different solutions. A number of them are worth investigating because they have attracted a large amount of users and because they can adapt more easily to the user's needs than the standards can. In this section, we will look at a number of these technologies, in particular those designed by Macromedia and by Apple.

Macromedia offers around 20 software products for the Web, ranging from text editors to full studios for creating multimedia presentations. The most interesting tools for our discussion are Flash and Director Shockwave Studio.

Flash is a piece of software that helps people create 2D vector-based graphics for the Web. It is currently the leading software product for designing 2D graphics and simple animations. Flash uses a proprietary binary format for publishing, which is very efficient in terms of compression. Although it is proprietary, the specification of this format is public, which means that many tools are available for editing content or for converting other graphical formats into this one and vice versa. Flash's binary format is popular because it is adapted to the workflow of the graphics designer. The graphical primitives used in Flash are approximately the same as the ones used in SVG and are similar to the elements used in MPEG-4 BIFS.

The combination of Director Shockwave Studio and Flash is similar to the combination of SMIL and SVG. Director is a piece of software that enables users to create multimedia presentations by embedding audio, video, text, and Flash content. It is a reference tool for creating multimedia presentations for the Web. Director also has associated binary file formats for editing and publishing. The designer can specify the spatial organization on the screen and create animations for the different objects. Director makes use of a scripting language called "Lingo." This language allows the user to assign quite complicated behaviors to different media objects. Among other possibilities, Lingo allows the graphics designer to employ interactive actions (mouse clicks and keyboard entries) to create simple synchronization between different mediums (key points) or to animate 3D worlds.

4.6.3. MPEG-4 and Interactive TV

Interactivity is the primary difference between MPEG-4 and MPEG-2. MPEG-2 is currently broadly deployed in digital television systems. Making interactive TV a reality in an MPEG-2-based environment implies that operators need to adopt one or more proprietary solutions, or solutions based on technologies not native to MPEG, and add them productively to an MPEG-2 delivery environment. This has led to the emergence of several proprietary add-on technologies competing for the business of ITV operators.

Each operator has a unique composite solution of technologies, usually determined by its MPEG compression platform, its Conditional Access System, and its Middleware platform (e.g., OpenTV). This may lead to the emergence of multiple vertically integrated solutions and markets that are mutually incompatible.

One promising technology for interactive television is specified by the DVB Project (Digital Video Broadcasting) and is known as the Multimedia Home Platform (MHP). In the United States, an equivalent approach is the Java-based Digital Applications Software Environment (DASE), which is an Advanced Television Systems Committee (ATSC) activity. Another similar approach has been undertaken by OCAP, the Open Cable Application Platform specified by the Open Cable consortium. This approach is also based on the MHP specification.

MPEG-4 and MHP: It is often asked how MPEG-4 relates to MHP (see www.mpegif.org [6]). DVB 1.0 specifies the transport foundation of the DVB family of standards for delivering media content over satellite, cable, and via terrestrial channels. So far, this specification has used MPEG-2 as the compression technology for audio and video, as well as for the systems portion. MPEG-4 is seen as a logical evolution, in which DVB will offer efficient means to deliver media services over IP. As of this writing, DVB has announced that it is considering the adoption of MPEG-4 AVC/H.264 and MPEG-4 AAC as extensions to the existing DVB specifications.

The Multimedia Home Platform is included in the DVB 2.0 specification and comprises a variety of next-generation delivery applications, including copy protection and copy management, as along with delivering DVB services over IP. The MHP defines a generic interface between interactive digital applications and the terminals on which those applications are executed. MHP specifies how to download applications and media content, which are typically delivered over any DVB-compliant transport stream. As an option, MHP is considering the presence of a return channel, which means that a receiver device such as a set-top box receives broadcasted data (e.g., through a satellite link, but it can also establish a communication link back to the play-out center by means of a dial-up connection or a similar Internet connection).

MPEG-4 can be seen as a natural complement to MHP applications. It can compress media objects to achieve a low bit-rate video stream. Furthermore, MPEG-4 provides scene description formats that can be delivered over IP by means of streaming mechanisms to set-top boxes. The application, interaction, and synchronization models of MPEG-4 allow dynamic content to be added to MHP-type applications. It has described the means to transport MPEG-4 media objects and streams over MPEG-2 transport mechanisms. This way it is possible to achieve a very fine-grain synchronization between the broadcast program and the MPEG-4 multimedia content.

Integrating MHP with MPEG-4 enables object-based interactive digital television services. The combination of MHP and MPEG-4 offers the chance to develop flexible and rich interactive applications for the interactive broadcast domain. The celebrated MPEG-4 features can be introduced smoothly and gradually, in a backward-compatible manner.

MPEG-J and DVB-J: The MHP architecture is defined in terms of three layers: resources, system software, and applications. Typical MHP resources are those elements that can be called upon by applications to perform certain functions, for example, MPEG processing, I/O, CPU, memory, and graphics handling. For the applications, the system software presents a standardized view of the resources offered by the platform. This way, MHP enables a high level of "platform independence." Generic Application Program Interfaces (APIs) are specified in MHP, based on DVB-J(ava), which includes the Java Virtual Machine (VM) as originally specified by Sun Microsystems. MHP applications can only access the resources of the platform via these specified APIs. This is a feature that guarantees the stability of the platform and its robustness.

MPEG-J(ava) offers a set of functionalities complementary to those offered by DVB-J. MPEG-J in MPEG-4 is a set of Java APIs that may be present on a MPEG-4 terminal. MPEG-J applications, sometimes called MPEGlets, are sent in a stream as part of a complete presentation. An MPEGlet controls the capabilities and resources of the MPEG-J terminal through the use of the MPEG-J API's.

4.7. Innovative Technology—FCB or Brave New World?

FCB stands for "Faster, Cheaper, Better," and describes the use of new and improved technology to foster existing business models and established value networks, by making those businesses more profitable, by improving the quality of the service, or by introducing more features for existing products. The "established business" in our context is television or a related industry, which also includes streaming media or video conferencing. These applications and many others are requiring better and better compression for video and audio. This is why the adoption of AVC/H.264 and AAC has received so much excitement in the industry, as these technologies fuel the compression of audio and video as used in TV-like applications and beyond. The economic benefit of improved compression can be easily calculated and further investment can readily be justified.

The FCB-type of innovation is sometimes referred to as "sustaining innovation," a term coined by Clayton Christensen [7].

A sustaining innovation is an innovation to an existing product or service that is meant to sustain its profitability by making the product cheaper to produce or to improve its performance or enhance its feature set. A few remarks on another type of innovation are in order here, which we will call "Brave New World" applications (with homage to Aldous Huxley).

As new technology becomes available, it must be picked up and embraced by people who have a clear vision of how to turn technological opportunities into innovative Brave New World products. By that term we mean applications that are creating new markets that were not in existence before. Browser software is an archetypical example of such a new application. It sometimes happens that technologies are ultimately used in products that address entirely different aspects of our lives than originally anticipated by the proponents of the technology. Take the overwhelming success of Short Messaging (SMS) in GSM phone networks. Nobody had anticipated this level of success for this technology. A similar observation may also apply to MPEG-4, but only the future will tell. At the time when the cinema was invented, one of its first applications was the filming of theatrical plays on stage. The idea was that the plays could then be shown in many places, far away from the location where the actors were performing. Some pessimists thought that this new cinema technology would kill the theatre, which did not in fact occur—the theatre lives on today. However, as it turned out, this type of cinema was rather boring to watch, as all the action happened in one place—on the stage. At the same time, there were creative people realizing that cinema technology, through the use of the camera, rendered possible an entirely different way of storytelling by using scene cuts and close-ups and even allowing the camera to move. This way, the cinematographers created a new and very different dynamic and a new language of images, which was not possible in theatrical plays.

Yet another wave of technological innovation is represented by the advent of television technology. After experimenting with the capabilities of this new technology, television started to develop its own culture and tradition, going beyond the immediate application of delivering movies via the television screen. Television has developed its own esthetics, and from its inception has differed from the tradition and style of the movie production industry. Television has replaced neither cinema nor the theatre. Instead, it has developed its own distinctive niche in the media world. The new markets and applications of television were created by bringing together new technology and inspired creativity.

The same may happen with interactive technology, as embodied by MPEG-4. The immediate idea to apply the new technology to shift scheduled television programming onto IP networks and offer video-on-demand may not even materialize. The streaming industry is still searching for killer applications for the technology. In the meantime, the parts of MPEG-4 that foster the progress of existing business models and markets, such as AVC or AAC, are in high demand. For the moment, the parts of MPEG-4 that are thought to be more bold and visionary, namely the interactive and object-oriented parts, are often despised as being stuff that nobody needs. However, it may only take a few creative minds to come up with innovative ideas and create something entirely new in terms of applications or esthetics. The technology needs to be better understood and embraced by creative people so they can create new digital content that people find attractive and exciting. Thus, educating the content creators, storytellers, movie producers and directors, writers, and so on about the capabilities of MPEG-4 will be the driving force for the establishment and sustainability of this new technology.

4.7.1. Some Final Remarks

You may read articles, or hear presentations given by experts in the field, in which MPEG-4 is accused of having diverted into technologies that nobody seems to need, such as scene description, interactivity, and all this object-based stuff. The often-heard criticism is that MPEG-4 has lost focus and therefore has not delivered technology at a competitive level compared to other standards bodies (ITU) and compared to various proprietary approaches (Microsoft, Real Networks). Its detractors say that MPEG-4 instead should have concentrated on developing technology for things like better compression of rectangular videos and generic audio.

These criticisms may sound very reasonable and down to earth, but they are also very conservative and lack vision. Back in 1994, when MPEG-4 started out pursuing the object-oriented track, it was felt on a fairly broad basis that this was the way to go. At that time, nobody seemed to have a clear vision of how a major step forward for compressing video could be made. After all, MPEG is not a research laboratory, but a standards body. It is true that very diverse ideas were brought to MPEG and quite a few obscure techniques were standardized. However, in hindsight, it is easy to criticize and also a bit unfair to beat up MPEG for its openness to new ideas and approaches. Maybe next month somebody will come up with an ingenious idea for how to make use of the interactive and object-based elements in MPEG-4 to venture into a new era of media services. As we've mentioned, it happens quite frequently that technology gets developed with a particular idea in mind and is then used successfully for something completely different.

When it comes to the critics of MPEG-4, consider the following history. For many years, the research and development in the domain of video and audio compression has been motivated by the vision of video telephony and video conferencing. While video conferencing technology has turned into a somewhat significant but limited market, video telephony has developed from a zero million dollar business to a zero billion dollar business and has been taken from the agenda for now. The video telephony vision may be re-juvenated by some sort of service in the realm of mobile communications. Most probably, it will then look entirely different than what was anticipated back in the 1980s. The recently cele-brated AVC/H.264 standard is a descendant of those ideas geared toward video telephony and video conferencing. MPEG-4 started out with a similar motivation toward very low bit-rate coding, adopting a lot of technology from the video conferencing world (H.263), but took another route for a while (object-based coding) and has only recently rejoined the mainstream (AVC/H.264). The result of all these activities justifies the engagement and investment, in spite of the original motivation, which did not lead to the envisioned commercial success. We cannot foresee the future, but we can enable it.

4.8. Bibliography

DVB Web site. www.dvb.org
Internet Engineering Task Force. www.ietf.org
R. Koenen (Ed.). *Overview of the MPEG-4 Standard.* www.chiariglione.org/mpeg. Retrieved March 2002.
MPEG Web site. www.chiariglione.org/mpeg
C. Pearce. *The Interactive Book.* New York: Macmillan Technical Publishers, 1997.
F. Pereira, T. Ebrahimi. *The MPEG-4 Book.* Upper Saddle River, NJ: Prentice Hall, 2002.
A. Puri, T. Chen. *Advances in Multimedia, Standards and Networks.* New York: Marcel Dekker, 2000.
The Media Standard. *MPEG Industry Forum White Paper.* 2002. Download from www.mpegif.org
J. Watkinson. *The MPEG Handbook.* St. Louis, MO: Focal Press/Elsevier, 2001.

4.9. References

[1] J. Watkinson. *The Art of Digital Audio* (3rd ed.). St. Louis, MO: Focal Press/Elsevier, 2000a.
[2] J. Watkinson. *The Art of Digital Video* (3rd ed.). St. Louis, MO: Focal Press/Elsevier, 2000b.
[3] Videatis GmbH. www.videatis.com
[4] Video Quality Experts Group (VQEG). www.vqeg.org
[5] W3C Consortium. www.w3.org
[6] MPEG Industry Forum. www.mpegif.org
[7] C. M. Christensen. *The Innovator's Dilemma.* New York: Harper Business Essentials, 2002.

CHAPTER 5

Business—Technology Interface

5.1. When Technology Meets Business

Technology, especially information technology, often involves numbers and formulas, machinery and components, and so forth. This is certainly true when it comes to MPEG-4, and while you have read and learned quite a lot about this technology by this point, you may be asking yourself, do I actually need this, and if so, how and where would I use it? Well, as we all know, technology is a key ingredient in any product, no matter whether it creates nice moving pictures for you, long-lasting concrete, fast cars, or wonderful textiles—it is always there. The trouble starts when the technical experts come along and propose—and in many cases rightly so—the development, introduction, adoption, or deployment of new technologies to improve the quality of products. Any and all of these proposals demand a certain level of investment of the usual resources, which, at the end of the day, all come down to money.

Here we are, right in the middle of an MPEG-4 book, talking about the common influences in business life from the point of view of an investor—someone who must decide whether or not to invest and deploy new technologies in order to improve the overall performance, standing, and indeed value of his or her company.

The concerns of an investor often lie, to a great extent, in the skepticism toward this new MPEG-4 technology and whether it is good enough, and whether your company's products and services will be successful or not. Technically, there is more than proof in the pudding that MPEG-4 will be a dominant and key player in the multimedia landscape, and that it is an exceptionally well-developed technology. But as is not uncommon in business, there are a few obstacles in terms of adoption, deployment, usage, and, indeed, migration to this new technology, which we will address later on. Economically, the prerequisites are also ready to be listed. Amongst them are obviously the availability of respective products and services offered under business models that make sense and the commercial basics surrounding standards-based technologies, such as licensing. But in every worry there is also a challenge and, with a diligent approach, risks can certainly be minimized and controlled. As a matter of fact, if you are a realistic optimist you will see the opportunity in the difficulty; if you are, however, a pessimist you sadly see the difficulty in the opportunity, which is of course not very helpful in business at all. The next question is related to desire for profit—how much can we make with this? How much can we save with this? And so forth. The kind of strategies centered around profitability, affordability, revenue, and market share growth, and, at some stage, in most cases exit strategies or end games, come to most people's mind. Exit- and end-games in the MPEG-4 world are not really dissimilar to any other technologies or enterprises. Either a company gets acquired or gets into a merger, competes a trade sale, or attracts major strategic partners, delivering more revenues. Obviously, this chain of potential events can be continued for quite some time. In addition, we are talking about an investment in the future, which can, if managed properly, certainly create long-term impacts on your revenues. After all, you are not interested in this technology because your mission is to utilize new technologies in your business; your mission is to successfully create revenues and profits. This is not meant to be a sales pitch, but clearly the main objective in creating, developing, and deploying new technologies is for our own and your organization's benefit.

Here is the true interface of technology and business. The important bit is obviously to understand and to differentiate between what you want to, should, and must have in order to stay competitive. Technology in some way determines your destiny in this respect, and you must carefully look at the potential business benefits, and indeed risks, associated with various technologies.

Equally important is the decision of whether to go a "standard" or "non-standard" route. This is where coherent decisions need to be made, and it is very important to look at all the pros and cons from as many perspectives as possible. It also, of course, depends on which side you are on (i.e., whether you are a vendor or a user). It may well be that a vendor will go down the opportunistic path and offer products, services, or solutions for both variants. Or the vendor might exclusively commit herself to one direction. A user will always go down the path of least resistance in the sense that as long as products and services are affordable and offer satisfactory quality, they are what he or she will opt for.

5.2. Arguments for MPEG-4

The beauty of MPEG-4 is that it is not only an extremely advanced and versatile technology, it also delivers new and exciting business opportunities.

Already at this point you may be thinking, technologists come up with more and more solutions to all our media problems by the hour. What's so special about MPEG-4? The answer lies in the simple fact that MPEG-4 is the multimedia standard that enables content to be created, delivered, and consumed in various qualities, for various devices, and is the only standard that gives you the opportunity to create interactive content. The other good news is that MPEG-4 is an international, open standard, which brings with it many advantages, as we saw earlier on. One major advantage, which plays an important role for business decision makers, is choice. To put it in simple terms, buyers are in charge. The many technology providers (i.e., the vendors that are offering their products) strive to deliver best-of-breed products to the marketplace, corresponding to their buyers' specifications and requirements. Flexibility, transparency, competitiveness, interoperability, and creation of larger markets are the key words surrounding this aspect of open standards.

With "non-standard," better known as proprietary, technologies or formats, buyers may have a choice of a variety of vendors, but the technology provider is ultimately always the same organization. Buyers run the risk of becoming dependent on the vendor and being captured in a monopolistic environment where many obstacles may need to be overcome over time. In other words, in addition to worrying about your business and pricing models, you will have to do the same with respect to your supplier, who may change, amend, or add to her model without telling you—not a pleasant thought. You may end up having to guess the roadmaps and plans of your supplier, which will divert your attention away from the essential parts of your business. Or you have to take technology licenses, which include much more than you require (for which you will end up paying, too). You may even find yourself in the tricky situation that your supplier becomes a competitor of yours, which might defeat the purpose of the whole relationship.

From a user's perspective, another important consideration in the global discussion of whether or not to use MPEG-4 is that it was developed by the Moving Picture Experts Group (MPEG). Emmy award–winning MPEG also developed MPEG-1 and MPEG-2, the latter of which currently represents a market worth double-figure billions of dollars.

As a technology user, without a doubt your demands and requirements for technology and services are increasing over time, and you are most interested in availability, reliability, scalability, and price. Standards deliver you all of these. This was only the technology side, we will get to the content issues a little later.

With this brief explanation of the key advantages of an open standard, and specifically MPEG-4, in mind, the next step is to appreciate what this means in the business context. Put simply, the use of MPEG-4 can reduce costs and increase revenues.

Let us boil this down to something even simpler. There are two main benefits, which have a direct impact on business:

- MPEG-4 is a technical evolution
- MPEG-4 is an international open standard

5.2.1. MPEG-4 Is a Technical Evolution

Let us look at the technical evolution of MPEG. It is creating new, alternative business models and embracing a broad variety of markets. In fact, it is pretty simple to explain and we have seen the beginning already in the MPEG-2 arena. If one looks at audio/video coding, it goes something like this: "We have something to encode, we have something to deliver, we have something to decode. Plus we serve both the professional and the retail segments." The rest, to a large extent, is strategy.

However, the situation has changed slightly in recent years. MPEG-2 has reached its limits to some extent, and there are other uses that need to be covered besides digital television and packaged media, for example, DVDs. With MPEG-4 having such vast possibilities for usage, like interactivity (which sadly so far has not really taken off), audio, video (in virtually all networks you can think of), etc., it is the prime technology to close these gaps.

A few chapters earlier, we were able to familiarize ourselves more with the technical advantages and finesse vested in MPEG-4, and a translation of this into business terms is not very difficult. If you are involved in this kind of market and happen to own or distribute some form of content, your prime aim obviously is to reach as wide an audience as possible. Until recently, you were able to work with MPEG-2. Your exposure was kind of limited to digital TV and distribution on DVDs. Certainly, you were able to utilize the additional channel of the Internet, but you actually had to change formats in order to do that, due to issues of bandwidth.

In order to better understand, let us look at aspects of content creation and delivery, which represent the most important parts of the process and are therefore a paramount consideration when it comes to acquisition and running costs.

For the purpose of simplifying, let us break this whole delivery scenario down into networks. Remember the orange juice example? We were talking about the transport of the OJ in the "concentrated" form, say by air, rail, or road—using any or all of these different delivery methods. The most popular transport networks in our multimedia scenario are broadband (Internet streaming), broadcast (digital television), and mobile networks (handheld video)—all different types of universal data-highways.

The delivery is a very crucial aspect of your business considerations. In this respect, there is no difference between you and the OJ producer—all you want is to make sure that your product arrives on time and in good condition. But this does not only depend on the actual delivery or its method. In today's technology climate, delivery requires that two main factors be taken into consideration. The first is that with broadband connections becoming more widely available, there is an accompanying increase in user/viewer expectations—in fact, many viewers are only interested in and driven by their demand for personally relevant information and content.

Second, where more bandwidth connections are available, more content can, in theory, be streamed or downloaded by viewers. Over the past few years, indisputably, the supply of content offered has increased considerably, as has the demand for it by customers. More and more people are enhancing their "daily dose of news," for example, by watching news clips on their PC, or they check out the trailers for the newest hit movies.

As a rule of thumb, the easier it is for consumers to receive and acquire content, the more interested and eager they are to get more and diversified content. This can develop into a very cost-intensive exercise for the content owner which is why better compression must be a major consideration. We will look into the cost aspect a bit later; however, one example would be that football enthusiasts will always choose the channel or network that delivers the broadest coverage (i.e., many different camera angles, etc.), and certainly the content owner charges a respective amount of money for the privilege. The fact remains, however, that the underlying risk is never really on the content consumer side, but rather on the content provider side, because the latter has to make an initial investment in the hope that some pays off. But while we are still on the subject of different usages, we should comment on what content actually will be consumed by users and in what circumstances.

In reality, the likelihood of watching a full-length feature film on a handheld device is extremely remote. Handheld devices are ideal media for the delivery of "quick content" such as trailers, news, music clips, stock quotes, or short personal videos. However, with devices like laptop computers, packaged media such as DVDs are already enjoying tremendous popularity—who hasn't watched a DVD on a plane flight or in a hotel room somewhere. And of course, there is the PC with its big, flat screen, where much longer streamed content can be viewed than on handheld devices. But so far nothing has come along that beats the experience of watching movies, sports, etc., on a quality TV set.

As stated earlier, the market must utilize a variety of formats in order to cover the aforementioned market segments. In today's technology landscape, with an exponentially growing jungle of content, market participants are becoming more and more aware of the necessity to re-purpose content. Thus, the ideal situation would be to create content for multiple usage scenarios right off the bat. In other words, stick to one format for all media deliveries. This is possible with MPEG-4, because as the multimedia standard for low, intermediate, and high bit-rate coding, there are solutions available for all of these types of content. By a "solution," we do not mean separate machinery for each of these purposes. One machine will do, and most codecs available in the marketplace today offer a variety of flavors when it comes to encoding. From straightforward, PC-based applications to highly sophisticated encoding platforms able to run parallel encoding jobs, there are enough options to choose from. It does not stop there though. As this technology evolves, progresses, and becomes more efficient, there will be a variety of new features and functionalities becoming available.

Actually, the equation is very simple. With better compression of data, less bandwidth is required, which keeps the cost down. So, with MPEG-4, we can eliminate inconvenient multi-format content creation for multi-network delivery—including IP—and can thereby reduce the actual delivery cost. Also, MPEG-4 can easily

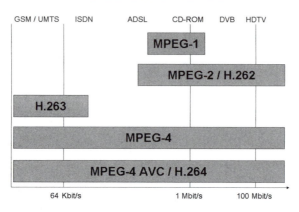

Figure 5.1 This figure shows the various video coding standards and their corresponding bit rates and networks/usages.

be integrated into existing MPEG delivery environments, which is extremely valuable in terms of saving costs. Not bad for a start! If one considers Figure 5.1, quite a lot is immediately evident—the broad spectrum as to where MPEG-4 and MPEG-4 AVC can be utilized. Interestingly enough, if one considers the various usage scenarios like DVD, digital TV, or HDTV and takes into account the unarguably large market in this area, then the conclusion that MPEG-4 will be widely successful can be theoretically drawn. Business-wise, it is extremely important for content owners and providers to be able to turn to one format that can cover all possible exploitation scenarios.

5.2.2. MPEG-4 Is an International Open Standard

Let's now look at the benefits of MPEG-4 as an international open standard. From the standpoint of continuity and stability, the fact that MPEG-4 is an international standard coming from a well-reputed organization is very important, as are its previous successes with the introduction of MPEG-1 and MPEG-2.

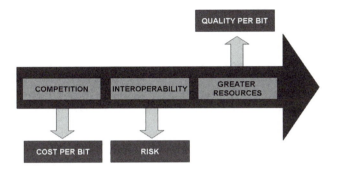

Figure 5.2 The benefits of the open standard MPEG-4 at a glance.
Competition pulls cost per bit south as interoperability reduces risk.
Greater resources drive up the quality per bit.

Market Maturity: In theory, markets actually function quite simply, based on concepts like supply and demand. But there are also underlying issues that make it possible for markets to function for the benefit of all concerned. One of them is the element of time. Although maturity does not necessarily come with time, in the technology world there are many examples where the use of standards has proven to be a key factor in establishing a continuous market, which has brought maturity to the technology itself as well as the products and services offered by market participants. Maturity is, of course, less bound to time, and more affected by the impact a technology has on a marketplace, or on a whole industry. Think about the impact DVDs (and, along with them, MPEG-2) have had since their introduction, or plain old CDs.

Extreme Durability: Another positive aspect of standards is durability. Also an element established by long-term use, durability is founded in robustness and completion. If one considers TV standards like NTSC and PAL, it is apparent that both have stood the test of time and have provided billions of users with moving pictures. Since watching is one thing, and hearing is another, the availability of MP3 (also an MPEG standard) is another good example of a durable standard, which has been successfully deployed all over the world.

Format Continuity: Once a format is agreed on and deployed, the markets require that it not become obsolete in the foreseeable future. The invention of CDs has delivered exactly that—a format that has stood the test of time. Over more than a decade, CDs have become part of our lives in many respects. Initially, we bought these small, silver discs to improve upon the sound quality of our good old LPs (another great example of format continuity), and now we are loading most of our computer programs from them, or utilizing them to store data. Or consider VHS video tapes—another format that has had a significant impact on our entertainment lives for a long period of time, and which is now being changed, slowly but surely, to DVDs.

Innovation: GSM, WLAN, 3GPP. Besides the factor of time, there is also the element of innovation, which is naturally present through the ambition of technologists to develop new technologies and improve existing ones. In order for these innovations to really work, and to deliver the other three aforementioned benefits of maturity, durability, and continuity, all of these elements are packed into agreed-on standards. A wonderful example of this is GSM. We all remember running around with a shoe box-sized mobile telephone, which we now easily slip into our shirt pockets and which we can use virtually anywhere in the world—all because of great efforts by technologists to provide a common standard. WLAN is no different in the sense that "wireless" is the latest industry buzzword, and judging from the overall spread and availability of this technology, one can rest assured it will have a prosperous future (even broadband in this context is not far behind!). Besides GSM, there is also 3GPP, another great standard initiative, which comes into play in next-generation mobile communications like 3G. As it happens, MPEG-4 Visual Simple Profile as well as MPEG-4 AAC audio are optional video and audio codecs within the 3GPP specification. MPEG-4 AVC Baseline Profile will become another optional video codec sometime during 2004.

Figure 5.3 puts the variety of standards into a timeline. It is very interesting to see what sort of quantum leaps the underlying technology has been going through over a relatively brief period of time. From still pictures to video pictures requiring less and less bandwidth while more and more bandwidth is being available is quite a journey. Plus, bear in mind the different kind of lifestyle

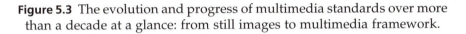

1990	JPEG	CODING OF STILL IMAGES
1992	MPEG-1	CODING FOR DIGITAL STORAGE MEDIA
1994	MPEG-2	CODING FOR DVD AND DIGITAL TV
1996	MPEG-4	INTERACTIVE MULTIMEDIA A/V OBJECTS
2001	MPEG-7	INTERFACE FOR CONTENT DESCRIPTION
2003	MPEG-4 AVC	ADVANCED VIDEO CODING
2004	MPEG-21	MULTIMEDIA FRAMEWORK

Figure 5.3 The evolution and progress of multimedia standards over more than a decade at a glance: from still images to multimedia framework.

today compared with the early 1990s. Today, you can get content and information anywhere, anytime, without a problem, which automatically means a bigger audience and therefore potentially more revenues. MPEG-4 is an enabler of the digital future.

What many people do not realize is the fact that open standards are part of our everyday life, as mentioned in some of the examples above. Just make a call on your mobile telephone and you are taking advantage of an open standard, i.e., GSM. Switch on your television and enjoy your favorite films, delivered to you in PAL or NTSC, both open standards. Consider the dominance and popularity of MP3s, also an open standard. There are countless other examples of open standards, many of which have survived the test of time and still play a significant role in today's technology landscape. In addition, open standards help bring the markets to maturity, as seen with MPEG-2, DVD, and CD technology.

5.2.3. Business Arguments for Open Standards

The discerning reader will agree that it is almost impossible to be best at everything. To illustrate, it's like having a decathlon athlete run 100 meters against the world-record holder in that specific discipline. The decathlon athlete has proven he is world class at all 10 events, but compared to the 100-meter runner, who is focused on his one specialty, he will always come in second.

In the open standard context, developers and manufacturers excel in their specific areas and not in others. The good news here is that "you never walk alone." That is, in the "standards ecosystem," many developments occur through joint activities, so you can partner up with the best in the business—pick and choose your partners, so as to deliver best-of-breed products. This very fact significantly lowers risk and exposure, making it easier to operate, including for new entrants to the field.

MPEG is really all about interoperability. Here lies the first theory, which in a wider sense has to do with the overall issue of how to make/save money with MPEG-4. It is of paramount importance that all market participants sit on one side of the table, i.e., technology providers/participants/vendors, and specialize in and focus on the particular discipline where they excel. With the existence of interoperability and specialization in certain distinct fields, market participants not only *inter*operate on the technical side, they also *co*operate on the commercial side.

Competition is obviously still ensured, because the streaming server software vendors, for example, can still compete amongst themselves, as can the codec providers, which is a good thing for any economic ecosystem. In essence, a climate of cooperation and competition can be created, which are both ingredients for a healthy economic climate in any industry.

Ultimately, of course, the customers sitting on the other side of the table decide whose products they will buy. With MPEG-4, they have freedom of choice since competition will "control" prices, which would not be the case if they choose proprietary solutions, where they would in effect be locked into the strategies and plans of a monopoly. So the first task is to create and foster the climate described above.

We could bring in many other examples where standards make life easier, from the lamp on your bedside table to the paper in your printer, fax, or copy-machine, but we will come back to this point later on. Let us now consider the most important business arguments for open standards, all of which, of course, apply to MPEG-4.

Competition: Competition is actually the key element in this whole equation, because to a very large extent your business decision will depend on how much this adventure will cost. Competition is actually a wonderful market mechanism, because it forces the market and its participants to operate within more or less realistic price boundaries. Many roadmaps, philosophies, and strategies collide here, which can result in a variety of different actions, but all of them are orientated toward being competitive at all times. What it boils down to is that competition within this standard ecosystem drives the cost per bit down, which benefits the customer. This is a logical process that has been clearly demonstrated, for example, in the MPEG-2 marketplace. It is far more convenient for a user to keep informed about the market, which guarantees her freedom of choice, rather than having to keep watch over one vendor, hoping that nothing changes.

Interoperability: One really odd aspect of the standard world—including MPEG-4—is interoperability. It's odd for the simple reason that vendors have to make sure amongst themselves that their tools and equipment do actually work together. So, on one hand you might find bitter rivals competing for valuable market share and revenues, but on the other hand, these rivals may be cooperating to make sure their work fits together. But the fact is that although many vendors compete with each other, they are all working toward the goal of being interoperable, because this is what a standard requires, and it is what makes standards work. So the motivation for a vendor to achieve interoperability with other market participants is clearly and directly linked to being competitive. Being competitive in today's technology landscape is extremely important. A product that might be offered at a great price, but does not work with other related products, is not of much use. Having said that, interoperability ensures that all vendors are working towards a common principle—they all strive to be best with their particular product and this is exactly what delivers the beauty of standards in that the actual, underlying technology improves over time. So, interoperability is tied to some large extent also into a continuous improvement of standard-based technology. In practice, this works very well, as can be seen from the highly successful and popular interoperability program initiated by the MPEG Industry Forum (MPEGIF). In fact, MPEGIF is currently expanding its reach in this respect by initiating a Logo Qualification Program, which will be available to its members who have success-fully completed specific interoperability testing. They will be able to apply the logo issued by MPEGIF, which will gain industrywide recognition that products bearing this logo have successfully proven to be interoperable. In other words, it will in all possibility be established as a seal of quality. It goes without saying that this will also become a strong sales argument amongst vendors.

Greater Resources: We have just learned about the competition driving the cost per bit down, and the coexistence of "rival" vendors through interoperability efforts. To these ends, many resources are deployed, be they on the business development side or the technical side. Focusing for a moment on the technical side, we should realize the following: Over time, the coding efficiency will drastically improve. The same thing happened, as we already know, with MPEG-2, with bit rates having been reduced by over 50% since the standard was frozen in 1996—all, by the way, with-out upgrading decoders. MPEG specifies and standardizes the decoding side only, which makes these encoding improvements possible. If this fact is paired with the huge amount of specialists from all over the world, it will be clearly apparent that these greater resources actually drive up the quality per bit.

So overall, competition, interoperability, and greater resources provide for an economically healthy, workable environment and deliver an extremely persuasive argument for going with open standards. An additional piece of good news is the fact that not one element in an open standard can be controlled by a single vendor—so no monopolies, but many shops for you to walk into and choose what you like most. That's the beauty of an open standard and what makes it work!

5.3. MPEG-4 in Action

5.3.1. Broadcast Industry

Bearing in mind that broadcasters need to be able to serve their content on multiple delivery platforms such as TV, Internet, broadband, DVD, wireless, VHS, and so on, they are in need of solutions that provide them with the utmost flexibility, scalability, functionality, speed, and reliability. Many of the systems currently in situ are not likely to be able to manage this additional workload in the most efficient way possible. This is exactly where MPEG-4 comes in. While MPEG-2 is currently regarded as the de facto video coding standard in digital broadcasting, MPEG-4 offers improved coding efficiency resulting in higher quality, particularly at low bit rates, of coded video and audio. With utilization spread across low, intermediate, and high bitrates, MPEG-4 offers a significant advantage compared to other video standards, enabling encoded data to be accessible over a wide range of media in various qualities. MPEG-4 is an extremely interesting format due to its coverage of many types of applications and wide ranges of resolutions, qualities, bit rates, and services. In addition, taking the latest developments into consideration, MPEG-4 will eventually succeed MPEG-2 as the dominant broadcast format.

With this diversity of usage, MPEG-4 can definitely help broadcasters satisfy their requirement for a coherent media asset-management solution and, at the same time, serve as the ideal format for their content delivery and storage. All of this combined offers a great potential to increase the value and return on investment of the broadcasters' media assets. We will look into this media asset management in more detail further on.

One goal of a broadcaster is to have a solution for easy and accurate search and speedy retrieval within a sophisticated digital broadcast chain, supporting indexing, browsing, and archiving. Content description (as specified in MPEG-7) and Digital Rights Management (with tools from MPEG-4 and MPEG-21) complement this picture.

Broadcasters also face the challenge of being multipurpose-oriented, i.e., their content nowadays is distributed not just via the traditional means, but also is delivered over broadband, IP, and mobile networks. MPEG-4 helps broadcasters meet this challenge by delivering the ideal multimedia standard to broadcasters. In fact, this cross-media exploitation is a unique selling point of MPEG-4. Broadcasters are interested in distributing their content using all the means described above, in order to maximize the value of their assets and use their resources and technology efficiently. Here is where MPEG-4, with its high coding efficiency for low bit rates, comes into its own. This is achieved, for example, through a variety of professional encoding products by numerous companies in the marketplace, which encode real-time and high-quality live or taped content at multiple bit rates on a hard disc, where content can then be archived and stored in different qualities for a variety of uses (IPTV, Internet streaming, mobile phone video).

MPEG-4 video coding is extremely flexible—it can be utilized for low, intermediate, and high bit rates, which is a great advantage compared to other video standards. MPEG-4 covers a wide range of applications, bit-rates, resolutions, qualities, and services, making it the ideal format for media delivery over different types of transmission or storage technologies.

Undeniably, the broadcast industry has changed dramatically over the past few years with the dawning of the digital age. Certainly, most broadcasters still follow the traditional methods of producing and creating, for example, television content, but there is a significant move toward the utilization of digital formats. Currently the most commonly used format is MPEG-2, which is known to all market participants. Also, regarding existing coding standards like MPEG-1, MPEG-2, or H.263, the fact is that MPEG-4 offers a better coding efficiency, which improves the quality of coded video and audio. Therefore, MPEG-4 will play a significant role in the interactive, digital television arena.

One of the characteristics of the broadcast application scenario is the delivery of television service over a unidirectional broadcast channel using a one-to-many communication method. The broadcaster's goal is to provide a media service to the customer that satisfies a minimum quality requirement for which a customer is willing to pay. In order to be cost effective, it is important to minimize the transmission bandwidth (via satellite, cable, or terrestrial means) that is necessary for the delivery of the service, that is, to minimize the cost for the service as each Megahertz of physical bandwidth has an associated price tag. Therefore, coding efficiency of audio and video codecs is of prime importance. Alternatively, the broadcaster can book a fixed amount of transmission bandwidth from a satellite service provider or cable carrier for a good price. In order to increase the revenue, the broadcaster can increase the number of offered programs if the coding efficiency of the audio and video codecs can be improved while preserving the minimum quality for the visual or audio service as perceived by the end user.

There is a certain asymmetry of the architecture in the broadcast scenario, which requires keeping the complexity and cost on the receiving end low. However, in order to achieve improved compression, it is feasible to accept some moderate increase in cost/ complexity for a future decoder or set-top box. A receiver must be able to access programming content without the use of a return path. Therefore, all pertinent information needed to understand the basic organization of a channel or channel multiplex and the data contained therein must be available in the broadcast data on a periodic basis. The acceptable delay from the time a user requests a change in programs (channel surfing) until an "acceptable" quality rendition of the requested material is presented is less than 300 to 500 ms.

Since there is a relatively low number of encoders necessary at the broadcaster's playout facility, additional complexity and the associated cost for the encoder is less of an issue. The encoding must be able to function in real time for delivering live broadcast of sports or similar live events. However, the broadcast scenario is not overly sensitive to delay incurred by the overall encoding-transmission-decoding signal path. As the consumer has no absolute reference to the actual time instance of events to be broadcast, a delay of up to several seconds is acceptable for the service without a negative impact in the perceived service quality. However, for very brief events, the latency should not exceed the length of the event.

The bit rates that can be expected for a broadcast channel range from hundreds of bits per second up to hundreds of megabits per second. Typical audio-visual broadcast services today use broadcast channels with bit rates in the range of 1.5 Mbit/s to 6 Mbit/s.

Media types to be used in broadcasting include text, still pictures, moving pictures, audio, and graphics. Current examples of multi-media broadcasting include TV station logos (watermarking), graphical overlays used in sporting events and stock tickers, and multi-window screen formats such as those used by Bloomberg Information Television or the sports and stock market crawls used by CNN Headline News.

Besides the more conventional form of media broadcast, there is a new business emerging called "data casting." This service is characterized by sending information that one assumes many receivers need or wish to receive. This is achieved, for example, by combining multiple data sets in a carousel structure, where each dataset is broadcast repeatedly. The repeat interval of such a carousel is based on the bit rate allocated to the service and the volume of data in the service. All forms of digital information can be multiplexed into such a digital data-casting environment. Not all data services require low latency. Some services, however, will require very low latency, such as downloads of small software or data snippets that run in set-top boxes (applets) or other end-user terminals. These can be accommodated in a large carousel that can conceivably contain vast amounts of data. This could be a way to distribute large chunks of operating software updates. Currently this mechanism is used in digital television services to update the operating system of TV set-top boxes over the air. The customer doesn't even notice that his or her box has received a new software version.

Typical video resolutions required are CCIR-601 (Standard Definition resolution) but may migrate to High Definition resolution in the near future. Audio is currently stereo but may migrate toward a multi-channel format (5.1 surround sound), where the expected quality is comparable to or better than that of an audio CD.

Virtual production techniques are becoming increasingly popular in TV production studios. These techniques are based on the well-known chroma-key method that has been in use for many years. Chroma-keying means that the actors perform in front of a colored background (usually blue or green), and a key signal is derived from a chroma-key unit, indicating which parts of the image contain the actors. A mixer then overlays the actors on another virtual background image, using the key signal to control a "soft" switch between foreground and background.

With traditional chroma-keying, the studio camera cannot be moved, since the registration between actors and background would be lost. One of the new features of virtual production is that the camera can be moved, because its position and orientation are measured, and the background image is adjusted to keep the correct registration. This is usually achieved by rendering the background on a graphics computer, and updating the position of the virtual camera to match that of the studio camera. In situations where the camera is allowed to pan, tilt, and zoom, but not translate, the background image can be stored as a 2D image, which is transformed to match the current camera angle. If the camera is allowed to translate, true 3D models of all virtual set elements are generally required. Virtual objects can also be inserted in front of the live action, by generating a key signal for each object that forces the mixer to switch to the virtual background signal within the object, regardless of the presence of the actor's key signal. This can be achieved by giving every object (including the actors) a depth value, which determines the way in which objects are overlaid.

MPEG-4 offers the possibility of broadcasting programs produced in this way, using object-based techniques. The final image composition then takes place in the decoder rather than in the studio mixer. This is likely to offer advantages both in coding efficiency and increased functionality (such as user interaction and stereo-scopic viewing of the scene).

It is also important to ensure that the audio signal presents the same spatial "story" as the pictures that go with it. As an actor who is talking moves within a space, the proportion of direct-to-reverberant voice sound changes and indeed even the spectral content of the sound may change. This is normally accomplished manually, but in the context of MPEG-4, where spatial information may be rendered at the consumer's end of the chain, it is important to generate this feature automatically, using tools such as those provided in structured audio effects (SAFX).

Virtual actors are sometimes incorporated into virtual productions. These are 3D models of people, usually animated by motion data captured from a real actor. The face and body animation features of MPEG-4 could be used here, as long as they offer sufficient control over the appearance of the virtual actor to satisfy the program producer.

Integrated Service Digital Broadcast (ISDB) is a concept for con-structing a complete digital broadcasting system, which offers a great variety of services with high-spectrum efficiency, flexibility, and extendibility. ISDB provides not only existing basic broadcast-ing services such as SDTV and HDTV, but also new services, such as multimedia TV, the TV newspaper (multimedia information services), and two-way information services. It enables viewers to make better use of television and offers services with multiple functions. It is controlled by a CPU, thus enabling the viewer to enjoy programs through personal filters and an intelligent agent for broadcasting. Figure 5.4 shows an example of the program menu the user can see just after turning on the switch.

5.3.2. MPEG-4 and Media Asset Management

Since we learned how to move pictures, there has been a con-stant and continuously growing necessity to archive content. In today's technology environment, where digital technology rules,

Figure 5.4 Example of the program menu of a terminal for receiving ISDB services.

broadcasters are faced with the requirement of optimizing efficiency, increasing revenues and market share, and reducing cost, while at the same time improving quality and, of course, staying competitive.

Businesses must be managed, but so must content! Now that we know a little bit about creation and delivery, let us look at another interesting and crucial aspect of the digital media arena—Content Management, which we will call Media Asset Management; after all, contents are revenue-generating assets. MPEG-4 directly impacts the production, archiving, and programming chain, where for example it permits broadcasters to browse through video archives with ease and speed, which is of paramount importance. There are browsing systems available on the market, where Standard Definition MPEG-2 to MPEG-4 smart file transcoding is used to produce a frame-accurate proxy and/or browse a version of the high-quality MPEG-2 archive. The bit rates utilized in these kind of scenarios are usually 300 Kbps and 800 Kbps. The displayed video is of high quality, particularly when the MPEG-4 Visual Advanced Simple Profile is used. From a business perspective, this is very attractive since, in essence, the content is "purposed" in two directions: storage of a high-quality video, and archiving. The latter is particularly attractive given that there is an extremely large amount of content available, which is growing every day, and content owners must utilize the principles of archiving not only for their own purposes, but as a contemporary content-selling tool, which clients can access through a number of different means.

Another benefit of an MPEG-4 media asset management system is that not only the broadcaster but also the viewers can utilize the system to locate, preview (at a very low bit rate), and choose content for viewing (in an appropriate bit rate and quality that fits the user's needs and environment).

It is certainly fair to say that the broadcast industry is constantly evolving, which requires market participants to deploy flexible, standards-based environments and management systems that can be easily accessed both internally and externally, taking into account the fact that content, and the way it is managed and presented, will always rule and determine the overall value proposition. MPEG-4 can deliver this important piece in the value chain and is on the way to establishing itself not only as an exciting professional add-on, but as the new de facto standard for these applications.

Let's now look at elements of content-based storage and retrieval as part of media asset management. The term "content-based" refers to systems whose objective is to provide access to content, or rather archived/stored content, based on attributes associated with the video or audio content. These attributes may be keywords (often a semantic description) but they can also be numerical attributes. Generally, the purpose of such libraries is to assist in the management of large collections of digital video assets. As an example, many of these systems rely on temporal and/or spatial segmentation of an audio-visual stream. Although the segmentation process itself is not part of MPEG standardization, the provision of mechanisms to efficiently access such temporal or spatial segments is within the scope of MPEG-4. The result is that in addition to accessing content using traditional methods such as fast-forwarding to a particular temporal value, it is also very beneficial to be able to browse through these segments based on associated textual and numeric attributes.

Many content-based media asset management applications will need to be able to speedily compare attributes associated with the assets stored in the database with a representative set of attributes defining a query. Often, in the case of browsing, the query is defined by one or more examples and their associated attributes. When it comes to rather large collections, the way to make this exercise feasible is to make sure the method does not involve the decoding of the entire audio/video stream. A fundamental component of such systems for this purpose is the use of a "decision support representative" (DSR). A DSR can be used to represent a large audio-visual asset in a very condensed form, allowing the user to decide on the appropriateness of an asset for his or her purposes. The exact nature of the DSR can vary from application to application (for example, single representative frames, or a small mosaic of frames, icons, etc.); however, it is desirable to have support for the efficient storage and access to the DSRs. What is important to realize is that MPEG-4 is the enabler for media asset management, providing the ability to browse through and/or access content in order to identify and choose specific content, for specific purposes at any point in time. MPEG-4 is not intended to be involved in the delivery of assets, since these can be on a variety of media, such as on film or tape.

5.3.3. Studio and Television Post-Production

When it comes to post-production, before source material ends up in its final form—for example, as a television program—it passes through various processing steps, which involve editing and multiple copying from one storage medium to another.

The ease of creating complex effects, such as color separation, overlaying (or chroma-keying), cross-fading, cutting-and-pasting, and a variety of other digital video effects, is increasing because of the transparency of digital recording operations and the automation using edit controllers as well as offline edit systems. The need for versions in different languages favors separation of program elements and requires separate storage of all intermediate versions. Regional variations of a program may also have similar requirements.

In reality, a pretty broad spectrum of operations, as the ones described above, is needed to produce the final product and caption it. This may involve several passes, for technical reasons, and may therefore require the intermediate storage of results to an appropriate medium (typically tape). It is entirely possible that as many as 10 to 20 passes may be needed on a single project, with 4 or 5 versions retained.

For TV production and post-production, the advantage of choosing a standard offering the possibility of content-based video manipulation is attractive for the following reasons:

- The combination of multiple sources of visual information to produce a single entity (i.e., program) often amounts to retrieving objects of interest from those sources and recombining them accordingly. With sources in the multimedia era becoming more and more diverse, this tendency is likely to increase.
- Lossy digital compression techniques that do not produce visually perceptible distortions are being increasingly employed in studios, particularly through the proliferation of storage devices (i.e., recorders) that use bit-rate reduction to improve storage efficiency.
- With Virtual Reality techniques emerging, it is anticipated that they will have a considerable impact on television and film production. These techniques are object driven and make extensive use of 3D audio-visual models. Efficient storage and transport of 3D object descriptions are essential where capacity is at a premium, e.g., on servers and networks for one-to-one service provision.

In post-production, it is not uncommon that each pass is made on a different, separated platform, each of which has quite different hardware and software features (CPU power, 3D-CG accelerator, real-time grabber, mixing capabilities, etc.). This especially applies to 3D-CG workstations with both fast rendering capability and fast mixers for online 2D layer composition. This clearly requires interoperable exchange formats supporting the import and export of extended video as well as scripting data. In addition, a common scripting language to use when supervising the different "post-production islands" from a central editing suite is strongly desired.

Continuing along this road, we come to the concept of content-driven manipulation of coded video in the studio. Although the ambition is to keep each video in its compressed form for as long as possible, some applications may require transcoding, which means that the compression used should be very efficient in this respect.

Thanks to the fact that digital uncompressed data can be copied straight (dubbing), it is possible to reproduce distortion-free video data as many times as required. Where lossy compression is utilized, however, the accumulation of coding errors limits the number of times that encoding/decoding operations can be undertaken before the quality becomes visually unacceptable.

An additional difficulty arises if further processing is needed between the aforementioned encode/decode operations. Very simple effects can be applied to simulate intergenerational processing, such as small spatial/temporal shifts and fades. However, when these kind of effects are combined with traditional compression algorithms at television transmission rates (i.e., MPEG-2 MP@ML@4.5 Mbit/s), the output video quickly becomes unusable (i.e., after 3 to 4 generations).

5.3.4. Digital TV

By using digital data, the viewing experience of consumers can be improved through more interactivity, for example:

- Video-on-demand
- Link between TV programs/advertising to Web pages with tailored data exchange (user's preferences)

- Access to Internet entertainment and information
- E-mail and messaging on TV sets with cordless keyboards
- Secure and authenticated E-commerce such as banking and shopping
- Interactive games
- Any specialized interactive application

MPEG-4 is designed to deliver the above-mentioned functionalities. Typically, these sorts of functions will be available through set-top boxes, which means that they can be classified as MPEG-4 applications. As you can see, there are far more interesting uses for set-top boxes than simply being a receiving device for moving pictures. In fact, there is a very strong tendency that STBs develop themselves into multimedia gateways; not only is the receiving of content on the agenda, but the storage of content, whether that may be temporary or permanent, is becoming prevalent. In addition, if one considers the various aspects of conditional access and the related possibilities, which we do not want to list here, then it becomes pretty much apparent what sort of impact the existence, evolution and progress of digital media technology can have right in the living rooms of millions of users. Surely, let's not get overly excited and assume this all happens overnight. The fact remains that there are millions of STBs deployed and operators do not tend to simply switch everybody over and hand out new STBs. It will take sometime and it is a specific transition and migration path to be followed, which is not only characterized by technology considerations, but also very much so by corporate and commercial considerations. One must very soberly distinguish between the availability of technology and its deployment—as in many things in life, it is all about timing, but the great news is that we can lean back and look forward of taking advantage of these technologies in the not-too-distant future.

As a rule of thumb, a set-top box will receive MPEG-2 transport streams carrying MPEG-2 video and audio. The decoded audio and video will then be rendered on a set of speakers and a screen, respectively, and can be described as the standard digital TV experience. In an MPEG-4 scenario, the MPEG-2 transport stream can also carry MPEG-4 streams, which have been specified in the standard to enable such an operation. In the conventional setup, the de-multiplexer would simply discard this information. This makes the bit stream carrying the additional MPEG-4 data fully backward compatible. On the other hand, on an MPEG-4-enabled set-top box, the MPEG-4 stream will be recognized by the receiver as such, and passed on to the appropriate MPEG-4 decoder. The MPEG-2 video and audio will be rendered through the MPEG-4 rendering mechanism, together with the additionally received MPEG-4 objects.

Use Case—Home-Shopping: There are many countries, where home-shopping channels are successfully in operation, giving the consumer at home the opportunity to purchase all sorts of products. This is not a talking-heads environment, but an object-rich scenery, which is perfectly suited to MPEG-4. For example, besides the moderator, there is a background (mainly a picture), there are logos, information about the products (text), and of course the product itself (as a still picture from a variety of perspectives).

Orders are typically placed via the telephone but they can also be placed through the configuration of a back channel (which may well be a telephone line), which makes the ordering more user-friendly, simply by interacting with the TV screen using the remote control. This makes shopping easier and more impulse driven, and therefore it becomes an interesting feature for shopping channel operators. This can all be achieved through sending a small MPEG-J application program to check if a back channel is configured, and if so, product-ordering information can be taken with special pop-up menus, and, via remote control, information about the number of items, the item specifics (size, color, options, etc.), and credit card number (note that this will involve security issues) can be taken. The back channel is opened (possibly by dialing a specific phone number), the order information is sent, and the back channel is then closed.

Use Case—Conditional Access: Subscribing to specific channels or pay-per-view services has been possible for quite a while now with analog set-top boxes. Using the same technology as described above, movies can be ordered and paid for. Conditional access can be set up to require a password, which will be verified via a back channel or compared with information stored on the set-top box hardware. Alternatively, a specially installed device like Smart Cards (used for access verification and/or decryption) can be utilized to control access.

5.3.5. Video Over IP

One buzzword that has come out of the woodwork recently is "triple play" in the telecoms industry, which can be translated, in essence, to mean the delivery of broadband Internet access, voice transmission/telephony, and video over IP, the last of which is a new addition to the telco service spectrum. However, the "video" part of this equation is becoming more and more of a necessity in order to stay competitive and to keep their subscribers. Overall, it is the same old song of attracting subscribers, keeping them, in turning them into revenue generators. Let's be clear on the dimensions of this—we are not only talking about big telcos, but telcos of all sizes that are embracing this new business and service-offering initiative.

The fact is, the infrastructure is in place and the underlying technology is as well, so many market participants are deploying these kinds of services, bringing motion pictures directly to your PCs, laptops, or mobile devices, utilizing your broadband connection, over wireless—on demand, scheduled . . . you name it.

It is a great opportunity for telcos to get involved in this field. On one hand, they have been forced to do so to some extent by deregulations in their original field of activity, but on the other hand, they clearly understand that consumers are demanding even more content, everywhere and all the time, which gives them a real chance to deploy and sell more services. The good news of course for the telcos is that this all goes down a tiny cable, which is already present in their subscribers' homes. Plus, from a consumer's view-point, it is simple to get and manage—three services out of one shop!

- Telephony
- Internet Access
- Video over IP

So how does this actually work and where does MPEG-4 come into play? The short version of the technical side is that there is a so-called operator head-end (the point where content is "injected"), a regional center (a kind of distribution point not too far from the subscriber), and then there is what is called "the last mile" (i.e., the distance to the actual subscriber). MPEG-4, and especially MPEG-4 AVC, can be perfectly utilized to encode/transcode the respective content at the head end, which is then transmitted over the backbone via the regional center to the subscriber, where the content is decoded on a set-top box or on the PC. There are already quite a number of sophisticated MPEG-4 encoder and streaming products available on the market, which will become even more efficient, functional, and versatile than they are today, once MPEG-4 AVC is being adopted and introduced in the market place.

As we learned earlier, MPEG-4 can be utilized here in a very efficient way, since it works for ostensibly all bit rates—whether it is for a standard broadband connection or a satellite connection.

The benefit of using MPEG-4 in this triple-play scenario—and it is anticipated that video over DSL will be one of the key drivers for MPEG-4 over the next 12 months—is that it is easy to integrate into the existing infrastructure and that it offers cross-media exploit-ation by making content available for a variety of different uses. Without a shadow of a doubt, video over IP is a valuable alternative to the traditional ways of broadcasting, since it gives even more consumers the opportunity to receive more content, more services, and more value for their money.

5.3.6. Mobile Communications Industry

We have already briefly touched upon the significant involvement of MPEG-4 in the mobile industry, mainly through the adoption as an optional video and audio codec with the 3GPP and 3GPP2 standards. Without going much deeper into these standards, it is important to understand the basic definitions in order to fully appreciate the impact of MPEG-4 within the mobile industry.

First, let us define yet another buzzword in the technology landscape—3G. It stands for third generation and is in fact a generic industry term describing the high-speed delivery of data over mobile networks. To put this into context, it all started with the first generation, analog, leading into 2G and 2.5G (GSM, GPRS, and EDGE, respectively), and now 3G. 3G, which is currently being rolled out worldwide, enables the sending and receiving of bandwidth-intensive data, such as video (streamed/on demand), high-quality audio, and all sorts of other rich multimedia data.

3GPP and 3GPP2 have been specifically designed for this purpose, enabling the creation, delivery, and playback of multimedia content within a unified framework and delivered over high-speed mobile connections to new, state-of-the-art mobile devices. While MPEG-4 has proven to work very well in the Internet arena, the technologists behind 3GPP decided to take advantage of this knowledge and have based their standard on MPEG-4. Therefore, as in MPEG-4, in 3GPP you can mix text, video, and audio in a single file and deliver it over your chosen network.

It should be mentioned at this point that MPEG-4 took a lot of input and basics from Apple Quicktime, which has been extremely successful over the course of many years. In fact, if you look at the overall impact of Quicktime, and consider its support for MPEG-4, you do not need to be a rocket scientist to work out how hundreds of existing applications can easily adopt and utilize MPEG-4, and indeed 3GPP. The availability is guaranteed; the various uses are commonly recognized, and content owners are able to create their content easily within their "usual" environment but in a new, more contemporary format to deliver said content via new, contemporary delivery channels. With millions of users currently, Quicktime is a prime example of MPEG-4 in action. The number is growing weekly, and with more content being available via all manner of transmission tools, MPEG-4 has found a prominent position in the mobile industry.

Of course, in the mobile industry it is of paramount importance to ensure interoperability, and virtually all the leading infrastructure companies providing content owners with the "engine room" for their services deliver solutions that work with devices and software available in the marketplace. For this reason, all the big names in mobile handsets, whether from Japan, the United States, or Europe, have been spending significant resources in order to remain or become interoperable.

But what will drive MPEG-4, and later MPEG-4 AVC, in the mobile markets? Here, a very interesting picture emerges in which content is not only created by professional content providers, but by the actual users themselves. Mainly this will entail short video clips with talking heads as in news, sports, music videos, and so on, but it will also include privately created videos from the last holiday, etc. For the operators, that means that they need to be able to serve both the "traditional" networks but also mobile networks. In fact, operators do like this scenario, from the simple point of view that it presents them with a sort of a Greenfield opportunity to get involved in a market that is currently being developed and expected to properly take off soon. Operators must be supported in terms of the content creation in order to provide a service with value additions to deliver more subscribers, or enable subscribers to upgrade. There are visible trends in the industry for this, with a number of 3G services being launched and quite a large number of video-enabled mobile handsets becoming available.

There are of course a number of obstacles, which are addressed through the utilization of MPEG-4. If one subscriber likes to send a video to a friend, utilizing her video-enabled handset and her operator's network, and this friend happens to not have a video-enabled handset, the subscriber can email the video to her friend (video mail), who can then watch the respective movie using MPEG-4-compliant player software.

5.3.7. Mobile Multimedia

The mobile industry is obviously not only characterized by mobile telephones, but also includes mobile computing—the use of a portable computer capable of wireless communication, which is not only used for local, stand-alone data processing, but also for wireless communication situations of a mobile user in motion.

In a typical mobile computing scenario, a mobile user communicates with a remote computer system using, for example, a laptop/notebook or a Personal Digital Assistant (PDA) via wireless communication links, which follow the same principles in terms of the delivery as described earlier.

Multimedia applications in the mobile sector are faced with challenges that do not exist in this form for desktop applications. The reason for this is that mobile technologies and applications must deal with less computational power, low bandwidths, and at times the poor reliability of the chosen transmission mechanism.

In addition to requiring a high compression performance, the ability to adapt is very important for mobile applications. The reasons for this are as follows:

- Diversity of mobile devices (for example PDA, sub-notebooks, notebooks, or portable workstations) with regard to available resources
- Diversity of wireless networks (e.g., WLAN, GSM, 3G/UMTS, or satellite) with regard to network topology, protocols, bandwidth, reliability, etc.
- The need to continuously provide the maximum in terms of quality and performance and the minimum in terms of cost

MPEG-4 is very appropriate for mobile multimedia applications since, because of its ability to accommodate very low bit-rate applications. More precisely and in summary,

- High compression performance can be achieved.
- Flexibility of encoding and decoding complexity, for example, temporal resolution, and different spatial resolutions and quality enable very flexible trade-offs between quality, performance, and cost.
- Object-based coding functionalities allow for interaction with audio-visual objects and enable new interactive applications in a mobile environment.
- Face animation parameters can be used to reduce bandwidth consumption for real-time communication applications in a mobile environment, e.g., mobile conferencing.

5.4. MPEG-4 in Business

5.4.1. Pricing

If one considers the current pricing for MPEG-4 products, it is evident that some market participants on the vendor side apparently believe they are in a business that sells power plants in volume, or believe that MPEG-4 products need to be priced for early adopters, who are sometimes willing to pay more than the average customer would. Many of these companies have been taking on a considerable amount of investment, which in turn, being faced with significant monthly costs for their operation per month, seems to drive prices up, never mind their expectations. In economic terms, they need to charge and present these sorts of prices to sustain their operation and deliver some form of return back to their investors. Of course, this is something that is apparent in any industry, however, and as always, timing is the important factor. Usually what happens is that when the market becomes more mature and the possible volumes are higher, prices will automatically come down. Obviously, growing competition contributes to that too. The bad news in this regard is that there may be more than a few corporate casualties along the way, which to some extent is normal in any industry that is experiencing change or consolidation in some shape or form. Critics may take this as an opportunity to judge MPEG-4 as failing, which is of course their right; however it is rather misguided to draw conclusions about the success or failure of a technology that is just now getting in gear. Certainly, this "gearing up" has taken some time. In terms of "age," MPEG-4 Video (Part 2), which was finalized in 2000, may sound like it's "old" considering the speed of technological progress these days. But look at it instead from the perspective of maturity, and the ability to improve over time. It can take a number of years for a technology to "mature." Just like MPEG-2, which has only now reached its limits, the quality of MPEG-4 is slowly improving over time. And, of course, with MPEG-4 AVC having been finalized in early 2003, the story of developing and making available the best, most flexible and scalable compression technology continues.

5.4.2. Specialization

With specialization, and staying focused on which market segments to serve, the likelihood of companies succeeding is much higher than it would be otherwise. The MPEG-4 market requires a healthy, coherent, competitive, and reasonable pricing for products in order to function well and deliver commercial satisfaction.

The intent here is to illustrate how the market could function possibly much better with the help of MPEG-4, generating more revenues for all concerned. The great advantage of MPEG-4 in contributing a "revenue-increasing element" to the business of content creators is the fact that consumers' requirements and expectations grow constantly. There is the never-ending demand for personal, anticipated, and relevant information.

Let us consider the evolution of media. Going back to the emergence of the TV set, besides the fact that the consumer could view only one program in the beginning, he or she needed to get out of a seat to interact with his/her TV—switch it on and off, turn the volume up and down, etc. The first improvement to this situation (besides more programs to choose from) came with the introduction, or rather the innovation, of remote control—the consumer could now interact from a much more convenient position than before. In the years that followed, there were video players/recorders that enabled consumers to record and watch content whenever desired. The evolution of this interaction has gone yet another step with Internet and DVD technology bringing information to consumers. But consumers want more, continuously. New technologies have always made it possible to go a step further; the same applies to MPEG-4. While MPEG-2, the currently dominant format in the digital media arena, has brought a lot of new functionalities to the consumer, e.g., DVD as mentioned above, it is impossible to create truely interactive content with it and deploy it on DVDs and a variety of interactive broadcast networks. This function, which MPEG-4 offers, is extremely attractive to content creators since it enables them to deliver the type of content required and demanded by users. So MPEG-4 makes money primarily because of technological superiority.

This same principle can then be deployed in another major growth market for MPEG-4. After having spent billions on obtaining the respective licenses from governments, the operators of 3G/UMTS networks are also taking advantage of MPEG-4 (or at least have the freedom of choice to do so through the 3GPP specification, as we learned earlier, that contains either MPEG-4 or H.263), as have the manufacturers of appliances supplying the relevant gadgets, since, the demand by customers has risen dramatically, sometimes even exponentially, in recent years. Where consumers at first were happy to speak to one another on a phone they could carry in their pocket (OK, initially it was more like a shoe box), soon they were able to send text messages, followed by still pictures, and now they can even send each other videos over their mobile phones. This emerging market, with a number of networks in place and others being launched in the months to come, particularly in Europe, will, by its very nature, deliver a considerable revenue to the MPEG-4 community—particularly to hardware manufacturers but ultimately to all participants in the production chain if one considers the growth potential for "home-cooked" videos.

The "personal creation market" has potentially the biggest growth potential among all perceived opportunities including news, sports, music, etc.

5.4.3. How to Make Money

The "how to make money" aspect comes into play through the simplistic and everlasting principle of satisfying demand. However, a demand can only be satisfied if the cost of doing so is within reason, and above all within reach, of the consumers' and customers' wallets, which leads us back to where we were a few lines earlier. In other words, MPEG-4 makes money when vendors provide content creators with the opportunity to capitalize upon the technical innovation MPEG-4 brings along by offering multiple narrowband as well as broadband platforms like the Internet, digital TV, and wireless, for the distribution of content.

In addition, as we have learned above, MPEG-4 and especially MPEG-4 AVC vest a significant bit rate saving in itself. Bit rate savings can be immediately equated to monetary savings. Also, one has to look at MPEG standards as such, and it is clearly visible that they were structured from day one with economics in mind—simple decoders, complicated encoders. Or, in other words—cheap decoders, expensive encoders. Certainly, this analogy is slightly

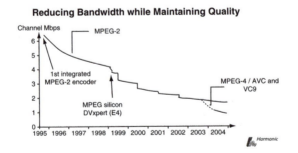

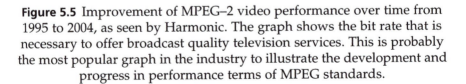

Figure 5.5 Improvement of MPEG–2 video performance over time from 1995 to 2004, as seen by Harmonic. The graph shows the bit rate that is necessary to offer broadcast quality television services. This is probably the most popular graph in the industry to illustrate the development and progress in performance terms of MPEG standards.

exaggerated, but at the core remains a fact—MPEG standards are made to make money. Also, it created a whole new industry from which no one would have probably expected this sort of perform-ance in terms of quality improvement.

So clearly, as in MPEG-2, we will be seeing the same sort of curve as in Figure 5.5 happening over the next few years with coding effi-ciency improving. Technology vendors and certainly content owners as well, will benefit from the fact that more bandwidth will be available, while offering new products requiring the use of less bandwidth—a very nice situation to be in and to take advantage of. MPEG-4 as a proven technology delivers much better economics and is a feasible facilitator for content owners to achieve their objective and provide big audiences with great quality content and to generate continuous revenues in doing so.

5.4.4. Key Factors for Migration

The many uses of MPEG-4 could fill hundreds of pages, if we were to cover all possible business models. However, there are certain key factors evident that make a migration to or intro-duction of state-of-the-art compression technology, i.e., MPEG-4, viable for your business, some of which we have already described above.

- Multimedia: Continuous demand for the delivery/availability of audio/video data through various networks and packaged media
- Security and surveillance: Public safety and national security are increasingly important, and providers have started switch-ing from analog to digital technologies
- Mobile: Similar to multimedia, audio/video data must be de-livered to people "on the go" through the latest wireless tech-nologies
- Bandwidth: Supply is rising, but so is demand. Even though prices are going down, bandwidth remains a major cost factor in the industry

The critical reader may now comment that all these wonderful things that we have been describing over the last few pages can also be provided through proprietary technologies It goes without saying that there is excellent multimedia technology being offered; however, as we mentioned before, the use of a single technology provider/vendor comes with a lot of disadvantageous elements for market participants. In addition, there are a few more considerations to be taken into account when looking at the past few years of digital media. For example, the open standard MPEG-2 is dominating the broadcast industry at the moment, and the likelihood of a proprietary format taking over is, frankly, extremely remote. Plus, MPEG-4 can offer interactivity, which will be playing a major role in years to come. So, let us look further into the various potential uses of MPEG-4 and start with some thoughts about compression technologies in the MPEG-2 arena.

One of the most discussed topics today is obviously which compression technology will become a true successor to MPEG-2. First, the departure of MPEG-2 is certainly not imminent. Second, with MPEG-2 being a true open standard, it can, from this perspective, only be succeeded by another true open standard. The good news is that this successor, MPEG-4 AVC, exists, and not as some kind of a futuristic, conceptual, and revolutionary idea, trying to capture market attention while being light-years away from reality, but is a highly sophisticated compression standard, available today. MPEG-4 AVC advances many techniques utilized in MPEG-2 and adds new tools that dramatically improve coding efficiencies with up to 40% to 50% gains over today's state-of the-art MPEG-2.

In business terms, all this can be characterized quite simply. If your existing business was technically a success while using MPEG-2, the likelihood of this continuing with MPEG-4 is a logical and reasonable conclusion. The very fact that you have been relying on MPEG-2 in the past makes a migration over to MPEG-4 easier, in large part because the same organization is behind it.

There are certainly implications to be considered here, since technology alone will never ever be the sole factor that makes your business a success. Technology is certainly a facilitator enabling businesses to be successful; however it will always boil down to your proposition, unique selling points, and overall offering. Just a few paragraphs earlier, we discussed some of the money-making aspects. Making money can obviously also be achieved through *saving* money. If you consider the gains in coding efficiency mentioned above, you will realize that this percentage can also be illustrated as your potential savings if the respective costs are taken into account. We will look into this interesting aspect in the next section, where we will deal with costs.

There is of course also Microsoft's Windows Media 9 (WM9) compression technology, which is without a doubt a very advanced, multipurpose technology. In addition, in a move toward some of the benefits of standardization, the Windows Media 9 specification was submitted to SMPTE for ratification in September 2003. Certainly, Windows Media technology is extremely well recognized, is commonly available, and is now moving more into the broadcast arena with (a) the decoupling of the transport stream and (b) the new Advanced Profile with interlace support and other essential elements required for professional-grade broadcast. (The previous WM9 Main Profile was PC-centric and clearly not targeting solutions for the broadcast community.)

The discerning critic will ask, where does all this leave an open standard like MPEG-4. The simple answer is in an interesting competition. In addition, it should be noted that currently, as far as the broadcast world in early 2004 is concerned, MPEG-4 AVC is ahead of Windows Media 9, since the aforementioned Advanced Profile has not yet been released.

Customers in the broadcast industry will soon have the choice between these two technologies, which in the end is good for competition and perhaps allows broadcasters to pursue slightly diverging business models. So there will be natural competition within MPEG-4 as to which vendor can actually offer the best implementation technically or the best acquisition model, paired with the competition on the overall technology level, i.e., proprietary vs standard-based technology. This attitude is already clearly demonstrated by a number of vendors, who, while being supporters of MPEG-4, have also now added Windows Media 9 support to some of their products. You may ask yourself, how is this coherently possible and viable to actually support two different technologies. Well, if one considers the current situation where we also have a major element of coexistence of various formats serving the industry, this will, to some extent, continue. This may sound like a contradiction, since MPEG-4 is being advocated throughout this book, but then consider the size of the market we are talking about. The multimedia, digital market is a multi-billion dollar industry, and therefore there are many corporate considerations, cross-company interests, and a variety of other factors that must be thought of

The name of the game is not for a technology vendor to decide what its customers want, but to offer them, and let them choose from, a variety of "flavors." Without a doubt, there is room for MPEG-4 and Windows Media 9 (Advanced Profile) to coexist in the huge digital media marketplace and ecosystem, which can therefore deliver the key elements of a demanding economic environment: advanced offerings, choice, and competition. The advantages and benefits of this are quite evident with respect to MPEG-4. But no matter how much one believes in MPEG-4, it has to be acknowledged that there are alternatives around, and it will be quite interesting to see the industry move forward.

In summary, the business aspects, especially regarding cross-media exploitation, are mainly tied to the creation element where an automated flow of encoding procedures will deliver a cost-effective solution. But there is much more to it, which leads us to the exciting opportunities MPEG-4 opens up in a variety of sectors. We cannot consider all of them in this book, but let us take a closer look at some of the issues related to content.

5.4.5. The Chicken and the Egg—How to Roll Out Coding Technology

We all know about the chicken-and-egg scenario, which has kept mankind pondering for many centuries. However, no matter how you look at it, all parties have their "logical" explanations, which, strangely enough, all seem to make sense. The trouble is that no one solution has emerged and been agreed upon, so mankind will no doubt have this interesting topic to talk about for years to come.

In the media world, we are faced with a similar kind of question. What was there first, the content or the players? First we have to consider what is actually content. "Content" is effectively an ongoing fully flexible event, whether in the past, present, or future, and whether it is real or fictional. A "player" is the medium through which content is shown and presented to an audience. In order to consider this sort of question properly, we need to go back in time.

In the early days, content was painted/written on cave walls, which, research has shown, was for information and entertainment purposes (please do not get overly excited and mark this point in time as the birth of pre-historic television). Transmission at that time was almost exclusively through word-of-mouth within communities, since at that time everything was pretty micro-cosmic. But already at that early stage, we are not able to answer coherently whether in fact the content was there first or the player.

We could play this little game through the thousands of years of mankind's existence and would not find an answer. However, if we start from this pre-historic beginning of content creation and play forward to today's media landscape, there are a few considerations about content and players, at which we want to look a bit more closer now.

First, let's step back into the present.

When the Internet became more popular, it was logical that pictures would start to move on the screen that everybody until then only thought of as a projector of numbers, letters and still pictures. Quite boring stuff, if we compare this to what is possible in today's technology landscape. All of a sudden, it seemed, the world community possessed the ability not only to watch TV but also videos, clips, etc., on their PC screens. Yet again, content had found a way of presenting itself.

The problem now became a pragmatic one (i.e., with broadband in its very early stages and nowhere near being deployed and the overall concept of transmitting moving pictures over IP networks was also still a dream). But the very fact of getting a PC monitor to be an acceptable medium for video content was pretty progressive. Critics may now say that, overall, the whole idea of watching TV on a PC screen is nonsense, but here are a few things to consider. Going back to our little timeline, users initially had to live with video CDs or the like until the Internet was able to offer an on-demand scenario. "Video-on-demand" was a pretty widely used buzzword at the time for a variety of reasons. For technicians, it was a logical consequence of their progressive technology developments, and for the business development people, it was a nice key word for securing finance and marketing appeal. With content now available online, the player machinery really gained momentum and began to roll. The big players on the circuit, i.e., Apple, Microsoft, and Real Networks, started to flood the market with very good products, and the market has done quite well since then, offering consumers a wide variety of choices.

Standards were not really an issue at the time, since in the early days of content, it did not really matter, as everybody was "doing their own thing." In today's content world, it is absolutely imperative to have some sort of focus as to which formats can or should be used. The standards issue came to confront broadcasters as well, when, after scratching their heads for a while, they decided to utilize the standards PAL and NTSC. To give you an idea of what might have happened if that had not been the case, in theory, it would have meant that users would have been required to have a different TV set for every different format a broadcaster was using to air respective programs—quite an irritating prospect if one considers the amount of channels available today.

The same situation is apparent with the players when it comes to Internet content, with one slight difference: Some of the companies offering players team up directly with content owners and providers, effectively blocking out users, who may not have that particular player. A standard would help a lot here. Having said that, it should be noted that two of the "big three" player providers (Apple and Real Networks) do support MPEG-4 in one way or another.

5.5. MPEG-4 and the Costs

Let's have a closer look at the cost of transmitting data by jumping into the IT money jungle. In order to make this exercise a little easier and illustrative, let us consider the cost in an Internet streaming environment at the server end.

Fact: Broadband adoption will dramatically increase Internet server costs. There will be a tremendous cost impact on video streaming Internet servers as broadband use grows. Much has been documented on the topic of consumer adoption of broadband Internet connections and the resulting requirement for increased video content. However, there has been no discussion of the impact of this paradigm shift on the cost to the Internet servers streaming the video. The increase in bandwidth utilization will require better and better compression techniques in order to meet the expectations of users and the cost requirements for bandwidth.

Internet Server Costs Impacted by Video: Every video played by a viewer must have a server streaming the video to it. The server must pay for every bit of the video that is streamed to a viewer. Streaming digital video requires a significant amount of bandwidth. The number of concurrent video streams from a server determines the amount of bandwidth consumed by the server.

There are two general types of digital video streams. The first, narrowband, is designed for viewers connected via standard phone-based modems—typically 27 to 50 kilobits per second (Kbps). The second, for viewers using a broadband connection, such as DSL or a cable modem, is typically 100 to 300 Kbps (and projected by futurists to someday be as high as 10,000 Kbps).

The calculations that follow will show that bandwidth is the single highest cost component for video servers. Ignoring dedicated line fees and other peripheral costs, currently 1 Megabit per second (1 Mbps = 1024 Kbps) costs approximately $18,000 per year. This means that top video streaming sites may have to pay as much as $24 million per year for server bandwidth, which is a considerable expense that somehow needs to be earned back.

Current Site Bandwidth Costs: Broadband users place a much larger burden on video servers than narrowband users. As demonstrated in the following calculations, even a simple site streaming only 100 concurrent users can expect a hundredfold cost increase as users convert to higher bandwidth streams.

Table 5.1 Costs for narrow and broadband connections for 100 concurrent streams

	Narrowband (modem)	Internet-Broadband	Video-on-Demand
Bits per second (bps)	28k	300k	1000k
Gigabits per year	81,000	900,000	3,000,000
Cost per year	$51,000	$548,000	$1,800,000

This increase in cost will be outside the budget for many companies who wish to stream video and action will need to be taken in order to stay competitive and maintain a viable business. Two of these required actions are

- Reduce the bandwidth of streams below full capacity
- Apply advanced compression to reduce the utilized bandwidth while maintaining quality

It is reasonable to expect that managers will reduce their costs as far as possible while retaining their required quality. Estimates using current compression techniques result in acceptable streaming rates of approximately 300 Kbps for base commercial usage and as high as 3Mbps for entertainment. As shown in the previous example, even the minimal 300 Kbps rate will not be within most budgets.

Increase in Broadband Internet Users Will Increase Demand For Video: Many marketing strategy and analyst firms track user Internet profiles. Combining their estimates, it is reasonable to expect that by 2004, more than 25% of American households (more than 16 million) will connect to the Internet via a broadband connection. In addition, the vast majority of businesses will connect to the Internet via broadband (this is estimated to be about 3 times the household access). Not surprisingly, surveys of users with access to broadband show that their expectation for more and better graphic and video content matches their added investment in connection speed. This means that in addition to the increases in the cost per user, the number of video users will increase. If the example is extended to grow from 100 users to 1000 simultaneous video viewers, the picture becomes even more desperate in terms of the costs involved for the provider.

Table 5.2 Server bandwidth costs for 1000 simultaneous video streams

	Narrowband (modem)	Internet-Broadband	Video-on-Demand
Bits per second (bps)	28k	300k	1000k
Gigabits per year	810,000	9,000,000	30,000,000
Cost per year	$510,000	$5,480,000	$18,000,000

Bandwidth Costs May Drop, But Increased Usage Will Offset: It is likely that bandwidth costs will drop over time. How fast? Traditionally, they have not dropped nearly as fast as semiconductor costs (which follow "Moore's Law"). But even assuming that bandwidth breaks with traditional trends and starts falling at the dramatic rates of Moore's Law, a quick calculation shows that because of the increase in Internet usage, even this aggressive cost drop will not solve the problem of server costs.

Current projections by the major marketing firms state that broadband utilization in U.S. households will potentially grow by around 80% per year over the next five years. As shown in the table below, this growth outweighs even a generous projected reduction in bandwidth costs. In fact, the huge increase in users will continue to increase the costing pressure on sites delivering streaming video.

Table 5.3 Increases in Internet usage will more than offset drop in bandwidth costs

Year	Simultaneous Users	Price per Gb	Yearly Bandwidth Cost
2000	1,000	$0.60	$5,688,000
2001	1,820	$0.42	$6,901,000
2002	3,312	$0.28	$8,373,000
2003	6,028	$0.19	$10,161,000
2004	10,971	$0.12	$12,332,209
2005	19,967	$0.08	$14,963,000

Yearly bandwidth cost reduction: 33.3%
Bandwidth per video stream: 300 Kbps

Compression Improvements Will Be Very Valuable: What is the value of compression improvement in this scenario? A quick calculation shows that the value is immense. In 2001, the example above shows a site with approximately 1,800 concurrent broadband users generating about 16.5 Terabits of streamed video at a cost of just under $7 million. Using these figures, the table below shows the dramatic cost savings that can be realized by better compression.

The example above is for a single site. Assuming 1000 of these large sites streaming video in 2001, these sites would have a combined bandwidth cost of $7 billion per year. An advanced compression

Table 5.4 Improved compression reduces server bandwidth cost

Improvement	Gb Streamed	Bandwidth Cost Savings
Current Technology	16,432,237	$ -
10%	14,789,014	$ 690,154
20%	13,145,790	$ 1,380,308
30%	11,502,566	$ 2,070,462
40%	9,859,342	$ 2,760,616
50%	8,216,119	$ 3,450,770

that reduces this bandwidth by only 10% could save these 1000 customers $700 million per year! This figure already sounds extremely good, but if one applies even a conservative estimate as to how much MPEG-4, and specifically MPEG-4 AVC, delivers as bit rate savings compared to MPEG-2—say 30%—the resulting monetary saving would be a staggering USD 2.1 billion!

There are more than 15 million commercial sites on the Internet today, so it is easy to project that there will be more than 1000 sites serving video in the coming years. Some will be large as in the example above, and many will be small, but it is clear that broadband will make bandwidth costs a concern for all.

Analysis Assumptions: For the sake of simplifying the examples, the following assumptions were followed: There is no accurate count of the current video servers in the United States or worldwide. It is cumbersome to do comparisons using bandwidth due to arguments of appropriate utilization (during peak hours this might be 80% while off hours are 10%), proximity to the backbone, etc. As such, we have converted bandwidth to a per-Gigabit download price using current bandwidth costs and assuming 100% utilization (our estimate is $0.63 per Gigabit). This defines a solid lowest cost data point for transmission. Calculations are focused on bandwidth used by broadband users for two reasons. First, there are accurate projections for the number of such users in the United States, and their interest in video has been documented. Second, the impact of narrowband streams is negligible when compared to broadband.

5.6. MPEG-4 Licensing

Most certainly, the next argument from MPEG-4 critics would be the acquisition cost and licensing aspects. Well, it's true, nothing comes for free; proprietary formats also have their price tag. In addition, one must clearly and categorically differentiate between patent licensing and technology licensing.

In an open standard, a number of patents are utilized to achieve a particular result. But the technologies or procedures underlying these patents first had to be created by someone. Creation means that research, developing, and testing were undertaken by a number of organizations, which in turn could also be characterized in terms of resources. Resources come at a price. Therefore, it is only logical that the patent holders should get their share of the action. In MPEG-2, this is illustrated quite well and indeed has proven to be a scheme that works. In addition to patent fees in open standards, the technology provider also would like to see some return on his investment in developing standard-conforming products. Thus, open standards come with a combination of patent and technology licensing.

A bit later, the licensing aspects of MPEG-4, which have been widely criticized, will be considered in much more detail, but one fact to keep in mind at this stage is that with such a vast number of possible uses for MPEG-4, it is virtually impossible to create an "all-encompassing" licensing scenario that takes on all possible business models.

With proprietary formats, it is a bit different since only technology licensing fees apply. However, they very often come without patent infringement indemnification, which is where we once again encounter a disadvantage of these kinds of technologies. Another factor is operating system independence, which is not always delivered by proprietary technologies; whereas MPEG-4, the open standard, can be obtained in all flavors that a market participant may want to utilize: Windows, Linux, OSX, Solaris, Pocket PC, Symbian, and so on.

A little earlier, we talked about patents and intellectual property rights. ISO, which we're familiar with by now, does not deal with licensing at all and operates under firm rules. MPEG, being part of ISO, also does not get involved in licensing, but takes technology proposals from companies to be adopted into the standard and requires contributors to make their patents and technology available on reasonable and non-discriminatory terms.

But how does the patent licensing of standards, or more precisely, of MPEG standards work? Very simply. There are so-called "patent pools" in which companies and institutions that have contributed to a standard bundle their interests and are represented by an administrator. In the MPEG world, there are actually two main players. MPEG LA, an independent license administration company, acts on behalf of the patent holders of MPEG-2 visual and MPEG-4 Visual as well as MPEG-4 Systems. The audio part for both is administered by Via Licensing, which is an independent subsidiary of Dolby Laboratories and which develops as well as administers patent licensing programs or patent pools on behalf of patent owners/licensors. An important fact to realize in this context is that patent pools are effectively a private initiative from the patent holders for the benefit of the market and are not conducted on behalf of either ISO or MPEG, which also do not endorse or support these efforts, the reasons for which is found in their rules of operation.

Patent pools, in essence, operate quite simply. The patent holders meet, agree on a joint strategy and mutually acceptable terms, and these are then announced with the administrator collecting the respective patent license fees from the market where applicable.

There have been quite a few critical voices regarding patent licensing who feel that all or part of the standard should be royalty free. If one really thinks about it, this would be akin to Chrysler giving away cars for free, which is highly unlikely. Let's stay with the car scenario for a minute. Car manufacturers are paying patent license fees to companies that have designed particular parts of the cars they manufacture. Similarly, it is perfectly reasonable that patent license fees are payable to the organizations that have contributed to a standard like MPEG-4, because, after all, they have made the whole thing possible. In addition, there is a legitimate desire for every industry participant to be remunerated for their efforts.

Another trouble with MPEG-4 and patent licensing is that, in some people's minds, it took quite a while to get the whole licensing scenario structured, announced, and released. While this may be true, it should be noted that the MPEG-2 market was already buzzing even before the patent licensing was in place. In reality, however, the delay of licensing terms being available has prevented the industry from deploying even more MPEG-4 products and solutions. Regarding MPEG-4 AVC, the good news is that the fundamental licensing terms were already released by the end of 2003 by two organizations who had organized a patent pool, and respective agreements are expected to follow in early 2004. By that time, the finalization of new products and services supporting MPEG-4 AVC will be well advanced with deployments starting sometime in 2004. So, from this perspective, MPEG-4 AVC holds the promise of great opportunities and potential. In addition to the "break" in deployments due to the licensing situation, at a certain point the industry seemed to hold back slightly and wait for MPEG-4 AVC to be available. As a result, 2004 will be a very important and interesting year for MPEG-4.

Overall, patent licensing by its very nature is reasonable and appropriate and contributes to an appropriate climate for technology being used by all market participants. Patents are considered important from an investment point of view and are revenue generators, just as regular products and services are.

On the following pages, we will take a schematic look at the various licensing terms for MPEG-4 Visual, Audio, and Systems as well as the brand-new MPEG-4 AVC.

5.6.1. MPEG-4 Visual

In this section, we will deal with both the visual parts in MPEG-4. The first is MPEG-4 Part 2, which is widely deployed in today's technology landscape, and the second is MPEG-4 Part 10, mostly referred to as MPEG-4 AVC (Advanced Video Coding), which has recently been finalized and is beginning to be deployed throughout the industry.

MPEG-4: The administrator for MPEG-4 Part 2 is MPEG LA, and the respective license covers MPEG-4 visual products from January 1, 2000, on (with an initial term until December 31, 2008). In a nutshell, the deployment of an MPEG-4 video encoder amounts to USD 0.25 per encoder, and the deployment of a decoder sets you back USD 0.25 as well. In addition, there are use fees applicable for different scenarios, and a variety of licenses are available from "pay as you go" to "all you can eat" licenses. For several usage scenarios, there are also thresholds with no license fee payments available.

Coverage and Patent Holders: The license for MPEG-4 visual covers all the current MPEG-4 visual profiles as defined in ISO/ IEC 14496-2:2001 (Part 22 Visual), 14496-2:2001/Amd.1:2002 (Studio Profile), or 14496-2:2001/Amd.2:2002 (Streaming Video Profile), which obviously includes the popular Simple and Advanced Simple Profiles. To put it more simply, it covers the deployment of MPEG-4 video encoders and video decoders from January 1, 2000, until December 31, 2008.

Here is the list of patent holders, whose patents are essential for the MPEG-4 Visual standard: Canon; Competitive Technologies; Curitel Communications; France Telecom; Fujitsu; GE Technology Development; General Instrument; Hitachi; KDDI; Matsushita Electric Industrial; Microsoft; Mitsubishi Electric; Oki Electric Industry; Philips Electronics; Samsung Electronics; Sanyo Electric; Sharp Kabushiki Kaisha; Sony; Telenor AS; Toshiba; and Victor Company of Japan.

License Structure and Fees: The structure of the MPEG-4 Visual license is actually quite simple and organized in a "pick-and-choose" manner with six categories in order to respond and cater to a variety of business models.

Category 1—Consumer-Recorded Video, which means MPEG-4 Video encoded by a consumer (with an appropriate device) but not

Internet, mobile, stored, or unique-use video. Examples are devices like PVRs (personal video recorders) and camcorders.

- *Consumer-Recorded Video decoders* (make, sell, and use) = $0.25 per unit*
  - Annual Cap = $1,000,000 per legal entity*
  - First 50,000 units/year = no charge**
- *Consumer-Recorded Video encoders* (make, sell, and use) = $0.25 per unit *
  - Annual Cap = $1,000,000 per legal entity*
  - First 50,000 units/year = no charge** (The royalty fee applies to the end product; licensee is the end-product manufacturer; *one royalty per single licensed product; all licensed products subject to the same cap; **available to one legal entity in an affiliated group of companies)

Category 2—Internet Video, meaning MPEG-4 Video received by or transmitted to a device, for example a PC, using the Internet.

- *Internet Video decoders* (license to make and sell; includes right to use by an end user only for decoding video transmitted by another end user) = $0.25 per unit*
  - Annual Cap = $1,000,000 per legal entity*
  - First 50,000 units/year = no charge**
- *Internet Video encoders* (license to make and sell; includes right to use by an end user only for encoding video transmitted to another end user) = $0.25 per unit*
  - Annual Cap = $1,000,000 per legal entity*
  - First 50,000 units/year = no charge** (Royalty is on functioning product; licensee is functioning product manufacturer; *one royalty per single licensed product; all licensed products subject to the same cap; ** available to one legal entity in an affiliated group of companies)

Category 3—Mobile Video. This means MPEG-4 Video transmitted to and received by a personal or portable wireless device, for example a mobile telephone.

- *Mobile Video decoders* (license to make and sell; includes right to use by an end user only for decoding video transmitted by another end user) = $0.25 per unit*
  - Annual Cap = $1,000,000 per legal entity*
  - First 50,000 units/year = no charge**
- *Mobile Video encoders* (license to make and sell; includes right to use by an end user only for encoding video transmitted to another end user) = $0.25 per unit*
  - Annual Cap = $1,000,000 per legal entity*
  - First 50,000 units/year = no charge** (Royalty is on functioning/end product; licensee is functioning/end product manufacturer; *one royalty per single licensed product; all licensed products subject to the same cap; **available to one legal entity in an affiliated group of companies)
- *Mobile Video decoder and encoder use*
  - $0.25/subscriber, subject to $1,000,000 annual cap or
  - $0.000333/minute, subject to $1,000,000 annual cap or
  - Paid-up $1,000,000 annual license (without reporting)
  - First 50,000 subscribers/year = no charge** This use royalty applies only where the video provider offers or provides MPEG-4 video for remuneration (direct or indirect but not including self-advertising/promotion); Licensee is the Video Provider (apparent source of the MPEG-4 video to the user; *each sublicense will be restricted to the environment for which it is granted; **available to one legal entity in an affiliated group of companies)

Category 4—Unique Use Video, which means MPEG-4 Video sold or transmitted to a subscriber who is neither classified in Category 2 (Internet) nor Category 3 (Mobile Video). Examples are cable, satellite, and other conditionally accessed television or video.

- *Unique Use Video decoders* (license to make and sell; includes right to use by an end user only for decoding video transmitted by another end user) = $0.25 per unit*
  - Annual Cap = $1,000,000 per legal entity*
  - First 50,000 units/year = no charge**

- *Unique Use Video encoders* (license to make and sell; includes right to use by an end user only for encoding video transmitted to another end user) = $0.25 per unit*
  - Annual Cap = $1,000,000 per legal entity*
  - First 50,000 units/year = no charge** (Licensee is functioning/end product manufacturer; * one royalty per single licensed product; all licensed products subject to the same cap; **available to one legal entity in an affiliated group of companies)
- *Unique Use Video decoder and encoder use* = $1.25 per decoder at earlier of (i) providing an MPEG-4 Visual unique-use decoder to an end user or (ii) providing MPEG-4 Visual unique-use video to an MPEG-4 Visual unique-use decoder
  - No cap, no threshold (Licensee is service provider, e.g., cable or satellite provider);
    - *Each sublicense will be restricted to the environment for which it is granted.

Category 5—Stored Video, meaning MPEG-4 Video that is paid for on a title-by-title basis and is stored either on physical media, like a DVD, or transmitted electronically in a form that allows end users to view it at least 20 times for at least one year.

- *Stored Video decoders* (license to make, sell, and use) = $0.25 per unit*
  - Annual Cap = $1,000,000 per legal entity*
  - First 50,000 units/year = no charge** (Licensee is end-product manufacturer; *one royalty per single licensed product; all licensed products subject to the same cap; **available to one legal entity in an affiliated group of companies)
- *Stored Video encoder* (make, sell, and use)
  - $.01/30 min to $.04/movie 5 years or less in age
  - $.005/30 min to $.02/movie older than 5 years
  - $.002 for 12 min or less
    - No cap, no threshold (Licensee is replicator or transmitter)

Category 6—Enterprise (ultimate parent entity and its 50% or greater owned subsidiaries)

- Enterprise may pay annual royalty (without reporting)
  - $5 million per year 2004/05
  - $7 million per year 2006/07
  - $10 million per year 2008
  - Covers all royalty payments of enterprise for consumer-recorded video, Internet video, mobile video, unique-use video, and stored video decoders but *not* stored video encoders
    - Elect by November 30 of prior calendar year

As time and the market as well of course, have gone on, there has already been a revision in the licensing terms. This happened at the end of April 2004. A revision in the sense that licensees that have already signed a license agreement based on the terms outlined above can freely elect if they wish to continue with their current agreement or switch to the new arrangement.

The process or the terms of patent licensing are also some sort of a moving target because market conditions may change or develop further. In the case with MPEG-4, it actually is designed by the licensors to make things easier and provide a more compact licensing scheme in addition to responding to the voice of the industry, which has been calling for changes in the terms, especially on the use fee front. What has happened here and what we will see again later on when we are looking into the Licensing of MPEG-4 AVC is that MPEG LA have effectively synchronized the terms for both MPEG-4 and MPEG-4 AVC in certain areas, which is actually a good thing.

Under the revised License, there are the following changes:

a) *Sublicenses for manufacturers* (the right to make and sell MPEG-4 Visual decoders and encoders) will be consolidated from the multiple categories representing different market sectors, as we have seen above, into one sublicense applying to all sectors. Royalties are to be paid by decoder and encoder manufacturers and will stay at the same levels as under the current license for each decoder and each encoder. For example,

- $0.25 per unit beginning after the first 50,000 decoders each year (annual cap of $1,000,000)
- $0.25 per unit beginning after the first 50,000 encoders each year (annual cap of $1,000,000)

(These thresholds are applicable to one legal entity in an affiliated group.)

These sublicenses cover decoders and encoders sold to end users directly or through a chain of distribution and fully functioning decoders and encoders for PCs. In addition to the right to manufacture and sell, they also include the right of end users to use the decoders and encoders for their own personal use, however not for the uses as described in the following paragraph.

b) *Sublicenses for Video Providers* will be consolidated into two subcategories. One subcategory is for the scenario when an end user pays directly for video services. The other subcategory is for the scenario when the video services are paid for by sources other than an end user:

Subcategory 1: Where an end user pays directly for video services on a subscription-basis (not ordered or limited title by-title), the service or content provider will pay the following royalties (per legal entity):

- 100,000 or fewer subscribers per year—no royalty;
- Greater than 100,000 to 250,000 subscribers per year—$25,000;
- Greater than 250,000 to 500,000 subscribers per year—$50,000;
- Greater than 500,000 to 1,000,000 subscribers per year— $75,000;
- Greater than 1,000,000 to 5,000,000 subscribers per year— $100,000;
- Greater than 5,000,000 to 25,000,000 subscribers—$200,000;
- Greater than 25,000,000 subscribers—$300,000.

End User pays on a Title-by-Title basis (for example where the viewer determines titles to be viewed or number of viewable titles are otherwise limited)—the applicable royalties are the lower of 2%

of the price paid to the Licensee (on first arms length sale of the video) or $0.02 per title for video greater than 12 minutes (there is no royalty payable for a title that is 12 minutes or less).

Subcategory 2: Where the MPEG- 4 video services are paid for by sources other than an end user, the license includes two categories:

"Free Television" (referring to MPEG-4 video that is television broadcasting sent to an end user and/or a consumer by an over-the-air, satellite and/or cable transmission, and which is not paid for by an end user)—the broadcaster will pay a one-time royalty of $2,500 for each encoder used in Free Television transmission.

"Internet Broadcast" (not Subscription or Title-by-Title, but delivered via the Worldwide Internet for which the End User does not pay remuneration for the right to receive or view it)—there will be no royalty during the first term of the License (ending December 31, 2008).

c) The maximum annual royalties payable by an *Enterprise* (commonly controlled legal entities) will be reduced to $3M for the sublicenses granting manufacturers the right to make and sell MPEG-4 Visual decoders and encoders (category a) above) and $3M for the use of decoders and encoders in providing video (category b) above).

So, these are the latest terms for MPEG-4 Visual, and especially on the Internet usage side, quite a few providers are happy now since there are no royalties to pay, which makes their business model easier for them and more attractive. A lot of market participants would have wished for PC based decoders to be free, but then their voice was not heard. The voice that was clearly heard was that the market did not agree at all to the former use fees that were based on time, rather than on revenue or a fixed price as it is the case now. The use fees were a major deterrent to the even broader adoption of MPEG-4, however the good news is that licensors have endeavored to provide an alternative approach with this revision. Also, last not least, these revised terms are probably much easier to understand and follow compared to the original terms, which were characterized by a number of subcategories and various scenarios and other stipulations.

The actual new license is anticipated to be available in the summer of 2004.

5.6.2. MPEG-4 Part 10 (MPEG-4 AVC)

The licensing for MPEG-4 AVC is not very transparent at first glance. Instead of one patent pool—as we have seen for MPEG-4 Visual Part 2, for example—there are in fact two patent pools offering licensing terms to the public. Or to be precise, they are in the process of finalizing licensing terms and agreements in order to have them available sometime in early 2004.

MPEG LA and MPEG-4 AVC Licensing: Let us start with the patent pool in the process of being organized by MPEG LA, since this organization was the first one of the two to issue a call for submission of patents in September 2002. After just over a year, in November 2003, MPEG LA announced, on behalf of the licensors, the terms of a joint patent license for MPEG-4 AVC and issued the final terms on May 18, 2004. At the time of writing this book, these

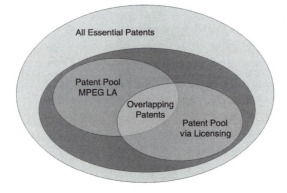

Figure 5.6 Qualitative relationship between the competing licensing pools for MPEG–4 visual in the context of essential patents. Note that there are patents that may be considered essential, but are not covered by either patent pool.

terms, which we will illustrate below, can only be considered for information purposes since no formal and final agreement has yet been published, although some are expected very shortly during the course of 2004. Also, as one can assume, companies can still apply to MPEG LA to have their patents (issued patents only) evaluated to determine whether they are essential for the MPEG-4 AVC standard, and therefore should be included in the respective patent pool.

What can, however, be said is that that the initial term of the license will be until December 31, 2010. Royalties for decoder-encoder manufacturer Sublicenses will commence on January 1, 2005; participation fees on January 1, 2006. Before these dates, no royalty payments will apply.

Coverage and Patent Holders: The proposed terms published by MPEG LA cover all of MPEG-4 AVC (ISO/IEC 14496-10), which means Baseline, Extended, and Main Profile. A number of organizations and companies have submitted their patents to MPEG LA whose applications were subsequently determined to be essential to MPEG-4 AVC. The following is a list of essential patent holders that are expected to participate: Columbia Innovation Enterprises; Electronics and Telecommunications Research Institute; France Télécom, S.A.; Fujitsu Limited; General Instrument Corporation, d/b/a Motorola's Broadband Communications Sector; Matsushita Electric Industrial Co., Ltd.; Microsoft Corporation; Mitsubishi Electric Corporation; Koninklijke Philips Electronics, N.V.; Robert Bosch GmbH; Samsung Electronics Co., Ltd.; Sharp Kabushiki Kaisha; Sony Corporation; Toshiba Corporation; and Victor Company of Japan, Limited. In addition, the following companies with essential patent applications have participated in the deliberations concerning the licensing terms that will be described below and are also expected to participate in the License subject to the determination that they have an essential patent: LG Electronics, Inc., LSI Logic Corporation, and Polycom, Inc.

License Structure and Fees: The licensing terms are classified into two main categories. The first is called Decoder-Encoder Royalties and deals with the product side of things, whereas the second category, Participation Fees, deals with services. Let us consider both categories in more detail:

Decoder-Encoder Royalties

End-product manufacturers will have to pay a royalty for what is referred to as a "unit," i.e., an encoder, a decoder, or both. The first 100,000 units each year are free. After that, for each unit, a royalty of USD 0.20 has to be paid. This royalty applies up to 5 million units per year being deployed. Above this figure, a royalty of USD 0.10 per unit must be paid.

As already practiced in the licensing model for MPEG-4 Visual (Part 2), the licensors have provisioned for an "all inclusive" license for companies (and their subsidiaries above 50% owner-ship). This right comes at a royalty fee of USD 3,500,000 per year in 2005/2006, USD 4,250,000 in 2007/2008, and USD 5,000,000 in 2009/2010. Furthermore, considering existing distribution chan-nels, a legal entity selling branded AVC products OEM for PC OS may pay for its customers as follows:

- For up to 100,000 units per annum, no royalty will be payable (available to one legal entity in an affiliated group)
- US $0.20 per unit after first 100,000 units/year
- Above 5 million units/year, royalty = US $0.10 per unit
- Enterprise cap: $3.5M per year 2005-2006, $4.25M per year 2007-08, $5M per year 2009-10

The above includes the right to make and sell encoders and de-coders as well as to their personal use by or between end users such as in connection with a video teleconference or mobile messaging. However, it does not include participation fees.

Participation Fees

The participation fees come in two main flavors and cover a number of possible applications for MPEG-4 AVC.

Where the end user pays directly for AVC Video

Title-by-title—For an MPEG-4 AVC video that is either on a physical medium, like a DVD, or ordered and paid for on a title-by-title basis—for example, pay-per-view (PPV), video-on-demand (VOD), or digital download, where the viewer determines titles to be viewed, or number of viewable titles are otherwise limited—there are no royalties payable for videos up to a length of 12 minutes. For videos longer than 12 minutes, royalties are either 2% of the price paid to the licensee from the licensee's first arms-length sale or USD 0.02 per title, whichever is lower. Categories of licensees include replicators of physical media, and service/content providers (such as cable, satellite, video DSL, Internet, and mobile service providers and operators) of VOD, PPV, and electronic downloads to end users.

Subscription—Systems (such as, for example satellite, Internet, local mobile, or local cable franchise) consisting of 100,000 or fewer subscribers (MPEG-4 AVC subscribers of course) in a year and providing MPEG-4 AVC video on a subscription basis (not ordered title-by-title) do not have to pay royalties. For systems with more than 100,000 subscribers, the annual participation fee is USD 25,000 per year up to 250,000 subscribers, USD 50,000 per year for 250,001 to 500,000 subscribers, USD 75,000 per year for 500,001 to 1,000,000 subscribers, and USD 100,000 per year for more than 1,000,000 subscribers.

Where remuneration is derived from other sources

Free Television AVC Video—Licensees will have two options here. Either they will pay a one-time fee of $2,500 per transmission encoder or they will pay an annual fee per broadcast market starting at $2,500 per annum, per broadcast market of at least 100,000 households, but no more than 499,999 households. For a broadcast market that includes at least 500,000 households, but no more than 999,999 households, $5,000 per annum will be payable, and $10,000 per annum per broadcast market that includes 1,000,000 or more households.

Internet broadcast—Since this market is still developing, there will be no royalties payable for Internet broadcast services (non-subscription, not title-by-title) during the initial term of the license running until December 31, 2010. After that, royalties shall not exceed the over-the-air free broadcast TV encoding fee during the renewal term.

As seen above in the decoder/encoder royalty description, as well as for the participation fee scenario, an "all inclusive" scheme is stipulated, amounting to a royalty fee of USD 3,500,000 per year in 2005/2006, USD 4,250,000 in 2007/2008, and USD 5,000,000 in 2009/2010.

Via Licensing and MPEG-4 AVC Licensing: Via Licensing has a very strong track record especially in administering the patent pools for a variety of audio standards. It came out much later (June 2003) with a call for submission of essential patents with respect to MPEG-4 AVC, and announced proposed licensing terms in October 2003. Final terms were announced on April 20, 2004. The current licensors in the pool hope to have the respective license agreement available in early 2004, so by the time you read this, there might already be an agreement available.

Currently, there is no information as to how long the initial term of this license will be, however there is a planned incentive for early adoption: Companies that execute a license agreement before September 30, 2004, will not have to pay royalties through December 31, 2004. This is based on the expectation of a license being available in early 2004.

Coverage and Patent Holders: The proposed terms published by Via Licensing cover all of MPEG-4 AVC (ISO/IEC 14496-10), which means Baseline, Extended, and Main Profile. The companies who have participated in the development of the terms are Apple Computer, Dolby Laboratories, FastVDO, Fraunhofer-Gesellschaft eV, IBM, LSI Logic, Microsoft, Motorola, Polycom, and RealNetworks.

License Structure and License Fees: First, let us consider what sort of products or services will be covered by this license. These will be end-use products in the event that they are sold directly or through distribution channels to end users. Not end-user products (for example, software development kits), or similar products are not subject to the license. In these cases, the party integrating or incorporating the products into its own end-user products is required to execute a respective license. In addition, the services of content provision, where content is replicated and sold/rented on a title-by-title basis to end-users, i.e., consumers, at their request and purchased/rented by them on a title-by-title basis, are also covered by this license.

It also should be noted which companies do not have to sign a license. Implementation providers (companies providing chipsets, board assemblies other than to end users, firmware code, software development kits, reference design hardware, and similar non-end-user products) are not required to execute a license. Users of end-user products (not limited to consumers), such as broadcasters, cable service providers, Internet service providers, and any other entity who only utilizes an MPEG-4 AVC-enabled product and does not replicate content or manufacture and/or distribute products containing MPEG-4 AVC technology, are also not required to execute a license. On the "who has to sign" side of things, companies engaged in the manufacturing of end-user products, replicating (for physical media), and those companies conducting transactions (for non-physical distribution) with regard to content that is subject to the replication fees, have to execute licenses.

The proposed license structure includes an initial license fee payment of USD 15,000, which will not be deducted from any royalty payments in the future. For companies with less than USD 2,000,000 per year in revenues, there are hardship terms available.

Also, there is a so-called "Threshold Royalty Free Program," which is designed for companies that manufacture and/or distribute less than 50,000 devices/products per year (that would be subject to the payment of royalties) and who, in this context, generate less than USD 500,000 of annual revenues from the combination of the aforementioned distributed devices/products and revenues generated through the sale/rent of content (that is subject to replication fees).

For companies that would qualify under these provisions, no initial fee nor payment of royalties for devices/products or replication fees apply. Although this program does not require specific product or revenue reports, it may require an annual certification to verify that the use remained under the stipulated limits. In addition, companies participating in this program need to notify the administrator when these limits are being exceeded.

In addition, there are two categories of royalties—the first one is for encoders/decoders and the second for what is referred to as replications.

Encoder/Decoder Royalties:

Encoder/Decoder, permanent end-user product—The royalty fee amounts to USD 0.25 per licensed product. The number of encoders and/or decoders with any single product is not limited, provided that they are not purchased separately. A permanent end-user product is defined as being able to decode content or use the decoder for not more than 20 decodes and/or 30 days after the first use.

Decoder, temporary end-user product—The royalty fee amounts to USD 0.0025 per licensed product. A temporary decoder is defined as being provided with content and intended to solely support decoding of that particular content. The temporary decoder must cease to function after not more than 20 decodes and not more than 30 days after the first use of the decoder.

Encoder/Decoder royalty cap—There is a provision for companies called an "enterprise cap" relating to licensed product royalties in the amount of USD 2,500,000 per year for the sale of all products. Excluded from this provision is PC software that is only sold through PC OEMs (Original Equipment Manufacturer) and which is installed by these OEMs on the storage medium of a PC. For companies selling its PC software through a PC OEM distribution channel, the enterprise cap for licensed product royalties is USD 4,000,000 per year. Alternatively, PC OEMs have the option to pay royalties for their hardware product, rather than the company that supplies the PC software paying separately for the installed software products. In this case, the standard enterprise cap as mentioned above would apply. In the event that a company opts for the enterprise cap at the beginning of the annual licensing period, it does not need to provide specific royalty reports.

Companies wishing to opt for the enterprise cap can do so for all parent, subsidiary, and affiliated companies that are under its common control, where control is defined as an ownership of more than 50% of the respective entity's voting stock or similar controlling interest that may exist under local jurisdiction.

Replication Fees

Content provision without replication fees—For content that is intended to be sold on a title-by-title basis, no matter whether it is to be distributed via a physical or non-physical medium, so-called replication fees apply. However, if content is provided on a title-by-title basis free of charge and not provided for sale and or rent, then no replication fees apply. As long as a user does not select, request, or authorize, on a title-by-title basis, the provision of content by any means or method, and pays on a title-by-title basis, no replication fees are payable.

Title-by-title, permanent basis—The maximum replication fee payable amounts to USD 0.025 per title replicated/sold on a permanent basis. The rates per title replicated and sold on a permanent basis are as follows (There are no caps fro replication fees of this kind.):

- If the length of the title is more than 90 minutes, the replication fee is USD 0.025.
- If the length of the title is between 31 and 89 minutes, the replication fee is USD 0.015.
- If the length of the title is less than 30 minutes, the replication fee is USD 0.005.

Title-by-title, temporary basis—Disregarding the length of the title, the maximum replication fee per title replicated/sold on a temporary title-by-title basis is USD .0025. There are no caps for replication fees of this kind. "Temporary" means that the end user can use the content or end-user product for no more than 20 decodes and no more than 30 days after the first use.

For all of the above, "title" is defined as a single video work, or a group of related video works (such as episodes of a television series), sold or provided to an end user bundled together, either as part of a digitally delivered bundle or replicated together on a single physical media carrier.

5.6.3. MPEG-4 Audio

Having learned about the licensing situation with respect to MPEG-4 Video (Part 2 and MPEG-4 AVC), let us now look into the licensing aspects of MPEG-4 Audio, which happens to be Part 3 of the MPEG-4 nomenclature. We will look into two aspects—the licensing of MPEG-4 AAC and MPEG-4 AAC HE (High Efficiency).

MPEG-4 AAC: In December 2002, Via Licensing was appointed as administrator for the MPEG-4 AAC licensing and the terms were finalized. Licensing began, with a license agreement in place, in July 2003.

Coverage and Patent Holders: The MPEG-4 AAC patent license grants rights for a variety of MPEG-4 AAC object types, including AAC LC (Low Complexity), AAC Scalable, and ER AAC LD (Low Delay). A number of companies hold essential patents with respect to the MPEG-4 Audio standard, including AT&T; Dolby Laboratories; Electronics and Telecommunications Research Institute (ETRI); France Telecom; Fraunhofer IIS; Fujitsu Ltd.; Nokia Corp.; Nippon Telegraph and Telephone Corp. (NTT); Philips Electronics; Samsung Electronics Co., Ltd.; and Sony Corp.

License Structure and Fees: The several licensing conditions specifically for encoder and decoder use will be outlined later, but before that, a few more important points and stipulations of the license will be covered.

For MPEG-4AVC, no use fees apply and also no fees are collected for the distribution of content in the MPEG-4 AAC format (no license is required for the distribution of MPEG-4 AAC bit streams). Only on the sale of encoders and decoders are royalties payable. Companies that are engaged in the manufacturing or developing of complete (or virtually complete) end-use encoder and/or decoder products, or of component encoder and/or decoder products that are directly provided to end-users, have to execute the license.

It should also be noted that the licensing of MPEG-4 AAC is more expensive than the licensing of MPEG-2 AAC. What must, however, be considered is the fact that companies can practice, and of course deploy and sell, MPEG-2 AAC products, provided they have executed an MPEG-4 Audio license. The reason for this is that the MPEG-2 AAC Low Complexity Profile is a compatible subset of MPEG-4 AAC, and therefore covered by the license.

On executing a license agreement, an initial, one-time fee of USD 15,000 is payable and is not deductible from future royalty payments.

There are three categories to consider in licensing MPEG-4 AAC— standard rates, PC-based software pricing for consumers, and professional products. There is a provision in the license that allows for the deployment of trial products. For decoder trial products, this trial is limited in terms of time for a period of up to 30 days. For encoder trial products, the trial is limited both in terms of time (up to 30 days) and use (the number of encoded items must not exceed 50). In order to better illustrate the respective fees, please have a look at the following tables.

The term "Channels" in these tables refers to an audio output channel. As you may know, stereo is a two-channel implementation, whereas mono is only one channel. The classification and breakdown into channels is pretty advantageous considering the fact that in MPEG-4 AAC, there are up to 48 full-frequency range audio channels. Pricing on a per-channel basis allows a much better differentiation between multi-channel (such as home theatre products) and simple mono or stereo products. The term "reset" basically means that the number of units sold or deployed in a previous quarter is disregarded, and every quarter is counted on its own in terms of units deployed, i.e., there is no roll-over or annual consideration.

Table 5.5 Standard rates

Volume (per channel/ quarterly reset)	Consumer Decoder or Encoder Channels	Consumer Decoder or Encoder Channels	Professional Decoder Channels	Professional Encoder Channels
Flat Rate	n/a	n/a	USD 2.00	USD 20.00
1 to 100,000	USD 0.50	USD 1.00	-	-
100,001 to 500,000	USD 0.37	USD 0.74	-	-
500,001 to 1,000,000	USD 0.27	USD 0.54	-	-
1,000,001 to 5,000,000	USD 0.22	USD 0.44	-	-
5,000,001 to 10,000,000	USD 0.17	USD 0.34	-	-
10,000,001 or more	USD 0.12	USD 0.24	-	-

Table 5.6 PC-Based software pricing—consumer

Volume (per channel/yearly)	Consumer Decoder Channels	Consumer Encoder Channels	Consumer Codec Channels
1 to 100,000	USD 0.25	USD 0.50	USD 0.75
100,001 to 500,000	-	USD 0.37	USD 0.62
500,001 to 1,000,000	-	USD 0.27	USD 0.52
Maximum annual payment	USD 25,000 (per PC software product)	USD 250,000 (per licensee)	USD 275,000 (per licensee)

Table 5.7 PC-Based software pricing—professional

	Professional Decoder Channels	Professional Encoder Channels	Professional Codec Channels
Flat Rate (per channel)	USD 2.00	USD 20.00	USD 22.00
Maximum fee per PC software product	n/a	Not to exceed 5% of end-user price, but not less than USD 10.00	Not to exceed 5% of end-user price, but not less than USD 10.00

In order to better understand the above and put it into context, the difference between "consumer" and "professional" products should be explained. Consumer products include devices like DVD players, TV receivers, set-top boxes, and portable music players, for example, and are non–revenue-generating products (from the perspective of the user). Professional products are those that are specifically used for the purpose of revenue generation, such as broadcast encoders and high-end audio applications, and are utilized in a production environment. The difference in price, and one reason for the non-existence of a volume cap in the licensing program, comes from the fact that consumer products potentially tend to be on the high volume, lower price side (which are therefore well served by the per-channel approach) and conversely, professional products tend to come in at lower volumes and much higher prices.

MPEG-4 AAC HE: Licensing terms for MPEG-4 AAC HE will have been released in January 2004 by its administrator, Via Licensing, and are illustrated in the following tables. Since, technically speaking, MPEH-4 AAC HE is a superset of MPEG-4 AAC, it is anticipated that the same license structure conditions will apply as in the present MPEG-4 AAC license.

Table 5.8 Standard rates

Volume (per channel/ quarterly reset)	Consumer Decoder or Encoder Channels	Consumer Decoder or Encoder Channels	Professional Decoder Channels	Professional Encoder Channels*
Flat Rate	n/a	n/a	USD 2.00	USD 25.00
1 to 100,000	USD 0.63	USD 1.25	-	-
100,001 to 500,000	USD 0.46	USD 0.92	-	-
500,001 to 1,000,000	USD 0.34	USD 0.68	-	-
1,000,001 to 5,000,000	USD 0.28	USD 0.56	-	-
5,000,001 to 10,000,000	USD 0.21	USD 0.42	-	-
10,000,001 or more	USD 0.15	USD 0.30	-	-

*If greater than two channels, total per-product fees are not to exceed 3% of end-user price, but not be less than $65 per product or more than $2,000 per product.

Table 5.9 PC-Based software pricing—consumer

Volume (per channel/ yearly)	Consumer Decoder Channels	Consumer Encoder Channels	Consumer Codec Channels
1 to 100,000	USE 0.32	USD 0.63	USD 0.95
100,001 to 500,000	-	USD 0.46	USD 0.78
500,001 to 1,000,000	-	USD 0.34	-
Maximum annual payment	USD 32,000 (per PC software product)	USD 312,500 (per licensee)	USD 344,000 (per licensee)

Table 5.9 PC-Based software pricing—professional

	Professional Decoder Channels	Professional Encoder Channels	Professional Codec Channels
Flat Rate (per channel)	USD 2.50	USD 25.00	USD 27.50
Maximum fee per PC software product	n/a	Not to exceed 5% of end-user price, but not less than USD 12.50	Not to exceed 5% of end-user price, but not less than USD 12.50

5.6.4. MPEG-4 Systems

Interestingly enough, the plan for creating a patent pool for MPEG-4 Systems was announced all the way back in September 2000, with final terms being released in July 2002 (alongside the final terms for MPEG-4 Part 2), and the actual licenses became available in February 2003.

Coverage and Patent Holders: The patent administrator for MPEG-4 Systems is MPEG LA. The license provides coverage for the MPEG-4 Systems standard is defined in ISO/IEC 14496-1 (Part 1 Systems) and currently includes patents owned by Apple-Computer, Electronics and Telecommunications Research Institute (ETRI), France Telecom, Koninklijke Philips Electronics, Mitsubishi Electric Corp., Samsung Electronics, and Sun Microsystems. The initial term of the license is from January 1, 2000, until December 31, 2008 (as with MPEG-4 Part 2; as commonly practiced in patent licensing, new licensors and essential patents may be added at no additional royalty during the current, initial term).

License Structure and Fees: The licensing for MPEG-4 Systems is structured in a similar way to what we have already seen for MPEG-4 Part 2.

Category 1—Consumer-Recorded Data, which means MPEG-4 Systems Data encoded by a consumer but not Internet, mobile, stored or unique use (for example, PVR or camcorder)

- *Consumer-Recorded Data decoders* (make, sell, use) = $0.15 per unit *
  - Annual Cap = $100,000 per legal entity*
- *Consumer-Recorded Data encoders* (make, sell, use) = $0.25 per unit
  - Annual Cap = $100,000 per legal entity* (The royalty applies to the end product; licensee is end-product manufacturer; *one royalty per single licensed product; all licensed products subject to the same cap)

Category 2—Internet Data, which means MPEG-4 Systems Data received by or transmitted to a device or product using the Internet

- *Internet Data decoders* (make, sell, use) = $0.15 per unit *
  - Annual Cap = $100,000 per legal entity*
- *Internet Data encoders* (make, sell, use) = $0.25 per unit *
  - Annual Cap = $100,000 per legal entity* (The royalty applies to the functioning product; licensee is functioning-product manufacturer; *one royalty per single licensed product; all licensed products subject to the same cap)

Category 3—Mobile Data, which means MPEG-4 Systems Data transmitted to and received by a personal or portable wireless device

- *Mobile Data decoders* (make, sell, use) = $0.15 per unit *
  - Annual Cap = $100,000 per legal entity*
- *Mobile Data encoders* (make, sell, use) = $0.25 per unit *
  - Annual Cap = $100,000 per legal entity* (The royalty applies to the functioning/end product; licensee is functioning/end-product manufacturer; *one royalty per single licensed product; all licensed products subject to the same cap)

Category 4—Unique-Use Data, which means MPEG-4 Systems Data that is sold or transmitted to a subscriber, and that is neither

MPEG-4 Systems Internet Data nor MPEG-4 Systems Mobile Data (e.g., cable or satellite)

- *Unique Use Data decoders* (make, sell, use) = $0.15 per unit*
  - Annual Cap = $100,000 per legal entity*
- *Unique Use Data encoders* (make, sell, use) = $0.25 per unit *
  - Annual Cap = $100,000 per legal entity* (Licensee is functioning/end-product manufacturer; *one royalty per single licensed product; all licensed products subject to the same cap)

Category 5—Stored Data, which means MPEG-4 Systems Data that is paid for on a title-by-title basis and that is either (i) stored, replicated, or encoded onto physical media or (ii) transmitted to an end user in a form that allows the end user to view, hear, or use such data at least 20 times and for a period of at least 365 days from the date of transmission

- *Stored Data decoders* (make, sell, use) = $0.15 per unit *
  - Annual Cap = $100,000 per legal entity* (Licensee is end-product manufacturer; *one royalty per single licensed product; all licensed products subject to the same cap)
- *Stored Data encoder* (make, sell, use)
  - $.001/30 min to $.004/movie 5 yrs. or less in age
  - $.0005/30 min to $.002/movie > 5 yrs. in age
  - $.0002 for 12 min or less
  - No cap (Licensee is replicator or transmitter)

Category 6—*Enterprise* (ultimate parent entity and its subsidiaries that own 50% or greater)

- Enterprise may pay annual royalty (without reporting)
  - $500,000 per year 2004/05
  - $700,000 per year 2006/07
  - $1,000,000 per year 2008
  - Covers all royalty payments of enterprise for consumer-recorded data, Internet data, mobile data, unique-use data, and stored data decoders, but *not* stored data encoders
  - Elect by November 30 of prior calendar year

5.7. Bibliography

dicas digital image coding GmbH www.dicas.de
MPEGIF White Paper "The Media Standard" 2002. download from:
http://www.mpegif.org.
Popwire Technology www.popwire.com
Report *Global Digital TV Technology & Markets*" by Nick Flaherty, Senior
Analyst InsideChips.com
VBrick Systems www.vbrick.com
Web site 3GPP www.3gpp.org
Web site Apple www.apple.com
Web site DVB www.dvb.org
Web site Harmonic Inc. www.harmonicinc.com
Web site Internet Streaming Media Alliance www.isma.tv
Web site ISO www.iso.ch
Web site Microsoft www.microsoft.com
Web site MPEG Industry Forum (MPEGIF) www.mpegif.org
Web site MPEG LA www.mpegla.com
Web site MPEG www.chiariglione.org/mpeg
Web site Nokia www.nokia.com
Web site Via Licensing www.vialicenisng.com

CHAPTER 6

Looking Ahead—Migration and Adoption Issues

In this last chapter, we will touch upon a few issues that are equally interesting and important to consider in the overall picture of compression, migration, technology advances, and competition, to name a few.

Throughout this book, we have been analyzing the technical ins and outs of MPEG-4 and have also discussed some of the business aspects surrounding this international standard. Most of our information has been based on past and present facts, observations, and yes, opinions; however, the more difficult task is to discuss or illustrate what may possibly happen in the future. The problem is that none of us has a crystal ball or other magic to foretell what's down the road. In technology, as in so many other industries, a vast amount of data is utilized to come up with certain views as to what the future may bring. All this information is based on statistical and empirical evidence. In our more limited context, the same situation applies. However, it is also possible to look at these things without having reams of figures as we try to determine the chances of success, the pros and cons, the timeframe of deployment, and so on. We can simply have a look at the implications of MPEG-2 to the multimedia world at the time and indeed over time as well as apply some of the knowledge gained out of this book plus common sense to the equation, and it is pretty evident that MPEG-4 can, should, and will play a major role in the multimedia world.

6.1. Migration and Transition

With respect to transition and migration, the key element is of course an actual decision to initiate change or a new beginning, which represents, in many cases, a challenge. Migration inevitably stands for change, for the introduction of something new. We will try to shed some light on some of the factors involved in the migration and transition process borne of a technological novelty, such as MPEG-4, that automatically impact the business and commercial side of things. In the context of looking at things from current market participants that are already in the multimedia business with having, for example, MPEG-2 systems deployed, the migration process is most likely a gradual one.

Gradual migration for this kind of legacy scenario will be most likely characterized by four different factors, either alone or in combination:

- Time
- Location
- Service selection
- Content selection

A gradual migration happens over a period of time, where current technology remains in place and is either complemented by new technology or two sets of technology co-exist temporarily. Regarding location, gradual migration can involve the deployment of new technologies in certain geographical regions with current technology remaining in place, for the time being, in other regions. Another approach to gradual migration, especially in the broadcast world, can be the selection of certain parts of the service provision, for example, specific channels (such as the VOD channel) that are fitted with new technologies, subsequently followed by others. The content selection approach is similar, except that specific content types (for example, news) are chosen. Besides the technological consideration, there are also a number of other factors such as:

- Economical and commercial aspects
- Customer- and competition-related
- Legal issues

These factors must be carefully considered in order to make a migration successful on all fronts.

Looking now specifically at MPEG-4, let us see how migration might work, and what strategies might be followed in the mobile and broadband sectors.

6.1.1. Mobile Communications Sector

In the mobile sector, the migration is characterized by a significant switch in the sense that not only data and pictures can be sent and received, but video is now also possible on a mobile handset. This does not, however, mean that everything will happen all at once. Even though 2.5G services (GPRS, EDGE) have been available for quite some time, not many handsets are enabled, and the content being offered is still limited. Having said that, and bearing in mind that the industry is gearing up for the deployment of 3G services, this opens up even more opportunities for mobile operators, be-cause traditional methods of revenue generation known, for example, from the broadcast industry, can also be applied to the mobile sectors. Not only can subscription services and transaction-based fees be generated, but e-commerce is also likely to soon be utilizing mobile handsets and generating additional revenue.

This is quite a significant step—especially with 2.5G services (GPRS, EDGE) currently available and 3G services becoming more widely available across the globe, the actual migration pro-cess is already well underway. Certainly, one has to admit, the technology inside the handsets and in and around the network infrastructure is still evolving, but that's only natural, considering how quickly a transition has taken place from plain voice to text messaging to Internet access to picture messaging, and now to video messaging and other multimedia services, the amount and range of which will definitely grow and expand over the coming years. The technology is available and deployed today, and there is plenty of room for further improvement.

Another, equally interesting aspect for the mobile sector is the fact that there is an additional opportunity for great business on the horizon: DVB-H, a specification issued by the Digital Video Broadcasting project group (DVB). DVB-H is the delivery of video content to mobile devices using the existing digital TV infrastructure. The good news is that DVB-H will in no way be a competitor to the services or delivery mechanisms we have described earlier. In fact, they will complement each other. So both mobile operators and the broadcasters are happy because there is another way for them to generate revenues and, in fact, probably charge a nice premium for that privilege, without affecting their existing business models.

Let us quickly define the difference between DVB-H and the video services currently available under 2.5G or 3G. In essence, and to keep it very simple, with DVB-H being "one-to-many" with longer videos (up to 30 minutes, maybe more) compared to the "one-to-one" scenario in 2.5G/3G, which are obviously on-demand driven, focused on rather short videos and not geared up to support millions of users at the same time.

But in this very difference lies the complementing aspect of both specifications. DVB-H is effectively a TV away from home, representing a much more efficient delivery channel for this purpose through its multicast nature. 3G, rather than of course 2.5G, is the ideal scenario when it comes to personalized, specific content delivery of on-demand mobile video. Also on the economic front it pretty much looks like DVB-H is the ideal delivery format of mobile video to mass audiences due to the network costs involved.

The obvious choice for the video coding part is MPEG-4 AVC, and quite a number of vendors are gearing up to provide products and services in this arena. From a logical point of view, DVB-H has an enormous potential, not only in combination with 3G, but also in conjunction with other services offered by operators and providers currently. New business models for the generation of revenues are available and content owners, as well as content providers and indeed operators can leverage the complementary aspects in their quest for revenues. In simple terms, DVB-H can open new revenues in the form of subscriptions from "fresh viewers" whereas the 3G revenue will be mainly driven by pay-per-view or other individual means.

6.1.2. Broadcast Sector

In the broadcast sector, there is sure to be a lot of movement. Everyone knows that technologies to succeed MPEG-2 are on the horizon, with MPEG-4 AVC being one of them, and, for reasons we highlighted earlier, the frontrunner. What will no doubt happen is that operators will bring in the new technology while holding onto the old one. They will wait and see which technology/standard will be the most dynamic and lucrative option and then make their choice. For the migration, that means that multiple standards have to be supported and that the overall term of migration can be pretty flexible. One must look at these things conservatively, because although we are passing a significant milestone in the evolution of video and multimedia services, this is not going to be a quick switch from the "old" standard to the "new" standard. It will happen, but gradually, utilizing a mixture of the various approaches, and taking a number of years.

There is, of course, always the question of whether it is a viable option for the broadcast world to migrate from MPEG-2 to MPEG-4 in order to benefit from the improved video coding. The net improvement may be considered too low to justify the cost of replacing MPEG-2-based set-top boxes with those that incorporate MPEG-4 coding technology. This poses a challenge for bringing new boxes to the marketplace. One solution may be to think about building set-top boxes that use a programmable processor. Changing decoders could then be accomplished by a simple change of software.

Soon there will be set-top boxes supporting MPEG-4 AVC, and some of them will most likely equally support MPEG-2. This is what is called Simulcast. The trouble with it is that transmission capacities are going to be compromised. There will be a variety of strategies that broadcasters will adopt in terms of migration, but we will probably see a good mixture of the elementary migration forms mentioned earlier. In addition, Windows Media 9, or better to say VC9, will be available on these set-top boxes as another alternative for the operators. There of course will be extra cost to go along with the overall service offering, which will include applications like Internet access, PVR, VOD, and so on. But customers will be happy to pay a bit more for their set-top boxes and/or upgrade to their subscription packages. The reason for this will be that on one side customers will want to be receiving the best possible service where possible. A lot of this is of course driven by the content provision, which continuously enhances in terms of presentation, for example. Sometimes the argument of watching the favorite sports from say four more camera angles is enough to convince the enthusiast to upgrade. Plus, certainly, the broader spectrum of content delivery as such. Say for example, you would not be able to watch your favorite show that starts at 8pm, you can actually come home later but still be able to watch it from the start without having recorded it. You can get it on demand. On the other side customers see the advantage of bundling a variety of services into one package from most likely one provider. With the pricing and the various combination of these sort of services becoming even more competitive, the popularity for a bundled package of Internet access and Digital Television will increase. All of the above is what operators and content providers have very high on their agenda, simply because the combination of customer requirement and demand paired with the providers ability to innovate and deliver guarantee a pretty functional and mutually convenient scenario. The roll-out of these sort of services has recently started. One good example for this is Video Networks, which has launched this kind of service in the UK.

As we mentioned early in this section, migration is about decisions and change. The deciding bit is very crucial, especially for broadcasters. The technical side of things is pretty much transparent from the perspective that some systems have been deployed in the past, so there is some experience to draw on when adopting new/evolved technologies.

The commercial and entrepreneurial decision in the context of migration also occurs in the realm of introducing brand-new services, which brings a whole different dimension to the "migration equation."

In any event, no matter whether existing services are being migrated or new technologies are being deployed and implemented through the introduction of new products and services, in most cases it involves the fresh investment of capital into new hardware, both regarding content creation on the operator's end, and, as we learned earlier, on the consumer end (need for new set-top boxes). In the case of MPEG-4 AVC this is clearly evident.

While the industry agrees that for the delivery the MPEG-2 transport stream will be used, which means in essence that the existing scenario will be further utilized and re-used, we will see some significant change on the decoder and encoder side. Both of them will have to be replaced. Certainly, this will not happen overnight, but the respective vendors, like for example Harmonic, have already positioned themselves with their respective products on the encoder side. Basically, operators that decide to go for MPEG-4 AVC will gradually migrate as described earlier and it goes without saying that the replacement of broadcast encoding systems will be an effort, but nothing compared to the migration on the set-top box side. Considering the millions of legacy MPEG-2 set-top boxes, that will certainly be very cost intensive. What we need to understand is that this is an investment into the future.

With stepping into the digital future, broadcasters most certainly face quite a few obstacles, such as the briefly described "replacement of set-top boxes" scenario as well as the challenge of continuing to offer state of the art services whilst improving the offerings at the same time. A lot of vision is required to distinguish between immediate and future requirements in order to stay competitive and ahead of the game. Having said that, as we learned earlier, there may be quite a significant investment necessary, which may be partially covered by increased subscription or initial set-up costs levied on the customer. Disregarding that, broadcasters find themselves in a situation, and indeed under pressure, where they must reduce costs to ensure their profitability. The significance of this becomes really clear, when one considers that in some markets, for example UK and Germany, customers can already get their set-top box for less than $3 by now, as part of a subscription package. There is certainly a shift in the pricing and a very sophisticated subsidy formula in place, as we can also see in the mobile telephone and other markets, but it is still a very competitive game that has to be played.

So, that is basically the superficial viewpoint. If one considers the long term perspective, it will become evident that, with the significant bandwidth savings through utilizing a highly advanced codec technology such as MPEG-4 AVC and its continuously improving coding efficiency over time paired with the introduction of new business model and additional revenue opportunities, this investment will perform well. Let us also not forget an important factor, that future decoders should not necessarily be considered "static" in the sense that what is loaded on them initially stays on it. Newly advanced technologies will make it possible to load "new" video decoders onto the set-top box. Why? Very simple, if one considers the overall length of the migration process it is very likely that set-top boxes being depleted will be fitted out to decode MPEG-2, with the ability to be re-programmed to MPEG-4 AVC as and when the provider switches over and moves along with this standard. Obviously, this would mean much less costs involved compared to exchanging lots of set-top boxes.

This whole migration issue is a logical, necessary, and useful step that the industry will undertake. As in many things in life and indeed business, very responsible decisions have to be made and the immediate road ahead may even be rocky. What counts is the end result. It is very interesting to see actually that MPEG standards have been designed with an economic thought. You may wonder now in what way—very simple, the technical complexity was shifted onto the encoder side of things whilst it was endeavored to keep the decoder side pretty straight forward and non-complex. If one looks at traditional broadcast encoding systems in place today, you will find that for most applications there is dedicated encoder hardware to ensure the most efficient encoding result possible. One cannot really say that price is not an issue as such, but by its very nature and complexity the pricing can also be quite high. On the decoder side, this sort of scenario would be absolutely bad news, because the more complex it gets, the more expensive. And that is what needs to be avoided.

So this foresight of MPEG plays certainly into the hands of the providers if we consider that aforementioned cost scenario in respect of deploying/replacing set-top boxes.

One business aspect, where there is obviously some concern in the broadcast world considering all these PVR models and VOD scenarios is directed at advertising. Advertising in the broadcast arena has traditionally been a significant contributor to the revenue generation of broadcasters. The food chain was and is very simple. Content owner sells a piece of content to a broadcaster, and the broadcaster "re-finances" part, or in some cases all, of that cost through advertising. In the case of Pay TV (i.e., where subscription and on-demand revenue is generated), it is slightly different but of course similar.

With all the technological advances we heard about before becoming a reality, the likelihood of a changing relationship between the content owners and broadcasters is not only probable, but inevitable. Revenues generated by broadcasters through advertising and in essence subsidizing the cost of content acquisition will go down. In other words, the technological evolution that we are describing here in this book and all the benefits and advantages that MPEG-4 is offering, are actually harming one of the most important revenue generators for broadcasters.

So, how can this be addressed? Looking back, adverts were mainly pretty static pieces of content that were mass-produced and positioned into the broadcast schedules on "long notices." That will have to change, simply from the point of view that a consumer being able to fast forward during the broadcast will simply do exactly that in order to avoid the adverts.

There is actually a huge opportunity in this challenge for all concerned. A number of variants spring to mind and are indeed under consideration by the relevant companies involved in that business. One very simple approach is to tell the consumer that his subscription or pay-per-view fee will be cheaper if he agrees to watch his content with adverts (technically this is obviously possible through the vast possibilities offered by conditional access systems). Another alternative could be to go down the Internet route and introduce pop-up like adverts, but here as we can all imagine the reception would not be very positive from the consumer side.

Something more sophisticated needs to be used. A few concepts are already on the drawing board, and they are actually quite easy to understand and follow. Let us try to be simple again and look into our local supermarket. Every product is positioned in a specific location for a specific reason. Impulse buying is what the supermarket wants to achieve and lead the consumer through his buying experience making it easy to source and find the products required but equally favored to sell by the supermarket. From a lot of statistical and empirical data, over time supermarkets came up with the idea of loyalty cards and other schemes. The result is that supermarkets today know exactly which brand of beer, cereal, soap, and toothpaste we prefer and are utilizing this sort of evidence and information to offer us a special deal on this, or a special deal on that. They can also pinpoint demographically and geographically interesting facts that people from area A aged between the age of 30-50 prefer brand X, whereas the same age group coming from area B prefers band Y.

You are asking yourself now probably, in what way this is relevant in our context? Simply, the same principles of targeted advertising based on knowledge is something that is of value for advertisers. Instead of, in the true sense of the word, broadcast one message to everyone, with today's technology advertisers can actually ultimately pinpoint and create a one-to-one relation with the consumer based on data that is and will be available to them. One of these inputs is obviously the content itself, information pertaining to the geographical location, age group, or other information available in the public domain about consumers enabling advertisers to provide adverts that are relevant to these consumers and therefore it is more likely that these adverts will have the desired effect.

There are quite a number of companies involved in this field not at least because this necessity has been identified, but also because this new constellation born out of the technological advance created new opportunities in this particular field as well.

In conclusion, migration is not only linked to technology- and business-related aspects, but also to corporate agendas and plans. We will consider this later in the chapter. Now we will examine compression's role in the industry.

6.2. Compression Remains Important

Disregarding the fact that the industry has reached a pretty good level as far as where compression is today, the drive and ambition to further improve this compression, in our case with the use of MPEG-4, will certainly continue. It is also agreed between the experts that coding efficiency will improve over time—of course a necessity in order to stay competitive. This very fact is still today continuing with MPEG-2 although MPEG-4 AVC, and of course VC9, is becoming available. Some experts believe that there is still about 20% improvement possible in respect of MPEG-2. Economically, this drive for improvement of course is impacting further in a positive way since, as we all know, reduced bit rates is good for business so to speak (i.e., less costs and more profits).

We also need to consider the overall concept or objective when it comes to compression. MPEG-2 came along and revolutionized the broadcast world from the analogue age into the new digital era. That is more than 10 years ago and MPEG is still ticking along nicely, since it still works for most applications. MPEG-4 AVC, is a step forward taking the whole industry onto a different level, because through the resulting bandwidth efficiency new dimensions are opened for market participants. HDTV is making a significant progress in this respect and to deal with all the ins and outs would be too extensive in our context. In addition, as we have learned in earlier chapters, video over DSL and video on demand are two of the main drivers for this migration and expansion of services.

There seems to be a common misconception that compression relates solely to a network delivery scenario, (i.e., for streaming, broadcast, VOD, etc). But compression comes into play in many places, from the hard drive on a PC, to the still omnipresent CD and the further evolving DVD, to storage devices in mobile handsets and digital video cameras. All of these have a continuous need for better compression while the technical abilities to work with respective content grow and develop.

Here we will return to the three elements we briefly touched on in the last chapter, as they perfectly illustrate why compression will remain important.

With improved and indeed improving compression, it is possible to:

- *Deliver content faster*—having available and utilizing the same bandwidth, the same content can be delivered via a network much faster. Speed of delivery and availability are key factors of a successful service provision.
- *Deliver content cheaper*—improved compression delivers bandwidth savings, which directly impacts the costs involved. This freed-up bandwidth can be used for other services or features such as interactivity.
- *Deliver better quality content*—utilizing the same bandwidth, picture quality can be increased dramatically through improved compression. The result is a much better experience for the user, which in turn is very important for business.

Having said that, we should also remember that without compression there is no practical transmission or delivery of digital video or audio over any type of network. This means that compression is the enabler that makes video/audio content available over a variety of networks. In this context, it does not really matter what sort of compression is utilized—in other words, any compression will do, whether it be standard-based or a proprietary technology. As a result, better compression enables the introduction of new business models that were not previously viable, widening the spectrum of how digital video and audio can be utilized in the ongoing quest to provide better products and services. With respect to MPEG-4, including MPEG-4 AVC, the much-improved efficiency, flexibility, and scalability of this standard will be adopted in traditional environments that are currently covered, at least partly, by MPEG-2—environments such as DVD, digital broadcast (cable, satellite, terrestrial), and VOD. Also, the wireless and Internet streaming industries will significantly benefit from better compression provided by MPEG-4 and looking ahead, the possibility of digital cinema enabled by MPEG-4 is likely in the near future.

If we were to look again particularly at the broadcast industry, we will find that compression is of course omnipresent and of major importance. But the best compression will be useless, to formulate this quite harshly, if the other important parts of the puzzle are not looked after in the same focused and advanced way.

Besides compression, one could list down the following factors that are important to keep in mind and of course work on to ensure a successful, maximum quality environment and service provision from a broadcasters perspective:

- Noise Reduction
- Video Pre-Processing
- Video Analysis
- Statistical Multiplexing
- Conditional Access
- Interfaces and Packaging
- Systemization
- Network Management
- Customer Support
- Integration Services and Training

This basically means that, in order to fully capitalize on the advances in digital broadcast, providers need to plan very thoroughly every step of the way, (i.e., the overall workflow), so that costs can be reduced and returns increased. It is certainly not helped if one only sweeps throughout he entire organization and cuts costs on every angle. The tide is going away from, for example proprietary middleware or video on demand systems, to fully integrated solutions.

So, all in all, it is clear that compression cannot be discounted or disregarded in any shape or form. It is a fundamental part of the multimedia landscape, and especially the broadcast sector, and plays an important role in the workflow chain influencing quite a few technological and economical items on the agenda, as we have seen. Compression is and will remain a strong driver for technology advance and improvement in the digital media sector.

6.3. Advances in Technology—What About Patents?

We all know at what a remarkable pace technology is evolving and progressing, delivering better and better products and services to the market and giving participants the opportunity to expand their offerings. Products and services in any technological industry are the result of development and research phases, and whereas to the outside world, i.e., the consumer, only the prices of products and services are visible, there is also, in most cases, a price on the results of the R&D work. There seems to be a strong trend in which Intellectual Property Rights and patents are rising on the priority scale and are being developed into potentially significant revenue generators by many companies. This practice has of course been occurring, and rightly so, for a very long time, but consider that if a company is looking for investment, its chances rise significantly if it can offer either patented or at least patent-pending technology. In fact, this can be seen as a "must have" in order to be entering a serious conversation with potential investors, especially in the aftermath of the dot com crash. Therefore, it is high on companies' agendas to develop patentable technology.

Once the IPR/patent has been "created," obviously the ambition is to protect it and prepare for the value extraction by defining respective policies, and then start to enter into the active promotion and licensing. This is a totally understandable, appropriate, and viable thing to do; if one has patentable technology, it would be foolish not to secure and protect one's rights.

In today's technology landscape it seems that virtually everything is getting patented. The potential danger is that market participants might develop products and services not knowing that they infringe upon existing patents, and instead of marketing they may have to engage in litigation. This all sounds pretty dramatic, and may be slightly exaggerated, but the intention is to raise the awareness of the potential problems.

Having said all that, in the standards world in which MPEG-4 exists, patented technologies are of course being used. That is actually a good thing because the underlying technology within the standard is in itself strictly defined, which offers extra comfort to organizations utilizing the standard. As described earlier, the creation of patent pools, like in the case of MPEG-4, provides a coherent structure of protection for both licensees and licensors. The issue facing the market in this context is found in the requirement to identify and implement patent-licensing terms and agreements that work for both licensees and licensors. In addition, timing (i.e., the availability of license agreements) is extremely important. With respect to MPEG-4 part 2, the situation has been very unfortunate and potentially may have some impact on the deployment of MPEG-4 AVC, although licensors are aware of the opinions and concerns of licensees and are trying to accommodate them when it comes to the respective licensing terms. Whether or not the market will accept that, or when indeed, is a different matter.

Currently, the market faces the following issues regarding the patent licensing of MPEG-4 AVC:

- Two patent pools are being organized, one by MPEG LA and one by Via Licensing, both of which we have described earlier in this book. This sets up a problem for the market simply because two patent pools issuing licenses for one and the same thing (i.e., what each of the patent pool administrators considers to be an essential patent) with different terms creates obvious confusion. For example, companies might find it difficult to decide which patent pool to sign up for, or they may sign up for both, which seems pretty impractical and incurs double the fees. But the latter is actually going to be the case—potential licensees will have to sign up for both pools in order to use this technology. Whatever the licensors motivations are or were, there is a strong opinion from some participants in the industry that it may well be better to have as many licensors as possible even if they are organized in two pools rather than one pool with a significant number of purportedly essential patent holders standing there on their own. It is, to some extent, an unfortunate situation, but that is the current reality.

- In addition, whilst final terms are available now and respective licensing agreements are released (expected to happen in early 2004), some market participants, and most notable some of the big players, will commit to MPEG-4 AVC only if, from their perspective terms have been improved, which means that adoption may get stuck before it has even properly started.
- As in MPEG-4 part 2, the so called "use fees" (as proposed by MPEG LA) are proving to be very unpopular.

Especially with regard to the use fees, there appears to be a very strong negative sentiment, and the market has made it clear, especially the traditional broadcast arena, that use fees are a complete non-starter. As an example, the World Broadcasting Unions Technical Committee (WBU-TC) issued a press release regarding MPEG-4 licensing in May 2003. WBU-TC is the collective technical body for the world's eight broadcasting unions reflecting the opinions of national broadcasters across five continents. In this press release, the WBU-TC states, "Video compression technology is a major factor for broadcasters, and other content service providers in the consideration of new services. Their decision about which technology to choose is influenced by performance, availability, and licensing costs." On the first two items, performance and availability, we have seen on numerous occasions that these are present and the remaining factor to be solved and implemented is licensing.

Generally speaking, the timing, and indeed the availability, of the final licensing looks far more promising than it did with MPEG-4 part 2, which was technically finalized at the end of 1998 and became a standard in early 1999 (additional extensions in early 2000). Final licensing terms were released in mid-2002 (license agreement available at the end of 2002). In the aforementioned press release, the WBU-TC also "believes that current licensing arrangements for MPEG4 Visual will be a major deterrent to its use." This statement refers to the use fees, which do not exist in MPEG-2, and are based on equipment fees.

Clearly, licensing costs are also a major factor in deciding whether or not to go with MPEG-4 AVC. It should be noted that this WBU announcement was made *prior* to any licensing terms being announced.

After licensing terms had been announced, the European Broadcasting Union (EBU), which represents 71 broadcasters in 52 countries in Europe, North Africa, and the Middle East, went to the public with a statement in November 2003, in which it made its recommendation "that EBU members should not adopt or use the AVC standard" and "that the DVB Project should not include the AVC standard in any of its Specifications." The reason for this opinion can be found in the fact that the EBU considers that the "licence terms and conditions for use of AVC are extremely unfavourable to broadcasters."

There is also concern, in the context of the MPEG LA license, as to what happens after 2010 when the initial proposed licensing term expires. This concern, however has been addressed by now in the sense that after the initial term is over, royalties will not increase by more than 10% each time the license is renewed. Although 2010 seems pretty far away, one has to consider the timing with which MPEG-4 AVC will enter the scene. Over the next 12 months, we can anticipate numerous deployments of MPEG-AVC in the video-over-DSL market segment, with HDTV possibly following in about 24 months from now, and mobile services being launched with MPEG-4 AVC potentially in about 36 months. In any event, the chain of events in terms of MPEG-4 AVC deployment is likely to go in the order of broadcast, video over DSL, cable, direct-to-home, low-bit rate, and finally handhelds.

At the time of writing this book, the situation with respect to MPEG-4 AVC licensing is clear to the extent that final terms are available and a license in sight, which are expected for early 2004. The identification of final terms that work for all has been the challenge, but it is clear that both licensors and licensees wish to find a consensus and arrangement that is acceptable for all concerned. We should be thinking positive that this will be the case, and maybe by the time you read this, these issues will be in the past with the present looking much better.

Let us finally look at some of the adoptions of MPEG-4 AVC that have already been taking place or are most likely to take place.

- Provisionally adopted by the DVD Forum as mandatory codec for the upcoming HD-DVD Video specification for DVD players
- Japanese Broadcasters adopt MPEG-4 AVC Video Coding for Mobile Digital Terrestrial Broadcasting
- More users await availability of patent licenses to start deployment
- Growing number of technology vendors offering support for MPEG-4 AVC

Overall, adoption of MPEG-4 AVC will continue; widespread adoption is only a question of "how," "where," and "when." We earlier looked at the technological and economical aspects of adoption, but, also from the perspective patent licensing, the corporate side of things needs to be considered. Companies are spending vast amounts on research and developments efforts and of course they would like to see a return. The objectives of this fact and the creation patents as revenue generators were considered earlier in this chapter. One needs to see the bigger picture and step outside the box as well as consider the current status quo, where it is evident that a lot of organizations are creating significant revenues through the provision of MPEG-2 products, but of course also the patent licensing. It is not a question of quality or any other technological feature, it is purely a question of timing as to when the market place decides that the time is there to fully embrace MPEG-4 AVC. If we remember the transition issues mentioned above it is also clearly evident that no one can expect that MPEG-2 is switched off over night and replaced by one of the new coding technologies like MPEG-4 AVC. That does not work technologically, economically, and logically. As everywhere in business, market participants follow different strategies, but bearing in mind the overall effort behind the MPEG standards and the continuous dedication to them by so many organizations, it is only a question of time until widespread adoption will be achieved. We are looking at this of course from the "non-competitive" angle, but we all realize that we will exist in a multi-codec world, which will be dominated by both MPEG-4 and VC9. The good news on that is that with the market being so huge, both technologies can perfectly co-exist.

Turning back to the standards world and the efforts involved, we probably all remember articles or presentations citing the thousands of man years of research and development that have gone into the development of MPEG-4. Obviously, this can easily be put in context with a monetary element and one would actually come out at a quite considerable investment undertaken by the participants in developing this standard, to say the least. In addition, work is of course on-going, and if we remember the structure of MPEG described in earlier chapters, it is also quite evident how much money is spent by the MPEG member companies every year through participating at the regular meetings. You can easily work out that the sum is again enormous when over 300 engineers meet four times a year for a week.

6.4. Conclusions

From a business perspective, as mentioned earlier, the main factor for successful adoption of MPEG-4 is that effective and competitive licensing terms are available, especially for MPEG-4 AVC. Knowing that technical superiority cannot, in theory, win over commercial disadvantage—MPEG-4 has proven to be robust enough in recent years to withstand all sorts of trouble, which makes us very confident for the days ahead.

The challenge for standardization in the future is to define a coherent and consistent patenting policy. It would be a great shame if many years of constructive research and development efforts go down the drain because of difficulties in the patent-licensing process. This kind of "brain drain" cannot be afforded on a long-term basis by any economy.

In the field of economics there is a term called the "tragedy of the anticommons," which occurs when many individuals have rights of exclusion to a scarce resource. The tragedy is that rational individuals, acting separately, may collectively "waste" the resource by under utilizing it compared to what some observers may believe to be a social optimum. An anticommons is contrasted with a commons, where too many individuals have privileges of use of (or the right not to be excluded from) a scarce resource. The "tragedy of the commons" is that rational individuals, acting separately, may collectively *over*utilize a scarce resource. In both the anticommons and commons situations, there is no hierarchy among owners such that the decision of one owner can dominate those of other owners, forcing them to use their resources in ways they would not, if they were permitted free will by the authority. So let's hope that MPEG-4 does not turn into another example of the tragedy of the anticommons. This may seem a bit harsh, however awareness has to be created in a sense that it would be a disaster of considerable dimension if the industry would manage to let MPEG-4 mutate into such a state. The probability is very remote, but a potential is existent.

Let us finally leave all that aside and quickly recap where we actually are and indeed can be with MPEG-4. MPEG-4 can be . . .

- The authoring format utilized on your DVDs
- The format used to deliver Digital Television (cable, satellite, DTT)
- The format that delivers video/TV over DSL directly to your home
- The format that you use for your home-made videos to save space on your hard-drive

- The format used to deliver TV content directly to your mobile phone
- The format in which you receive your on-demand video to your mobile phone
- The format used in your digital camera or camcorder and other consumer elctronics
- The format of your music or radio

In addition there are obviously the various usages not visble to the consumer in which MPEG-4 plays a role, such as Media Asset Management and archive systems, etc.

With this book, we have tried to bring you closer to MPEG-4 by providing a broad variety of technical and business-related perspectives, but there are certainly some elements we were unable to expand upon in more detail, and could only scratch the surface. From a technological point of view, it is very much apparent what advantages and efficient functionalities are enabled by the MPEG-4 family, and the continuing development and improvement of the standard-based environment will assure that this remains the case. There is also every indication that new potential applications will surface, leading more market participants to embrace MPEG-4. The result will be that the overall multimedia landscape will only benefit and prosper further in the years to come.

6.5. Bibliography

dicas digital image coding GmbH www.dicas.de
MPEGIF White Paper "The Media Standard" 2002. download from: http://www.mpegif.org.
Popwire Technology www.popwire.com
Report "Global Digital TV Technology & Markets" by Nick Flaherty, Senior Analyst InsideChips.com
VBrick Systems www.vbrick.com
Web site 3GPP www.3gpp.org
Web site Apple www.apple.com
Web site DVB www.dvb.org
Web site Harmonic Inc. www.harmonicinc.com

Web site Internet Streaming Media Alliance www.isma.tv
Web site ISO www.iso.ch
Web site Microsoft www.microsoft.com
Web site MPEG Industry Forum (MPEGIF) www.mpegif.org
Web site MPEG LA www.mpegla.com
Web site MPEG www.chiariglione.org/mpeg
Web site Nokia www.nokia.com
Web site Via Licensing www.vialicenisng.com

Glossary

3GPP   The abbreviation for "Third Generation Partnership," which was formalized in 1998. For more information, see also www.3gpp.org.

3GP File   A 3GP file is specified in the 3GPP standardisation and designed for utilisation in the mobile sector. It is essentially based on the MP4 file format.

AAC (Advanced Audio Codec)   AAC is an audio codec and specified in the MPEG-4 standard. AAC is an optional audio codec in the 3GPP specification and the mandatory audio codec in MPEG-4. See also http://www.chiariglione.org/mpeg/faq/mp4-aud/mp4-aud.htm.

Add-on   An add-on is "software for software." Effectively, it expands on the functionalities and capabilities of a piece of software.

AC-3   AC-3 is a audio codec developed by Dolby Laboratories and used in most cinemas and on DVDs. For further information, please visit www.dolby.com.

Active Streaming Format (ASF)   ASF is a very versatile Windows Media file format, which can contain objects such as audio, video, HTML, ActiveX, etc. ASF as a format has been designed by Microsoft specifically for streaming audio/video content. However, today, ASF is somewhat outdated and not fully supported anymore. The omnipresent Windows Media format is the legitimate successor for ASF. For more information on Windows Media, please visit www.microsoft.com.

ADSL (Asymmetric Digital Subscriber Line) ADSL is high-speed, always-on Internet connectivity provided through regular copper telephone lines. Most offers available are based on flat fee subscriptions. Asymmetric stands for the fact that ADSL supports different data rates for the upstream and downstream.

AIFF File (Audio Interchange File Format) AIFF, developed by Apple, is commonly utilised for uncompressed PCM audio. For more information, please visit www.apple.com.

AMR (Adaptive Multi Rate) AMR is an audio codec for very low bit rates, which was standardised by the European Telecommunications Standards Institute (ETSI) in 1999. AMR is an optional audio codec in the 3GPP specification.

API (Application Programming Interface) API stands for a function (or a variety of functions) enabling software users, especially developers, to interact with other software, especially in a development environment (usage in Software Developers Kits).

Applet An applet is effectively a small application. There is, for example, the Java programming language, which enables the inclusion and illustration of animations (also interactive ones) into a webpage, provided the computer platform utilised supports Java.

Application An application is software designed for specific, dedicated purposes. Examples are Web browsers, video editors, video encoding, word processing, etc.

ASF Format (Advanced Streaming Format) ASF is a format designed by Microsoft specifically for streaming audio/video content. For more information, please visit www.microsoft.com.

Archive An archive is a collection of information or content that is stored on any kind of storage device in a way that it can be retrieved any time.

ASP (Application Service Provider) An ASP is a commercial entity that offers access to specific software applications over Internet connections on a rental and/or pay-as-you-go basis for a specific period of time.

ASP (Advanced Simple Profile) The Advanced Simple Profile is a set of tools used for the video encoding.

ATM (Asynchronous Transfer Mode) ATM is a protocol that defines the delivery of fixed sized packets via a single route in comparison to other mechanisms where the composition of a file is achieved through sending packets over various network routes.

ATSC (Advanced Television Systems Committee) The ATSC is a non-profit organisation established for the development of terrestrial digital television standards for the United States. For further information, please visit www.atsc.org.

Audio Channels Audio channels are the number of more or less independent audio streams. Mono sound uses one audio channel, and stereo uses two audio channels.

Audio Precision Audio precision is the number of bits used to represent the amplitude of a sampled audio signal. The higher the precision (i.e., the more bits per sample), the better the sound. Higher precisions result in a bigger file size and higher bit rate. However, more than 16 bits per sample are only used for professional recording and mastering studios. Consumer devices such as a CD player offers 16 bit of audio precision. Conversational services, such as digital telephony or similar provide intelligible speech at 8 bit per sample.

Audio Samplerate Audio samplerate is the number of sample values per second used to represent an audio signal by time discrete values. The higher the sample rate, the better the sound. Higher sample rates result in a bigger file size and higher bit rate. Typical sample rates for consumer devices such as a music CD is 44.1 kHz. Professional audio equipment uses 48 kHz. Cutting edge digital recording studios are currently moving on to 96 kHz. Digital radio services often use 35 kHz sample rate, which is considered to provide sufficient bandwidth for radio.

Authentication   A process that takes place before a user can enter certain parts of a Web site, or can receive a stream of content etc. There are various levels of authentication, depending on what parameters the respective provider has set.

Automatic Update   Allows the automatic download, and in many cases, the installation of updates or plug-in software without user interference (i.e., no Web browser needs to opened and the installation happens "in the background").

AVI File   Short for Audio Video Interleave, the file format for Microsoft's Video for Windows architecture. This is, in fact, a very old specification that Microsoft is not really supporting anymore. Actually, AVI has not been formally been specified but happened to be around at some point in time. The format has become so ubiquitously used that it will live on for quite some time even outside of the control of Microsoft.

B-Frame   B-frames have their name from being bi-directionally predicted from at least two reference frames. That means for decoding a B-frame at time instant k the previous frame at time instant k-1 and the next frame at time instant k+1 are needed (see Figure below).

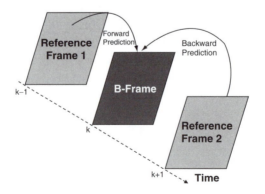

Even though B-frames are based on predictions coming from two neighboring frames a B-frame is not itself used as a reference frame for predicting other frames. This would lead to an aggregation of coding errors, which kills coding efficiency or image quality. B-frames are an effective video coding tool to improve coding efficiency. All coding schemes offering premium coding performance have a B-frame mechanism employed. However, using B-frames for coding requires more memory in the encoder and in the decoder as an extra frame (reference frame 2) needs to be stored during the decoding process. Furthermore, B-frames introduce extra delay, which is unacceptable, for example, in conversational applications. There, no B-frames are used. This holds for H.263 and its precursors as well as for MPEG-4 Simple Profile. For television services based on MPEG-2, there are typically 2 successive B-frames between two reference frames to further increase coding efficiency. Another price to be paid by B-frames is that frame exact editing in the coded bit stream is no longer possible. In order to reconstruct the red coloured B-frame in the figure, both reference frames are needed. If either one of them is gone due to cutting the video material, the B-frame is gone as well. In MPEG, the reference frames for coding a B-frame can either be P-frames or I-frames.

Back Channel   A back channel provides the ability to add, for example, interactivity to a broadcast or other transaction-related features such as authentication, payment details for services, etc. This is, in essence, achieved through an Internet connection between the viewer/user and the broadcaster and is an additional communication channel between the two.

Back-End   The back-end is effectively the engine room for content delivery where a variety of hardware (e.g., servers, storage media, network infrastructure) and software (database, transmission, encoding applications) are situated.

Bandwidth   In simple terms, bandwidth can be compared, for example, with the diameter of a water pipe. The larger the diameter, the more water gets through. By definition, bandwidth describes the amount of bits that can be transmitted over a network connection over a specific period of time (for example Kbits per second, etc.).

Bit   Bit is the abbreviation for binary digit and can either be 0 or 1. There is no other data description mechanism in technology that is smaller than a bit.

Bit Rate   Bit rate is described as the rate with which bits can be transmitted over a specific period of time.

BPS   BPS is the abbreviation for bits per second.

Broadband   Broadband comes in a variety of flavours, such as, for example DSL, ADSL, or cable, and they are high-speed, always-on Internet connections that are much faster than traditional Internet connection such as Dial-up or ISDN. Broadband is now very much deployed around the globe to business and homes alike.

Broadcasting   Originally a term that referred to the transmission of television and radio transmission; more recently it refers to all various forms of real-time transmission of media including (e.g., cable, satellite, and Internet distribution).

Buffering   When streamed media enters a user's computer faster than it can be played back, it is saved in memory without burdening the player too much.

Byte   Short form for "binary term." One byte is made of eight bits, which is approximately the amount needed by a computer to store a typed number or letter.

Cache   A cache is a temporary storage in a computer system for various data delivering quicker access to data. Applications are the access to recently used or often required or accessed data. A cache can also be used to store "anticipated" data (i.e., data that the system expects to be requested by a user soon).

Capture Device   A capture device transforms analogue audio or video data to digital data.

CBR (Constant Bitrate) In video coding, the bit rate of the compressed video is fixed as a certain rate. This usually results in variable perceived quality of the video.

CELP CELP is one of the most technically advanced audio compression algorithms. It is part of the MPEG-4 specifications. See also http://www.chiariglione.org/mpeg.

CIF CIF is a video resolution, the so called "common interchange format." The size is 352 x 288 pixels.

Codec A codec is a program that encodes and decodes digital data with the purpose of data compression.

Color Formats When video data is stored digitally there are several different formats to store the color value of a pixel. For example, RGB24, RGB32, and YUY2 are often used.

Content Delivery Network (CDN) A content delivery network (CDN) provides network architecture for the guaranteed delivery of broadcast content or other value added services. This infrastructure can also reduce network congestion or excessive burdens on servers.

Compression Compression is used to reduce the size of a file in order to make it suitable for a required bandwidth or for effective storage. There are two types of compression—lossy and lossless. MPEG standards are lossy compression techniques, where the decompressed file is not totally identical with the original file. An example of lossless compression is ZIP, in which the decompressed file and the original are identical.

Convergence Convergence is, for example, when voice, data, and Internet communication is happening over one dedicated line, as a result of which technical maintenance and administration costs are reduced.

Core Profile Core profile is a set of tools used for the video encoding. In MPEG-4, the core profile specifies the coding of non-rectangular objects.

Conditional Access Conditional access means the restricted access to certain broadcast programs achieved through the encryption of content on the broadcaster side and decryption on the recipient side (via a so called changeable "point of deployment module" in a set-top box and a serial number, which is registered in a central access control database). The reason for this sort of access control lies in the requirement for privacy and the desire to generate additional revenues (Pay TV).

CRM (Customer Relationship Management) CRM in this context is special software that is specifically designed to learn more about the requirements of customers and assist in adjusting our steering a sales process in a specific direction.

Cropping Cropping is the process of cutting the borders of a picture or video.

Data Virtually anything from numbers, to words, to images, to sounds that are possible to transcribe into bits. Once this has happened, the information can be stored, read, or transmitted over a network.

Datacast A datacast is the one-way delivery/transmission of data from the broadcaster to the viewer. An example for this is digital television.

Deblocking Deblocking is a process running as part of either the video encoder or the video decoder. The purpose of deblocking is to minimize the detrimental visual effects of block-like artifacts in decoded videos. Those blocking artifacts mainly occur as the video encoder starts to remove relevant visual information. This happens if the bit rate or available bit budget is insufficient to represent the video content and, hence, the quantization is acting too hard on the video samples.

Deinterlacing Interlacing is a classical technique for bandwidth reduction dating back to the time of analog video and television. Interlacing works on the basis that only every other line of a video frame is shown during one time instant (i.e., alternating half images

consisting either of the odd or the even lines of the image are shown alternatingly). The effect is that interlacing achieves a high temporal resolution (50 half images per second or 56.94 half images per second) without requiring extra bandwidth. The high temporal resolution is beneficial for showing sports events or similar high motion events.

Deinterlacing denotes the process of inverting the process of interlace (i.e., of putting two images of the half resolution together to one image). This can be done in many different ways, all of them producing various degrees of visually annoying artifacts (cheap deinterlacer) or almost flawless and crisp images with full resolution.

Deringing   Deringing is a process of minimizing the effect of ringlike artefacts in decoded videos.

Digital Media   Any kind of images, text, video, and sound in digital format that are available for download or transmission over various networks.

DirectShow DirectShow is part of Microsoft's DirectX framework. DirectShow is the media streaming architecture. See also www.microsoft.com.

DirectX Microsoft DirectX is a set of application programming interfaces (APIs) for creating games and other high-performance multimedia applications. See also msdn.microsoft.com.

DivX DivX is a widespread video technology that utilises MPEG-4 to compress digital video.

Download A download is the transmission of data by a user from a remote server over various networks (e.g., the download of media files from over the Internet).

DRM (Digital Rights Management) Digital rights management allows content owners to protect their property by applying certain rules and technology. For example, with DRM, content owners can set specific periods of time that viewers can access content or set specific means as to how content can be viewed.

DSL (Digital Subscriber Lines) DSL is a form of high-speed Internet access delivered through a regular telephone line to homes or offices, etc.

DTV (Digital Television) Originally "reserved" to describe digital terrestrial broadcasting, it is now also used to describe all form of digital television (i.e., which is delivered via cable, etc.). There is also DTV Multicast, which means that a variety of programs are transmitted via a single transmitter, and the viewer can choose from what is offered.

DV DV is a standard for digital video recording. DV videos can be imported by special DV codecs via FireWire.

DVB The Digital Video Broadcasting Project (DVB) is an industry-led consortium of over 300 broadcasters, manufacturers, network operators, software developers, regulatory bodies, and others in over 35 countries, who are committed to designing global standards for the global delivery of digital television and data services. For further information, please visit www.dvb.org.

DVD (Digital Versatile Disk)   DVD stands for digital versatile disk and physically looks like a regular CD; however, a DVD can store 4.7 Gigabytes of data.

DVR (Digital Video Recorder)   A DVR is in essence the same as what is known as a video recorder, except that a DVR records media, such as audio and video onto a hard-disk. DVR functions, like play, record, fast forward, etc. are controlled and managed through software.

E-Commerce   E-commerce or e-business is undertaking of commercial transaction between suppliers and consumers via a network such as the Internet.

Encoding   Encoding means the transfer of digital media from one format to another.

Flash   Flash is a vector graphics-based animation software, which has become a de-facto industry standard when it comes to the development of interactive, rich media Web site content. For more information, please visit www.macromedia.com.

Format   A format is a specific way or arrangement as to how information can be stored. Some examples for formats are MP3, MP4, DVD, VHS, etc.

FPS   FPS is an abbreviation for frames per second.

Frame   A frame is a picture of a video. Normally you have 20 to 30 frames per second.

GIF (Graphics Interchange Format)   GIF stands for graphics interchange format. It is a format that is mainly used in Web pages and in which images are constructed in colored pixels, where each pixel represents and corresponds to a particular are of the image.

GMC (Global Motion Compensation)   GMC is a MPEG-4 video encoding tool.

Graphics   Everything other than text on a web page can be classified as graphics; even text that is created using graphics software is considered a graphic as opposed to plain text.

Head-End   A head-end is the place where a variety of transmission signals are aggregated and from where all these signals are fed into the cable system to be delivered to viewers.

Hint Track   The hint track is one track of a MP4 file. It contains information needed by some streaming servers.

HTML (Hypertext Markup Language)   HTML stands for Hypertext Markup Language and is a simple, tag-based language used to create Web pages on the Internet.

I-Frame   An I-frame is a single frame in a video clip that is compressed without making reference to any previous or subsequent frame in the sequence. This frame is compressed using techniques that are similar to still image compression techniques, such as those employed in the JPEG compression standard. For professional video editing systems that use compression as a means to extend hard disk capacities or required transmission bandwidth, so-called I-frame only video codecs are used. This way, a frame-accurate editing of a video clip is still possible. However, using I-frame only codecs for video compression is by all means a luxury as such a codec is inferior in compression efficiency as compared to a codec that uses B-frames or P-frames. For television systems, an I-frame is sent typically every half second in order to enable zapping. I-frames are the only frames in a video data stream that can be decoded by its own (i.e., without needing any other frames as reference).

IETF (Internet Engineering Task Force)   The Internet Engineering Task Force (IETF) is a large open international community of network designers, operators, vendors, and researchers concerned with the evolution of the Internet architecture and the smooth operation of the Internet. It developed the ''Recommended

Practices," with the force or standards that determine how the Internet infrastructure operates. It is open to any interested individual. For more information, please visit www.ietf.org.

Input Device Any device through which a user can make choices in respect of content or can create or manage content can be classified as input devices. Examples include digital camera, mouse, keyboard, remote control, function panels, etc.

Interactive TV Interactive TV is a form of television that allows the viewer to actively influence, contribute, and respond to a broadcast program.

Infrastructure Every broadcast ecosystem runs a variety of applications and requires specific software, hardware, and networks. These can be collectively or independently allied infrastructure.

ISP (Internet Service Provider) An ISP is a company that provides Internet access to private individuals, businesses, or any other organization.

Interlaced Each video frame is sent as two separate fields. The first field is displayed on the odd numbered scan lines of the TV— the second field is displayed on the even numbered scan lines.

Intranet An intranet is a private network deployed within an organization for its specific use, such as data sharing or other applications.

ISDN (Integrated Services Digital Network) An ISDN line is a digital telephone line for voice and/or data. Data transmission (128K) is faster than via a regular telephone line (56K) but slower than DSL.

ISMA The Internet Streaming Media Alliance is a non-profit organization formed to create specifications that define an interoperable implementation for streaming rich media (video, audio, and associated data) over Internet Protocol (IP) networks. For further information, please visit www.isma.tv.

Java   Java is both a programming language (for writing software that can run on a server, on a specific device or in a browser) and a software-only platform (that runs on top of other hardware platforms). For more information, please visit java.sun.com.

JPEG (Joint Photographic Experts Group)   JPEG is a lossy format that compresses images to significantly smaller file size retaining a high degree of color fidelity. It allows a user to choose to what degree an image should be compressed. The smaller, however, a file is compressed, the more color information is lost.

Keyframe   A keyframe is the same as an I-frame.

LAN (Local Area Network)   A local area network is a data communications system capable of high-speed data transfer rates that is operated within a set geographical area (i.e., in a building, several buildings, or a campus).

Latency   Latency or delay is the time that data requires to transit from input to output.

Media   Audio, video, or image data can be classified as media.

Memory   Memory is the actual amount of data that can be stored on a chip or hard-disk. Chip memory is rather for quick access to data, whereas hard-disk memory is mainly used for archival storage purposes.

MPEG (Motion Pictures Experts Group)   MPEG, established in 1988, is a working group of ISO/IEC and has developed several standards for the coded representation of audio and video. MPEG has delivered standards such as MPEG-1 and MPEG-2 as well as, more recently MPEG-4, MPEG-7, and MPEG-21. For more information, please visit www.chiariglione.org/mpeg.

MP3   MP3 is a file format, in which audio has been compressed in accordance with the MPEG-1 standard (MPEG-1 Audio Layer 3) delivering CD quality audio. MP3 files can be downloaded via the

Internet and played back on handheld devices (MP3 player) or on a PC.

Metadata   Metadata is information specific to a particular audio, video or image that containing information about (e.g., the artist, format, copyright, compression methods, date, or any other asset descriptors deemed necessary by the content creator).

Middleware   Middleware is in essence software that runs between a client (for example, a set-top box) and a database and has the function of managing both of them jointly or if required independently (without affecting the other).

MHP (Multimedia Home Platform)   MHP is an open standard that was defined by the DVB and defines a generic interface between interactive digital applications and the terminals on which those applications execute. It enables digital content providers to address all types of terminals ranging from low-end to high-end set top boxes, integrated digital TV sets and multimedia PCs.

MJPEG   MJPEG or motion JPEG is a non-interframe compression technique in which every video frame is compressed using the JPEG standard. The resulting movie is in essence a sequence of JPEG images.

Modem   A modem is a device that connects computers, for example, to access the Internet utilising a telephone line.

Motion Estimation   Using consecutive frames within a video sequence, the motion occurring in the video material is determined.

MP4 File   The MP4 file format is the official MPEG-4 file format.

MOV File   MOV is the quick time file format, which means to view the content of this file (which can be audio and/or video) Apple's Quicktime player is required. The MOV file format is the basis for the MP4 file format. For further information, please visit www.apple.com.

MPG/MPEG File   MPG is the container file format containing MPEG-1 or MPEG-2 encoded video/audio (also for raw MPEG-1/MPEG-2 video).

MPEG-1   MPEG-1 is a standard for video and audio compression developed by the Moving Picture Experts Group, which is mainly used for Video CD (VCD) playback.

MPEG-2   MPEG-2 is a standard for video and audio compression with several profiles developed by the Moving Picture Experts Group, which is mainly used for DVD playback and broadcast quality video (used in Digital TV).

MPEG-4   MPEG-4 is a standard for video and audio compression with several profiles developed by the Moving Picture Experts Group, which dramatically advances audio and video compression, enabling the distribution of content and services from low bandwidths to high-definition quality across broadcast, broadband, wireless, and packaged media. MPEG-4 also provides a standardized framework for many other forms of media—including text, pictures, animation, 2D objects, and 3D objects, which can be presented in interactive and personalized media experiences.

MPEGIF (MPEG Industry Forum)   The MPEG Industry Forum is a non-profit organization with the objective to further the adoption of MPEG standards by establishing them as well-accepted and widely-used standards among creators of content, developers, manufacturers, providers of services, and end users. See also www.mpegif.org.

Multicast Stream   A multicast stream is effectively a transmission from one point as the sender (broadcaster) to multiple viewers (i.e., it allows many recipients to share one source). Multicasting comes into play when large amounts of data need to be transmitted to a broad audience.

Network   A group of two computers linked together can be described as a network. These computers can be linked by telephone lines, fiber optic cables, or wireless connections. When a computer is connected to the Internet, it is part of a network

NTSC   USA video standard with 4:3 image format, 525 lines, and 60 Hz.

NVOD (Near Video On-Demand)   NVOD makes it possible for a viewer to choose a particular content from a program selection and view same not instantly but within a few minutes after having made the selection

On-Demand   On-Demand means that a viewer can view/access a selected program at any convenient time

Operating System   The operating system manages all vital elements of a computer, such as memory, resources, input devices, and output devices. Middleware, for example, requires an underlying operating system do that it can properly run a set-top box.

P-Frame   P-frames have their name from being predicted from a previous reference frame. That means for decoding a P-frame for a given time instant another previous reference frame at an earlier time instant is needed (see Figure below).
   Even though P-frames are based on predictions coming from previous reference frames, a P-frame can again serve as a reference

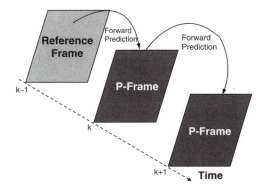

frame for predicting later P- or B-frames. P-frames are an effective video coding tool to improve coding efficiency as compared to a pure image encoder, which compresses each frame individually without making reference to any other frame. All coding schemes offering premium coding performance have a P-frame mechanism employed. However, using P-frames for coding requires the encoder and in the decoder to store the reference frame. For conversational applications, video encoders tend to us P-frames exclusively in order to avoid introducing extra delay, which is unacceptable. This holds for H.263 and its precursors as well as for MPEG-4 Simple Profile. A price to be paid for using P-frames is that frame exact editing in the coded bit stream is no longer possible. In order to reconstruct a P-frame the pertaining reference frame is needed. If either is gone due to cutting the video material, the P-frame is gone as well. In MPEG, the reference frames for coding a P-frame can either be P-frames or I-frames.

Packet   In a data transmission between computers, data is not transmitted per se but packets are (packets are pieces of data). These packets all contain relevant information including where this packet comes from and where it is supposed to go. Whilst the sending computer sliced up the data into packets, the recipient computer puts them back together.

PAL   European video standard with 4:3 image format, 625 lines, and 50 Hz.

PDA (Personal Digital Assistant)   A PDA is a hand-held computer that is able to run a variety of programs known, such as e-mail clients, video players, etc. and often includes also a mobile telephone.

PCM File   A PCM file stores raw uncompressed audio data.

Personal Video Recorder (PVR)   A PVR operates ostensibly like a DVR, but because it is orientated towards consumers, it may include more consumer specific functions, such as an electronic program guide, etc.

Platform The term platform is pretty widely used in the technology world to define the operating system that runs on a computer.

Plug-In A plug-in is an add-on; it is a smaller software program working in conjunction with a larger software program expanding or enhancing certain functionalities.

POD (Point of Deployment Module) A POD is a hardware decryption security device, mostly the size of a credit card that is put into a respective slot in a set-top box enabling controlled access and making set-top boxes independent of the cable system they are deployed in. PODs are an essential part of conditional access systems.

Profile Profiles are a set of coding tools. Profiles are used for compatibility definition.

Progressive Download A progressive download allows the viewer to watch or interact with the media while it is being downloaded at the same time.

Protocol Data cannot just be transmitted as and how required. Since there are so many different hardware platforms and operating systems used by computers that need to be connected, data transmission must happen within a specific set of rules, which are called protocols. Examples for protocols are TCP/IP, PPP, RTP/RTSP, or FTP.

Proxy A proxy is a server that is situated between a client and another server used to improve user experience and reduce bandwidth by way of trying to locate requested information either locally or if not found sends the request out to another server.

Pull Pull means that content is delivered at the specific request of a viewer. VOD or Web-browsing, for example, can be classified as pull.

Push Push means that content is delivered disregarding the interest of a viewer (i.e., the viewer cannot control what is sent). Broadcasting can be classified as push.

QCIF   QCIF is a video resolution and a quarter of CIF. The size is 176 x 144 pixels.

QP (quarter pixel estimation)   Quarter pixel estimation is a coding tool.

Quantization   Quantization is the action of information reduction to get a higher compression result.

Quicktime (QT)   QuickTime is Apple's equivalent of Video for Windows for the Macintosh. Apple also makes QuickTime for Windows. QuickTime is also used to refer to the Quick-Time Movie file format, a widely used format for digital audio, video, and other multimedia. See also www.quicktime.com.

Resolution   Resolution is the ratio of pixels used to display an image of a video and described in dots per inch (dpi). It relates to the clarity and detail of an image, and the higher the dpi, the clearer and precise the image.

RGB (Red, Green, Blue)   The colors are represented as red, green, and blue components. Most computer monitors use RGB pixels.

Router   A router is a piece of hardware that controls the path on which data gets transmitted from the sender to the recipient. Besides that, routers monitor the traffic on the network allowing only authorised computers to transmit and/or receive, address additional security aspects, or deal with network errors.

RTP/RTSP   RTP/RTSP are network protocols designed for real-time streaming.

Scalability   Scalability is the ability to increase the functionality of a software program or, for example, the ability to increase the capacity of a broadcast system without great expense or resources.

SDK (Software Developers Kit)   An SDK is a collection of software tools, API, and utilities enabling developers and programmers to implement and create applications for specific platforms and usages.

SDP file   The SDP file is the session description protocol. It is needed for some streaming connections.

SDSL (Symmetric Digital Subscriber Line)   SDSL is a form of high speed Internet access delivered over a regular telephone line. SDSL cannot operate simultaneously with voice connections over the same wire and does support the same data rates for upstream and downstream.

Serial Digital Interface (SDI)   SDI is an industry-used abbreviation for the ITU R BT 601 standard, which describes the SDI is an industry standard defined by SMPTE, which describes the interface of component digital video, which is used to connect video production equipment to transfer SD video.

Server   There are two definitions of a server; a server can either be a software program/application that manages the transmission of data or a piece of hardware (i.e., a computer) that runs server software.

Set-Top Box (STB)   A set-top box is an electronic device, which is used, in most instances, to receive and decode digital television broadcasts. In addition, they can also be used to access the Internet (instead of using a PC) and can further offer additional functions such as IP telephony, VOD, and other high-speed Internet TV services.

SMS (Short Message Service)   Mobile telephones are able to send and/or receive SMS.

Society of Motion Picture and Television Engineers (SMPTE) The Society of Motion Picture and Television Engineers is a professional membership organization that sets standards for the film and television industry. For more information, please visit www.smpte.org.

SP (Simple Profile)   The simple profile is a set of tools used for the video encoding in MPEG-4.

Storage Device   A storage device is a hardware equipment to store a variety of data, such as, for example, hard-disks, portable hard disk, digital tapes, etc.

Streaming   Streaming means the transmission of video and/or audio in packets from a server to a recipient. On the "other end," these packets are put together again on arrival and can then immediately be played back even when not the complete piece of content has been transmitted. Continuously, packets are re-assembled into data, which is then played back. Streaming is not equal to a traditional download since all packets (i.e., the data) are discarded after playback. Timing is of the essence in streaming, which is why a protocol called RTP (real-time transport protocol) is utilized.

SVOD (Subscription Video on Demand)   SVOD is a service, which is provided on a recurring basis and comes, in most cases, with a subscription fee. The viewer accesses the required and chosen content and can view same as often as desired during the subscription period or view as many programs during this period.

Tag   A tag is a programming language tool that contains formatting directions.

Transmission   Transmission is a term used for television style broadcasting but also used for the digital communication between computers over telephone lines or cable.

Unicast   Unicast means that a data communication takes place between a single sender and a single recipient.

Unicast Stream   Unicast stream is an IP based point-to-point connection.

URL (Uniform Resource Locator)   A URL represents the global address of a document or resource on the Internet. The first part of a URL describes the utilised protocol (for example, HTTP or FTP) followed either by an IP address or a domain name.

VBR (Variable Bitrate) In video coding, the bit rate of the encoded video stream varies over time. Sometimes the video is encoded with a fixed quantization factor resulting in varying bit rates and varying perceived quality. Sometimes the video is encoded with a fixed perceived quality, which usually results in varying bit rate.

VCD (Video CD) Video CD is a standard for storing audio and video information on CD discs. A 74-minute video sequence can be stored on a single disc.

Video for Windows A format developed by Microsoft Corporation for storing video and audio information. For further information, please visit msdn.microsoft.com.

Video over IP Video over IP is a method of transmitting video, audio, and data signals as packetized data over an IP network.

VOD (Video on Demand) VOD is a service in which a viewer has full control of a selected program that was chosen for viewing. The program can be stopped, paused, fast-forwarded, and rewound.

VOB File (Video Object File) A VOB file is the data container mainly used on DVDs and can contain audio, video, text, etc.

Voice-over IP Voice-over IP is in essence telephony via the Internet or networks based on Internet technology.

VPN (Virtual Private Network) A VPN is a secure, private network that utilizes a public network, for example the Internet, as a carrier.

W3C (World Wide Web Consortium) The world wide Web consortium (W3C) is an Internet standards body and develops interoperable technologies (specifications, guidelines, software, and tools) to lead the Web to its full potential. W3C is a forum for information, commerce, communication, and collective understanding.

Webcast   A webcast uses the Internet to transmit live or delayed audio and/or video data to users; it can be compared with traditional TV and radio broadcast with the main difference being that the Internet is the transmission carrier.

WAN (Wide Area Network)   A WAN can be an assembly of smaller networks, for example even two LANs, whereas the geographical limit are not set as for a LAN (i.e., it can in theory even spread worldwide).

WLAN (Wireless Local Area Network)   A WLAN is in essence the same as a LAN, the network connection is not maintained via cable or fixed line connections but totally depends on wireless networking techniques.

XML (Extensible Markup Language)   XML is conceptually related to HTML, but it is in itself not a markup language. It is a language to create other specific languages and is used for the definition of specialized markup languages, which are used to transmit formatted data.

YUV   YUV is the color space used in the PAL analog television standard.

YUY2   YUY2 is a color format very similar to YUV.

Index